World Finance and Economic Stability

World Finance and Economic Stability

Selected Essays of James Tobin

James Tobin

Formerly Sterling Professor Emeritus of Economics, Yale University, USA and Nobel Laureate in Economics 1981

Edward Elgar

Cheltenham, UK • Northampton, MA, USA

Published by
Edward Elgar Publishing Limited
Glensanda House
Montpellier Parade
Cheltenham
Glos GL50 1UA
UK

Edward Elgar Publishing, Inc.
136 West Street
Suite 202
Northampton
Massachusetts 01060
USA

A catalogue record for this book is
available from the British Library

Library of Congress Cataloguing in Publication Data

Tobin, James, 1918–
    World finance and economic stability : selected essays of James Tobin / James
        Tobin. p. cm.
    Includes bibliographical references and index.
        1. Monetary policy. 2. International finance. 3. Fiscal policy. 4. United
    States–Economic policy. I. Title.

    HG230.3 .T63 2002
    332–dc21

ISBN 1 84064 926 7   2002066598

Printed and bound in Great Britain by MPG Books Ltd, Bodmin, Cornwall

Contents

v

PART IV   POLITICAL ECONOMY

Foreword

The past year and a half has been a painful time for the world economy. In some countries, decades of progress have been reversed in a matter of months, so soul-searching is entirely appropriate. But we should also take stock of our accomplishments. At the Council of Economic Advisers and throughout the government, microeconomic issues command the majority of our time and attention. Fortunately, most economists, of whatever origin, value efficiency, appreciate the role of markets and incentives, and agree on the methodology for analyzing policy options.

My focus here will be on macroeconomics, where controversy reigns, rather than microeconomics, where economists generally agree. The Employment Act of 1946 and its later amendments, which established the CEA, gave the federal government the responsibility for stabilizing short-run economic fluctuations, promoting balanced and noninflationary economic growth, and fostering low unemployment. The Act envisioned the CEA's main role as giving the president advice on macroeconomic policy. But with radically different strategies advocated to attain the Employment Act's goals, the choice of advisers and paradigms arguably makes a real difference.

Consider some of the key questions on which macroeconomists disagree. Macroeconomists disagree on whether markets work adequately to create jobs on a continuous basis for those able, willing and seeking to work; they disagree on whether monetary and/or fiscal policy affect aggregate demand and whether active policy intervention can improve macroeconomic performance in practice; they remain at odds on whether budget deficits are good, bad or irrelevant; and they differ in their views on whether anticipated inflation imposes enormous economic costs or just minor inconveniences. In addition, there are sharp disagreements on which 'supply-side' policies are appropriate to boost economic growth.

Is there a Yale paradigm? And if so, what follows from it? Let me take a stab at a characterization, recognizing in advance that my description of the Yale approach may seem like a caricature that ignores the diversity and subtlety of opinion at Yale and the evolution of views over time (after all, it is almost 30 years since I last sat in a Yale classroom). The Yale macroeconomics paradigm, as I have taught and hopefully practiced it, combines a Keynesian understanding of economic fluctuations with a neoclassical

perspective on long-run growth. In the most difficult battles in the macroeconomics war, Yale economists – Okun before my time, Tobin, Brainard,
Nordhaus, Stiglitz in my time, and Shiller, Fair and Bewley after my days
at Yale – have served with distinction on the Keynesian side with Chris
Sims, whom I view as neutral, telling what to do econometrically. The
IS/LM and aggregate demand/aggregate supply models, hopefully still
staples in Yale's classes, provide the simplest description of the short-run
paradigm, while the neoclassical growth model, to which Tobin, Phelps,
Nordhaus and other Yalies contributed, provides the essential analytical
tool for long-run analysis.

The Yale macroeconomic paradigm provides clear answers to key questions dividing macroeconomists, along with policy prescriptions. Will capitalist economies operate at full employment in the absence of routine
intervention? Certainly not. Are deviations from full employment a social
problem? Obviously. In the words of my friend and teacher Jim Tobin, 'It
takes a heap of Harberger triangles to fill an Okun gap.' Involuntary unemployment is an extraordinarily costly social waste and the failure to address
it can exacerbate structural unemployment by denying new entrants the
skills and experience to succeed. On the question of whether monetary and
fiscal policy can succeed in moving the economy toward full employment
Yale answers 'yes' in both cases, except in exceptional circumstances such
as a liquidity trap. (After the Great Depression further real-world examples
of limits on monetary policy due to a liquidity trap seemed unlikely, but
Japan, unfortunately, provides a modern example.) In addition, the Yale
paradigm recognizes that the exchange rate regime matters to policy
impacts with a system of flexible exchange rates enhancing the effectiveness
of monetary policy and diminishing the effectiveness of fiscal policy as a
stabilization tool.

Do policy makers have the knowledge and ability to improve macroeconomic outcomes rather than make matters worse? Yes, although there are
lags and uncertainty with which to contend. On the perpetual question of
whether budget deficits matter and if so why, the Yale answer distinguishes
between cyclical and structural deficits. Structural deficits matter because
they diminish national saving, crowd out private domestic and foreign
investment and reduce future national income. On day one of macro,
however, Yalies learned that the automatic tendency of tax collections to
fall and transfers to rise during an economic downturn, creating larger
deficits in the Federal budget, serves as a vital economic shock absorber
that cushions private spending and mitigates fluctuations. Those stabilizers
should never, ever be disconnected. Are the costs associated with anticipated inflation high or low? Although most Americans apparently loathe
inflation, Yale economists have argued that a little inflation may be neces-

sary to grease the wheels of the labor market and enable efficiency-enhancing changes in relative pay to occur without requiring nominal wage cuts by workers. The attempt to push inflation too low could permanently raise unemployment and reduce the scope for monetary policy. Moreover, inflation's most serious impacts, through distortions in the tax system, can be addressed through indexation of the tax system, while small savers can be protected by inflation-indexed bonds.

Finally, what can be done to promote long-run growth? Yale's focus has urged increased national saving to enhance capital accumulation, and the promotion of human capital and R&D. These strategies, however, require current sacrifice to achieve future gain.

Having described the key elements of the Yale approach to macroeconomics, let me go on to claim that the Yale paradigm is alive, well and succeeding in Washington. Yale is certainly well represented. Two former Yale professors and two Yale PhDs have served on President Clinton's Council of Economic Advisers (CEA); three Yalies (2 PhDs and a mere undergraduate) have served on the Fed. There are highly placed Yalies at the Office of Management and Budget (OMB) and Yale PhDs occupy influential senior posts at the Fed, although that stalwart of stalwarts, Ted Truman, who has worked to solve every international financial crisis for the last 25 years, has moved to the Treasury. In addition to Yale economists, Yalie lawyers have had some say about economic policy since they serve as Chair of the National Economic Council, Secretary of the Treasury and sit in the oval office. Correlation is not causation, but if macroeconomic policy is succeeding, and I believe that it is, perhaps, along with good luck, the Yale paradigm deserves some of the credit.

I think it is easy to make the case that the US macroeconomic performance has been excellent – the best we have enjoyed since Jim Tobin went off to Washington in 1961 to help translate the Yale paradigm into policies which resulted in a 106-month expansion, the longest in recorded American history, with the records dating back to 1854. In the case of the current expansion, last December marked its 93rd month, making it the longest peacetime economic expansion on record. The expansion must continue through next February in order to break the record established in the 1960s. Throughout the expansion, job creation has been vigorous, with over 18 million jobs created since the beginning of 1993, unemployment has fallen to levels not seen since 1969, an accomplishment that seemed unthinkable only a few years ago, real growth has been solid, albeit below that of the 1960s when both productivity and labor force growth were higher. And remarkably, inflation has declined. The consumer price index rose by only 1.6 per cent during 1998, its second smallest increase since 1964, with other measures of inflation yet more muted. By this time in the expansion of the

1960s, in contrast, inflation was rising sharply and was much higher than now, approaching 5 per cent And this year the federal budget moved strongly into surplus, reaching $69 billion, the largest surplus as a share of GDP since 1957. Moreover, surpluses are projected well into the future, amounting to about $4.5 trillion over the next 15 years, according to administration estimates. Back in 1992, the budget deficit was $290 billion and expected to rise much further without policy changes.

While economic expansions have usually worked like tides lifting all boats, less skilled and disadvantaged workers have typically benefited disproportionately. During the expansion of the 1980s, however, low-income workers lost ground because the benefits of an expanding economy for these workers were offset by long-term trends depressing wages at the low end of the earnings distribution. However, the strong labor market we are enjoying now is again producing gains both in jobs and in earnings for these workers. The poverty rate has declined, with poverty for black Americans at a historical low, and in 1998 unemployment among blacks fell to its lowest level since 1973. After years of decline, the real wages of blacks and Hispanic workers, including young workers, are rising strongly. In 1998, for the first time since at least 1979, the real wages of male high school drop-outs rose almost 7 per cent. A strong economy in which job opportunities are plentiful is also a critical complement to programs and policies, like welfare reform, that are intended to encourage work. As the welfare rolls have plummeted since 1993, the labor force participation rate among single mothers aged 16–45 with children under 18 has increased by almost nine percentage points, and employment rates have also increased, suggesting that those leaving welfare are finding jobs.

I believe that the macroeconomic performance that I have described and the policies that have been pursued since 1993 reflect a sensible translation of the Yale paradigm into economic policy. The major short-term problem facing the economy in 1993 was high unemployment and sluggish recovery from recession. America's most important long-term problems included stagnant real wages, reflecting slow productivity growth, along with rising income inequality. In addition, the policy mix was disastrous from the standpoint of long-term growth: the Federal budget deficit was large and rising, with debt growing faster than GDP, and growing foreign borrowing that had transformed the USA into the world's largest debtor. National saving had fallen substantially during the 1980s, as both private and public saving plummeted, and stood at a paltry 3.1 per cent in 1992, its lowest level in the postwar period.

What was to be done? The Yale paradigm dictated that, in principle, either monetary or fiscal policy could be used to get the economy moving. However, with national saving low, fiscal policy already excessively lax from the standpoint of long-term growth, and deficits poised to grow nearly explosively, tighter fiscal policy, with smaller structural deficits, seemed the appropriate prescription. Moreover, a failure of the administration to come to grips with mounting Federal deficits risked the possibility that Congress might pass a Balanced Budget Amendment. By requiring that the budget balance in all but exceptional circumstances, this Amendment risked long-term damage to US macroeconomic performance by decoupling the automatic stabilizers. Such an outcome would have been disastrous. The overall economic situation was strikingly similar to that Jim Tobin faced in 1962, but the constraints created by a growing federal deficit, along with the enhanced effectiveness afforded to monetary policy by the demise of the Bretton Woods fixed exchange rate regime, led to some rewriting of the playbook.

Consistent with the Yale paradigm, the administration settled on a strategy of fiscal contraction coupled with (they hoped) an appropriate and well-executed policy of monetary accommodation by the independent Federal Reserve. The Fed's job would be to move the economy to full employment and to keep it there, offsetting the potential contractionary pressures resulting from mounting fiscal tightness over time. This strategy had its risks: contractionary fiscal policy could exacerbate unemployment in the absence of an appropriate monetary policy response, so that increased saving, instead of translating into higher investment, might instead be dissipated through declining output. (Indeed, to address this risk the administration initially proposed a short-term stimulus package, which luckily was not needed.) A further concern was that the cuts needed to reduce the deficit could diminish the resources for public investments – in human capital, in infrastructure and in R&D – which are also essential for growth. Cuts in spending that would be counterproductive to growth had to be avoided and ways devised instead to marshall additional resources for research, education and other investments in people in the face of increasing fiscal stringency.

The strategy was implemented, with the passage of the Omnibus Budget Reconciliation Act of 1993 and the later Balanced Budget Act of 1997, and I think it is fair to claim that it worked, even better than the textbooks might have predicted. The passage of a credible, phased in, deficit reduction package, coupled with the expectation by financial markets that the Fed would act appropriately to keep the economy growing, brought long-term interest rates down quickly, providing an immediate short-term economic boost. The expectation of fiscal tightening perhaps paradoxically may have speeded the pace of recovery. As anticipated, investment spending surged, with industrial capacity growing more rapidly over the last four years than in any other year since 1967, when the series began. In contrast to the other long expansions of the postwar period, this one has been overwhelmingly investment-driven. The national saving rate has more than doubled, reaching 6.6 per cent in 1998 even though boosts in wealth due to the strong stock market have essentially eradicated personal saving. Surpluses in both the structural and actual budget have at long last been achieved.

The emergence of large budget surpluses creates the opportunity to boost national saving yet further, helping prepare for the demographic transition at our doorstep. Saving more now would enlarge the pie later, easing the burdens on future workers resulting from the need to support retirees. In addition, a decline in national debt would free government resources needed to finance Social Security, Medicare and other retirement benefits by reducing debt-servicing burdens. The preservation of these surpluses, and their use to pay down debt, requires that Americans forgo current consumption and tax cuts now in order to enjoy greater consumption later. Polls suggest that, with a strong economy, Americans are prepared to make such a sacrifice. Thankfully, the potential disaster of a Balanced Budget Amendment was avoided, although policy makers must always remain on guard to ensure that the automatic stabilizers are not disconnected and they would be by legislative proposals that have recently been unveiled to force debt reduction along a predetermined future time-path.

This expansion provides an illustration of the *IS–LM* model in action: policy shifted the *IS* curve left, and the *LM* curve right by more; the results worked just fine. Actually, the results have been better than the textbooks would have predicted because one of the pleasant surprises of this expansion has been the continued good behavior of inflation. Policy makers have taken advantage of that surprise to push both inflation and unemployment below levels that were thought to be achievable.

The Yale paradigm has always recognized that good policy requires a sensible approach to handling uncertainty. Structural shifts occur and the impacts of policy actions are uncertain. During the current expansion, standard statistical estimates of the NAIRU suggested that the economy had entered incipient inflationary territory by the end of 1994, when the unemployment rate fell to 5.5 per cent; yet actual inflation continued to fall well into 1998 as the unemployment rate declined another point. The Phillips curve had veered off track, and a key policy question facing the Fed was how to gauge the risk of inflation and decide what level of inflationary risk to tolerate. Ideally, an explanation for the forecast errors would have been identified. Possible suspects include a variety of arguably temporary supply shocks, an inflation-mitigating increase in capacity, resulting from the recent rapid pace of investment, and possible shifts in the reduced-form Phillips curve relationship between inflation and unemployment due to a shift in the Beveridge curve – a favorite Yale tool for characterizing the extent of structural mismatch in the labor market. Conceivably, global competition had eroded the bargaining power of workers, with unusually low quits and high anxiety about layoffs among workers causing a shift in the Phillips curve.

How should such uncertainty be handled? Recognizing that estimates of NAIRU have a wide band of uncertainty, a sensible monetary policy strategy, and the one that was followed with spectacular success, entailed probing the frontiers, balancing the gains from lower unemployment against the risks attendant upon higher inflation, and revising views about tradeoffs along the way, taking new data into account. The success of monetary policy in the current expansion epitomizes the Yale view that discretionary monetary policy guided by trained common sense can improve economic outcomes even though it cannot precisely fine-tune the economy.

I have touted the scope for Yale economics, properly applied, to promote prosperity, using the United States as an example. I conclude on a cautionary note, stressing that the Yale model also contains sobering lessons for macroeconomic management. Decades ago, economists recognized an unfortunate implication of the Yale macroeconomic paradigm: that the simultaneous attainment of financial market openness, monetary policy independence and exchange rate stability – three desirable macroeconomic goals – was simply impossible! Countries would have to forgo at least one or risk financial crisis. Recognizing this policy dilemma, Tobin suggested the desirability of reducing capital mobility through a small transactions cost to throw sand in the wheels of global capital flows. A few countries took measures to restrain capital inflows; some forswore independent monetary policy, living with the unfortunate consequences; and some adopted flexible exchange rates. But many countries tried to have it all. As Yale economists forewarned, an international financial crisis resulted.

How should we proceed from here? What macroeconomic advice should policy makers offer to small open economies to help them achieve prosperity? What should be done to strengthen the underpinnings of the international financial system to make it less crisis-prone? And how can we improve the mechanisms available for dealing with future crises that may arise? This remains the unfinished agenda. Not surprisingly, Yale economists have already taken the lead in addressing these questions.

I am confident that in the next century the creative ideas generated by Yalies will help improve macroeconomic policy and promote prosperity not just in the United States but around the globe.

JANET YELLEN
Chairman, President's Council of Economic Advisers

Acknowledgements

The publishers wish to thank the following, who have kindly given permission for the use of copyright material.

American Philosophical Society for articles: 'Financial Globalization', in *Proceedings of the American Philosophical Society*, 143(2), June 1999, 161–7 and 'Jan Tinbergen (12 April 1903–9 June 1994). *Proceedings of the American Philosophical Society*, 141(4), December 1997, 511–14.

Council of Europe for extract: 'Private Markets vs. Public Sectors, 1999', from Parliamentary Conference, Strasbourg, 31 May–1 June 1999.

Federal Reserve Bank of Atlanta for article: 'The Monetary and Fiscal Policy Mix, 1986', in *Economic Review*, August/September 1986, 4–16.

Institute for Research on Public Policy for article: 'Currency Unions, American v. European', in *Policy Options*, Institute for Research on Public Policy, Montreal, May 2001.

John Wiley and Sons Inc. for chapter: 'Can We Grow Faster?' in *The Rising Tide: The Leading Minds of Business and Economics Chart a Course Toward Higher Growth and Prosperity*, edited by Jerry Jasinowski, John Wiley and Sons, Inc., 1998, pp.27–46.

Kluwer Academic Publishers for article: 'Keynesian Insights for the Japanese Economy', published as 'Reflections on Japanese Political Economy', in *Economic Theory, Dynamics and Markets: Essays in Honor of Ryuzo Sato*, edited by Takashi Negishi, Rama V. Ramachandran and Kazuo Mino, Kluwer Academic Publishers, 2001, pp.468–71.

Macmillan Publishing Ltd for article: 'Supply Constraints on Employment and Output: NAIRU versus Natural Rate', presented at International Conference in Memory of Fausto Vicarelli, Rome, 21–23 November 1998 and published in *Economic Theory and Social Justice*, edited by G. Gandolfo and F. Marzano, Macmillan, 1998; and 'Foreword' to *Global*

Capital Flows: Should they be Regulated?, by Stephany Griffith-Jones, Macmillan Press, 1998, pp.xi–xiii.

MIT Press for chapter: 'The Political Threat to Social Security' in *Should the United States Privatize Social Security?*, edited by Henry J. Aaron and John B. Shoven, MIT Press, 1999, pp. 146–53.

New Republic for chapter: 'The IMF's Misplaced Priorities: Flawed Fund', with Gustav Ranis, in *New Republic*, 9 March 1998, 16–17.

Oxford University Press for 'Prologue' to *The Tobin Tax: Coping with Financial Volatility*, edited by Mahbub ul Haq, Inge Kaul and Isabelle Grunberg, Oxford University Press, 1996, pp.ix–xviii.

Springer-Verlag for prologue to *Current Issues in Monetary Economics*, edited by H. Wagner, Physica-Verlag, 1998.

Stanford University Press for chapter: 'False Expectations', in *The New Russia: Transition Gone Awry*, edited by Lawrence R. Klein and Marshall Pomer, Stanford University Press, 2001, pp.65–72.

Yale University press for article: 'Growth Through Taxation', *The New Republic*, 25 July 1960, 15–18.

Every effort has been made to trace all the copyright holders but if any have been inadvertently overlooked the publishers will be pleased to make the necessary arrangements at the first opportunity.

Introduction

The US economy suffered two quite distinct shocks in year 2001. First was the business cycle recession, raising unemployment from 4 to 6 per cent and depressing production, prices, incomes and asset values – familiar events which Americans had been spared for most of the previous decade. Recovery is coming, it is generally agreed, with revival of demand for goods and services by consumers, businesses, governments and foreign customers. Supply is no problem. The nation has the workers, materials, productive capacity and technology to respond to much higher demands.

How to stimulate spending? By still lower interest rates? The Federal Reserve cut its key rate 11 times last year, from 6 per cent to 175 per cent. Or should the Fed husband those remaining 175 basis points of the Federal Funds rate for possible future needs? It seems weak strategy, deliberately keeping monetary policy too tight. To avoid a liquidity trap, the Fed should try to lower longer-term rates and loosen bank credit.

By cutting taxes again? A large cut? The earlier one was estimated to add up to $1.6 trillion in this decade and permanently to deprive the federal government of two of the 16 percentage points of national incomes it now collects. Later in 2001, refunds of $300 per federal income taxpayer were distributed. Debate continues on further federal fiscal stimulus to demand.

The second blow was the terror of 11 September, wholly beyond expectation and experience; it is still potentially terribly dangerous and costly. The worldwide war against terrorism and the protection of the homeland are the highest priority uses of the nation's resources today. President Bush has proposed in his budget for fiscal year 2003 (which begins in October 2002) additional military spending of $48 billion (about one-half of 1 per cent of GDP) and new outlays of $38 billion (two-fifths of 1 per cent) for homeland security. To protect the American people against terrorist attacks, to the degree of safety we took for granted before 11 September, if at all possible, will take large expenditures for many years. At stake are buildings, airways, railroads, ships, ports, communications, theaters, stadiums, utilities, highways, bridges, public health, mail deliveries – almost every aspect of civilized life.

Why does the president delay acceleration of appropriations and spending for war on terrorism and homeland security until next fiscal year? Start now! By fortunate happenstance, these measures would also be very good anti-recession demand stimuli. Other stimuli, most of those debated by president and Congress. would contribute nothing to the nation's prime priorities. Indeed, dollar for dollar, government purchases of goods and services augment demand more than the tax cuts and dollar subsidies generally discussed, of which the recipients will generally choose to save at least part. And of course the direct demands of government are followed by the further spending of those who receive income by meeting the governments' needs – the once famous Keynesian multiplier.

The urgency of action on homeland security is especially great because much of the agenda is the job of state and local governments. The challenges and opportunities for these governments are critical. They will need to cooperate with each other and with the federal government. Yet the recession has drastically cut state and local revenues, while their politics and constitutions keep them from borrowing. President Bush and his homeland director should engineer generous new grants to state and local governments, meeting their regular responsibilities as well as the new needs of homeland security. It is important to sustain Medicaid and to attach to it financing of prescription drugs.

Further tax giveaways to individual and corporate taxpayers would be most inappropriate at this time. For one thing, it is quite uncertain that much of them would be spent while stimulus is needed. They would be temporary, and the beneficiaries other than the poor and liquidity-constrained might prefer to save funds for the future. Anyway, it is an illusion to expect that a temporary burst of spending will jump-start the economy like an automobile battery or prime it like a pump. The state of American business is probably little different today from what it would have been without the $300 or $600 income tax refunds of 2001. More important, the president is calling on the American people to make sacrifices to win the world war and protect the homeland. They are willing, indeed eager. Surely those sacrifices do not include still a third set of tax cuts within this president's young term. At this rate, with tax cuts the invariable prescription for whatever ails the national economy, there will not be any taxes left to cut. The advocates of tax cuts allege that tax rates are the highest in history. But it is illegitimate to count social insurance contributions because these are transfers from person to person and are not used to finance government activities.

President and Congress are right to place the emergencies post-11 September ahead of customary concerns or fiscal prudence, letting the federal budget go into deficit and the federal debt rise. One action of federal deficits and the path of the debt is to share costs and hardships equitably across generations. It is reasonable to shift some of our present burdens to taxpayers of coming decades. The straightfoward way to do this is to offset some of today's urgent expenditures and deficits by suspending some of the tax cuts scheduled for later years in the legislation of 2001. If 11 September-type disasters had occurred during the full employment, steady growth and prosperity of the 1990s, the new demands of war and homeland security would have had the same priority, but the labor and other resources required would have had to be drawn from other uses. That would have entailed tight money and high interest rates and restrictive fiscal policy as well, including most likely tax increases. It would have been painfully obvious, as it is not now, that the disaster imposed sacrifices on the American people. If and when full recovery from the present recession somehow occurs, our economy will be in that situation. The Kennedy–Johnson tax cuts of 1964–5 worked as intended to restore and sustain full employment, but they overstimulated demand once the burdens of the Vietnam war took priority. Now, too, it could easily happen that tax cuts welcome in present circumstances will turn out to be embarrassingly excessive in more prosperous times, given the burdens and threats of terrorism. This is especially true given the political obstacles to raising tax rates once reduced, even when the cuts were initially advertised as temporary.

This is no time for an ideological campaign to reduce the shares of government activity in the economy. Let governments handle the requirements of world terrorism and homeland security they can do best. Inevitably, they will buy most of the goods and services they need from the private sector. But if it is better that airport screeners be public employees, so be it.

The attack on Pearl Harbor on 7 December 1941 was, like the terrorist attacks of 11 September 2001, a wake-up call, suddenly focusing the nation on its vulnerability to foreign enemies. The president, Franklin D. Roosevelt then, George W. Bush now, led the nation's response.

In both cases the economy happened to be performing below par at the time of attack. In 1941, the American economy had still not recovered from the Great Depression of 1929–33. Although the 1929–30 levels of production and income had been restored, unemployment, at 10 per cent, remained stubbornly high. A setback to the recovery had occurred in 1937–8. Like George W. Bush today, FDR needed both economic stimulus and war fighting. On both counts economic mobilization was the answer, and FDR wasted no time. He asked immediately for new military appropriations of more than $100 billion, in an economy with 1941 GNP of $125 billion, of which federal purchases amounted to only $17 billion, with $14 billion for defense prompted by worries about Europe. American industry responded with miracles of innovation and production, notably ships by Henry Kaiser and planes by Howard Hughes. Car and truck factories were converted to build tanks and jeeps. The manpower of the armed forces expanded quickly thanks to the draft, selective service already in force.

GNP grew by 12 per cent from 1941 to 1942, 18 per cent the following year. By 1943, labor shortage had displaced unemployment, which fell to 4.6 per cent in 1942 and to 2 per cent the next year. Price and wage controls and rationing were necessary to keep inflation in check. By 1945, half of United States GNP was war production, but what was left for civilian use exceeded the whole of pre-Depression GNP.

There can be no doubt that expansion of government spending on goods and services can provide 'stimulus' in the process of carrying out the nation's priority programs. However, maybe the economy needs more demand stimulus than it needs added military spending. This could be matter of debate. The technology of a two-ocean World War II is a lot more demanding of manpower and other resources than what we have seen of the international war on terrorism. Perhaps this will change drastically by taking seriously missile defense, dear to the president's heart. Otherwise, homeland protection would be the main challenge and stimulus.

PART I

Financial Globalization and World Money

1. The global economy: who is at the helm?*

GLOBALIZATION: HOW NEW? HOW COMPLETE?

Globalization is a fashionable term, used to describe world economic trends somehow associated with revolutions in electronics, computation and communication. The Internet is a striking example. Kids can sit before computer screens and communicate at lightning speed all over the globe at negligible marginal cost.

According to many American workers, globalization is not so benign. They associate it with competitive invasions of imports and immigrants, endangering their jobs and wages. Imports are still only 13 per cent of US GDP. Foreign trade is on an upward trend, but this is nothing new. Imports grew from 5 per cent of GDP in 1959 to 6 per cent in 1972 to 10 per cent in 1985. As wages have advanced in the USA we have lost competitive advantage in a series of products: among them apparel, consumer electronics, motorcycles, shipbuilding. We still have jobs for 95 per cent of our labor force, but the jobs are not in the same industries they were 10, 20, 50 years ago. Thanks to technical progress, they are better jobs. When I was a boy, a quarter of the nation's labor force was in agriculture; the figure is 3 per cent today.

US foreign policy has sought free trade ever since Franklin Roosevelt and Cordell Hull began negotiating reciprocal trade treaties. In those days Democrats were free traders and Republicans were protectionists, having passed the notorious Smoot–Hawley tariff in 1930. The two parties' roles are somewhat reversed today, and the president depends on Republican votes to continue in the Roosevelt–Hull tradition. They were not enough this year. The key to the success of those negotiations over the years was the commitment to generalize to the whole world any tariff concessions agreed in bilateral negotiations: every country gets the treatment offered to the 'most-favored' nation. (Apparently one reason people oppose 'most-favored nation' treatment for China is their misapprehension that this

*   This paper is, with a few revisions and updates, one delivered to the World Affairs Council of Springfield, Illinois, 23 October 1997.

means China would get especially favored access to our markets. In fact it means that China would get the same treatment as almost everybody else, instead of being subject to the high Smoot–Hawley tariffs of 1930.

Regional free trade agreements are a breach of the most-favored-nation principle, allowable by the terms of the General Agreement on Tariffs and Trade (GATT) and now by its successor the World Trade Organization (WTO). The European Common Market organized in the 1950s was the big breach, favored by the USA for political reasons. NAFTA (North American Free Trade Agreement) is our own venture into regional free trade, discriminating against countries outside the region. President Clinton now aims to expand NAFTA to AFTA (ASEAN Free Trade Area), embracing the whole hemisphere. Reversing his stand for worldwide free trade, embodied in the WTO, in his last 'fast track' campaign, Clinton now goes for regionalization instead of globalization. Some economists who are free traders oppose this Clinton initiative on these grounds.

The issue in these cases is whether expansion and liberalization of trade within a region justifies the withholding of concessions from the rest of the world. A practical problem is the enforcement of regionally discriminatory agreements, for example preventing cars with large Japanese content from being assembled in Mexico and entering the USA on the favorable terms available to imports of Mexican goods. This awkwardness would be avoided by faithful adherence to 'most-favored nation'.

Globalization is in many ways proceeding faster in finance, where the electronic revolutions are the most applicable, than in trade. It is easy and cheap to move funds across countries and currencies. The worldwide volume of gross transactions is enormous, one and a half trillion dollars per day. Most of these movements are reversed within hours or days or weeks. *Net* movements of investment capital have grown since World War II, but not spectacularly faster than world trade and production.

Wealth-owners and portfolio managers are still quite nationalistic. In 1950, Americans' asset holdings included 2 per cent foreign assets; by 1990, the foreign share had risen, but only to 4 per cent. For equities the rise was from 1 per cent to 3 per cent, and for direct investment 4 per cent to 7 per cent. Foreigners' holdings are somewhat larger shares of American assets, and have grown faster. Since foreign assets offer opportunities for hedging and diversification of risks, it is surprising that cross-national holdings are so modest.

Obstacles to international capital movements have been reduced, in the Third World as well as the First. (I must say however, that my own bank is slow and expensive when confronted with a check or wire transfer in a foreign currency. I assume that recent MBAs (Masters of Business Administration) at Goldman Sachs are spared these annoyances.)

Obstacles to doing financial business in foreign markets have been reduced. For Wall Street and the City of London this is the joy of globalization. The sun never sets on world money markets.

The result is narrowing of interest rate differentials (risk-adjusted) between national markets. Yet the possibilities of divergent national monetary policies and interest rates have not been completely erased. Certainly national economies' business cycles are far from perfectly synchronized.

Labor markets are much farther from being globalized. Even in the European Union, where citizens of any member are legally free to be employed anywhere, in fact labor is much less mobile than across the states of the USA. In the world as a whole, restrictions on immigration are severe. The USA has been the most liberal First World nation, but we are quite selective and now we are trying to close doors. Economists know that to some extent trade in commodities is indirectly mobility of labor, but this process is weak and slow.

THE UNITED STATES ECONOMY, GREENSPAN AT THE HELM

A tour d'horizon of the world economy today is not very encouraging. Of the advanced democratic/capitalist economies, the USA is the star performer. Alan Greenspan deserves much of the credit; he is certainly the outstanding central banker of the age. The success is the persisting combination of low inflation and low unemployment. As recently as 1995, the Federal Reserve itself, along with most economists, thought this was impossible. Many are still doubtful that this macroeconomic paradise can last. The unemployment rate is now one and one half points below the 6 per cent that was thought to be compatible with stable inflation. That one point less unemployment is worth $150 to $225 billion of GDP per year (2 to 3 per cent). Fortunately Chairman Greenspan was willing to be pragmatic and to let the economy reduce unemployment so long as no speed-up of price rises was evident – rejecting advice to deal inflation a 'preemptive strike'. Alan Greenspan's bark is worse than his bite. Maybe the bark keeps the economy within bounds without the need for active monetary tightening.

Unlike the central banks of the other leading economies, the other six of the G-7, the Federal Reserve considers, and indeed is required by statute to consider, both unemployment and production on one side and prices and inflation on the other in making monetary policy. Prevailing doctrine and practice in Europe and Japan, and also in Canada, is to gear monetary policy solely to prices and inflation. In the USA too there are important voices urging such a rule, among economists, members of Congress and Federal Reserve officials. Many favor mandating price stability, inflation stability at zero, not any other number. Given Greenspan's well-advertised belief that statistical price indexes overstate inflation by at least one full percentage point, it would be illogical for him to take this view. As far as current monetary policy is concerned, the cost in jobs and output of eliminating the remaining two or three points of inflation would far outweigh the social gains. Fifteen years ago Chairman Paul Volcker in effect declared 5 per cent inflation to be effectively zero.

Its macroeconomic success does not mean the USA has no economic problems. We are all aware of the increased inequalities of income and wealth, the persistence of poverty and inadequate health care, the prospective aging of the population and financing the retirements and health care of the baby-boom generation.

Most of these problems would look more tractable if our long-term sustainable growth rate were higher. Contrary to widespread misunderstanding, our macro success in this decade was not that the sustainable growth rate turned out to be surprisingly high but that the achievable *levels* of real (inflation-corrected) GDP and employment are higher than was thought possible. We were able to enjoy a longer and stronger recovery from the 1990–91 recession than expected, during which our year-to-year growth could be temporarily high. But we cannot have unsustainably high rates of growth indefinitely. Sooner or later the economy must run out of workers and industrial capacity. And then growth is limited by the normal increases in the population of workers and in their productivity, according to current estimates amounting together to 2.25 or 2.5 per cent per year.

Many observers are impatient with this analysis. They want the USA to grow faster indefinitely. (As a statistical matter, maybe the same errors that lead the Consumer Price Index and other price measures to overstate inflation lead our measures of output to understate its growth equivalently. The trouble with this correction is that, extended backwards 3, 6, 9 decades, it implies we were incredibly, dreadfully poor. Anyway neither our present affluence nor our dissatisfaction with it and with its pace of increase can be altered by statistical correction.)

Various panaceas are touted to speed up growth. Jack Kemp seems to believe talking it up will do most of the job. Republican supply-siders propose tax cut after tax cut. Steve Forbes promised that his flat tax would double the growth rate. Unions want protection against imports. Bob Dole promised a rise of a full point if his cuts in income taxes were enacted. He also expected miracles if only the Constitution were amended to require budget balance.

There is a defensible argument that a balanced or surplus budget, whether or not constitutionally required, could accelerate output for a few decades. It would raise national saving and investment. More capital per worker would raise labor productivity. This is valid if the additional saving is in fact invested and not dissipated in recession and unemployment (a job for Greenspan), and if the budget austerity does not sacrifice public investments in infrastructure, education, science, research and development of equal or higher social value. At best, the contributions of additional private and public investment to growth are slow and difficult. There are no magic wands.

I hear more and more about a New Era, an idyllic paradise of rapid productivity growth, ever lower unemployment, Dow to 10 000 in year 2000, and general good feeling. One prophet is my most successful graduate student, Wall Street guru Ed Yardeni. New Era optimists think the growth of the 1990s recovery is sustainable. I subscribe to the more modest perception that the inflation-safe unemployment rate really has returned to 5 per cent or lower, even perhaps to the 4 per cent claimed by us Kennedy economists in 1961.

It may be true that, quite apart from any policies of government, the pace of technological progress will prove to have speeded up on its own, eventually bearing fruit in GDP growth rates of 3 to 4 per cent per year. The spectacular progress in electronics has yet to show up in sustainable aggregate productivity numbers, but maybe it will. Or maybe it eludes our old-fashioned measuring tools.

So far as the US economy is concerned, the answer to the question in my title is: Alan Greenspan is at the helm.

JAPAN, RUDDERLESS

Economic performance in other advanced democratic capitalist economies are disasters and disgraces, steadily worsening.

Consider Japan, where savers earn 1 per cent on deposits and long-term-government bonds bear 1.5 to 2 per cent interest. Those low interest rates are no reason to rejoice. They are a symptom of an economy in deep prolonged depression. No one sees enough profit to want to borrow and invest even at those rates. The situation reminds me of the 1930s in the USA, where similar rates were also symptoms of a depressed economy.

In such circumstances monetary policy is impotent; rates cannot go below zero. Worse still, the climate breeds deflation, making positive real rates that deter investment. In Keynesian economics, this was known as the 'liquidity trap', beloved in college macroeconomics courses but long since put aside as an antique curiosum. But here are the Japanese, making it relevant once again!

Keynes also pointed out the solution: fiscal policy, that is deficit spending – tax cuts, public works. Japanese policy is as perverse as that of
Hoover, and Roosevelt too before he learned better, trying to balance a
budget that the depression itself throws into deficit.

The Bank of Japan seems to be trying to lift interest rates to stem the fall
of the yen. Low rates encourage Japanese wealth-owners and portfolio
managers to move funds overseas into dollars, depreciating the yen, raising
the Japanese trade surplus and the American trade deficit, and arousing the
anger of the US government. But raising rates would prolong and deepen
the slump.

The sorry Japanese macro performance is at the root of the currency
crises of Southeast Asian countries. Their currencies were tied to the dollar
and became overvalued as the yen fell relative to the dollar. This blow to
their exports resulted from Japan's macroeconomic weakness, which at the
same time directly curtailed their biggest export market.

EUROPE, THE INVISIBLE HAND AT THE HELM

Consider Europe. In October, Germany's central bank, which sets the monetary tune for most of Europe, raised its discount rate. Why? There was no
provocation from inflation, steady at 2 per cent, and unemployment was in
double digits and rising. The explanation that the Bundesbank needed to
align itself with neighboring central banks was laughable, as those acolytes
confirmed by matching the Germans' upward boost. Possibly the
Bundesbank wanted to start the new single-currency regime off in 1999
with the new European Union central bank hewing to a tough strong-euro
line.

Norbert Walter, the chief economist of the Deutsche Bank, Germany's
leading private bank, proposed in a *New York Times* op-ed piece an ingenious solution to US and German labor market problems. The USA faces
shortages of skilled workers; Germany has a glut of them. Move those
German unemployed to America. They possess high skills, good educa-
tions and excellent work habits. The question arises why these sterling
craftsmen cannot be put to work nearer their own homes. Maybe this
article was just a fanciful critique of German policy, but I am afraid not.

High unemployment in western Europe is a disaster comparable to
unemployment in the Great Depression, although it is less of a human
tragedy because today's Europe is rich enough to buy off the chronically
jobless with generous welfare benefits. The official excuse for the unemployment is then to blame it on the welfare state itself, along with other institutions that create costs and inflexibilities for employers. European

unemployment is structural, we are told, not 'cyclical' or 'Keynesian'. That is, unemployment is alleged not to be the result of a shortage of demand for the goods and services workers produce or susceptible to any monetary or fiscal policies designed to augment demand. Any attempt to reduce unemployment by demand stimulus, in the orthodox view, would fail and would ignite inflation instead. This was the diagnosis in the 1980s when unemployment rates were 6 or 8 per cent, and it is still the diagnosis with unemployment at 11 or 13 per cent. Keynesian remedies have not been tried, anyway have not been tried on a concerted all-Europe basis. Their irrelevance is just inferred from the failure of high unemployment to generate galloping wage deflation.

The offending welfare-state institutions are the same ones of which these continental European countries boasted prior to the mid-1970s, when their unemployment and inflation rates were both lower than those on this side of the Atlantic. After the two recessions which followed the oil shocks of the 1970s, the USA adopted monetary and fiscal policies for recovery and the Europeans chose deliberately not to. Since then their welfare state institutions have been weakened, not strengthened.

Whatever the diagnosis of the unemployment, whatever the needed combination of further structural reform and Keynesian demand stimulus, surely there are feasible remedies. But European governments are complacent about the status quo.

Britain is an instructive exception. When Britain was pushed out of the European Monetary System in 1992, its monetary policy, exchange rate and interest rate thus released from submission to the Bundesbank, Britain prospered and reduced its unemployment rate to 6 per cent. Thatcher reforms had probably neutralized some of the structural problems of the continent.

The Treaty of Maastricht schedules the advent of the euro, the single common currency, for January 1999, now only 13 months away. It is not going to be easy to meet the deadline, but my bet is that it will happen, not for the entire European Union but for most of the 15 members, including the central core of Germany, France, Italy and the Benelux countries, and just possibly the United Kingdom too. Hardly any members will meet literally all the Treaty's requirements for admission to the European Monetary Union (the USA would pass easily, by the way). Since France and Germany, the indispensable leaders, are among the literal non-qualifiers, there will be no way to exclude such suspiciously 'soft' candidates as Italy, Spain and Portugal. Somehow the requirements will be fudged.

The Treaty's requirements for admission to the European Monetary Union reflect the economic philosophy of EU governments and central banks. A country's inflation rate must be no more than one percentage point above that of the least inflationary member. Its public debt must not exceed 60 per cent of GDP, or its budget deficit 3 per cent. The budget limit will continue into the new regime, under penalty of a fine of one half of 1 per cent of GDP payable to the Union central bank, called the European Monetary Institute (EMI).

The reign of the Bundesbank over Europe put into practice an extreme version of Adam Smith, the confident theory that capitalist market economies work just fine if governments stay out of the way, balance their budgets and gear their monetary policies exclusively to price stability. Markets will generate as much output and employment as is compatible with labor-market and welfare-state institution and with systems of taxation and business regulation. Under the European Monetary System, each member's currency was tied to the Deutsche Mark, and each member's inflation and interest rates were essentially those of Germany. Each member's output and employment had to adapt to these realities.

Maastricht solidifies this system by removing, almost irretrievably, the option of withdrawal from the system. Once euro supplants franc or pound or, for that matter, Deutsche Mark, France or Britain or Germany can no longer move up or down the value of its currency relative to other members'. Indeed, member nations will have no tools of macro policy – not exchange rate revaluations, not interest rates, not fiscal policies. The EU as a whole will also lack macroeconomic tools. The EU is not a government like the central governments of other federations, USA, Canada or Germany. The Union does not have enough of a budget to carry out countercyclical fiscal policies even if it wanted to. Conceivably, the EU's new central bank could run a monetary policy like America's 'Fed'. But EMI's mandate will not allow it.

Who is at the helm? Maybe for the time being the Bundesbank, to be succeeded by the EMI. Maybe just the Invisible Hand.

LESS DEVELOPED AND TRANSITIONAL ECONOMIES

The same faith in the optimality of the self-adjusting mechanisms of market economies has suffused the strictures we of the First World have been imposing on countries in process of development or of transition from communism. We want them to balance their budgets, cut public expenditures, privatize state-owned enterprises, open financial and commodity markets to foreigners, establish securities markets, make their currencies freely convertible and tighten monetary policies. Much of this is good advice.

But the stress on open financial relations with the rest of the world is often premature. Stock markets may be a central institution of capitalism. But a country does not become a successful capitalist economy by setting up stock exchanges any more than by painting its name on 737s. Paper-economy institutions are exciting to bright young MBAs and offer opportunities for these elites to become rich in a hurry, without producing wealth for their countries.

Likewise, currency convertibility and free movement of funds in and out put the cart before the horse. After World War II, Western European nations maintained controls over movements of funds for many years, in some cases until the 1980s. In spite of or because of these practices, these countries enjoyed remarkable recoveries and growth, in standards of living, in international trade in goods and services, and in real capital investments to and from other countries.

The experience of Mexico in 1994 and since suggests that playing by the rules pressed on the world by the US Treasury, the International Monetary Fund and other lenders does not immunize a country against financial crises, the aftermaths of which are lengthy punishments with painful consequences for innocent bystanders, millions of ordinary citizens. Mexico had austere fiscal budgets, conservative monetary policies, and non-inflationary wage pacts, but this good behavior did not save Mexico from several years of deep depression once fashions in Mexican and American financial circles turned against the peso. Mexico had made some mistakes, but had committed no crimes big enough to merit its punishments. The speculators, in contrast, were made whole with the help of credit from the USA and the International Monetary Fund (IMF).

The same drama, considerably amplified, with South Korea in the dock, is now under way on the world stage.

FINANCIAL MARKETS, HAZARDS AND REFORMS

Financial markets set up in small developing economies are thin, so speculative crises can be difficult to arrest. When herds of speculators want to sell, prices have to fall a long way before buyers appear. Events in securities and currency markets in the 'tigers' of East Asia are recent reminders. Even the director of the IMF, Michel Camdesus, agreed with this diagnosis in a speech reported in the IMF Survey of 1 December. Reminiscences of Wall Street's Black Monday ten years ago remind us that panics can occur even in our 'thick' markets. Well-functioning markets depend on 'fundamentalists' who take a long view of values and step in for bargains when short-horizon speculators create opportunities. In their absence markets give distorted signals to savers, portfolio managers and the CEOs of corporations.

How can market participants who intend to hold securities for the long run be encouraged while short-period seekers of quick gains are discouraged? One way, embodied in US tax law, is to tax gains on long-held assets at lower rates. (Gains on assets held until death or charitable gift are not taxed at all.

Another device is a transactions tax. It has the right incentive effects automatically. The tax is the same for a given purchase and sale round trip regardless how short or long the trip; therefore its burden, relative to the annual rate of return on the asset, is much less for long holdings. John Maynard Keynes suggested this tax for stock markets in his great book of 1936, *The General Theory*. I have been proposing it for currency exchange transactions ever since 1971. It is often called the Tobin Tax, and at least one magazine writer has wondered, 'How would you like to have a tax named for you?' The purpose of the tax, whether applied to transactions among the big three, dollar, yen and Deutsche Mark or euro, or to transactions involving lesser currencies, is to diminish speculative volatility and also to create more room for international differences in money market interest rates. This would enable national monetary authorities to respond to cyclical differences in economic conditions.

Once again, who is at the helm of the global economy? There was a time when the Group of Seven leading capitalist democracies, their presidents or prime ministers, aided by their finance ministers and central bankers, were supposed to be. But the G-7 seems to have abandoned this objective. So the answer is *nobody*.

This year is the 50th anniversary of the Marshall Plan, described by Secretary of State George Marshall in a 12-minute speech at Harvard Commencement. I happened to be there, to receive my PhD, Marshall to get an honorary degree. The anniversary led to a great deal of nostalgia about those immediate postwar years. They were the occasions for great statesmanship and leadership, not just the Marshall Plan but the building of many other important international institutions – the United Nations, the International Monetary Fund and the World Bank, the General Agreement on Tariffs and Trade, and NATO. These set the stage for the reconstruction of Europe and Japan. Nothing comparable has happened in the wake of our victory in the Cold War. In those days there were farsighted pilots at the helm.

2.   Financial globalization*

Globalization is a fashionable word to describe trends perceived to be dramatically and relentlessly increasing connections and communications among people regardless of nationality and geography. These trends are a general source of amazement and excitement, often of pleasure, often of fear. In the economic sphere, markets are less and less segmented by national boundaries. Both buyers and sellers face wider horizons of opportunity, and by the same token new sources of competition. Globalization affects markets of three kinds: (1) commodities – goods and services of all varieties; (2) labor – workers who produce goods and services; (3) assets and debts – securities, bank loans and deposits, titles to land, and physical capital. Markets of the third type are the subject of my discussion of financial globalization. The speakers who follow will have much to say about other kinds of markets and other aspects of globalization.

Trades of financial assets are the easiest to globalize. Nothing is involved beyond exchanging pieces of paper or making entries in electronic ledgers. The communications revolution makes transactions easy, fast, and cheap. No movements of physical goods or of people are involved. No frontiers have to be crossed. The only barriers are national regulations. As these have been liberalized in country after country, international financial flows have flooded into national securities markets and banking systems all over the world. These flows could be the vehicles by which savings in the advanced capitalist democracies are channeled into productive capital investments in the developing countries of Asia, Africa, and Latin America. Or they could be causes of currency crises, recessions and depressions, unemployment and deprivation in those countries. Or both.

The 1990s have been a decade of disturbances in international finance, beginning in Europe in 1992, followed by Mexico in 1994–5, climaxed by East Asia in 1997–8, Russia this year, and perhaps Brazil in the near future. Is the problem that liberalization in developing and transition economies is still incomplete? Or has it gone too far? That is the big debate today.

Despite the apparent pace of recent financial globalization and its spectacular technological support, it is in fact nothing new. Finance was much

*   This chapter first appeared as 'Financial Globalization', *Proceedings of the American Philosophical Society*, 143(2), June 1999, pp. 161–7.

more completely internationalized in the nineteenth century, particularly the period 1870–1914, the heyday of the gold standard. All countries made their currencies convertible into gold at fixed prices per ounce; for example, the pound sterling was worth about the ratio between the gold value of sterling set by Isaac Newton and the gold value of the dollar set by Alexander Hamilton. There were virtually no restrictions on international financial transactions. In particular, the United Kingdom lent overseas as much as half its national saving, financing the economic development of the Americas, Australia, India, and other realms of the British Empire in Asia and Africa. The Bank of England served as a sort of world central bank and lender of last resort. This regime was destroyed by World War I, the debts it left in its wake in the 1920s, the unwillingness or inability of the United States to take over Britain's pre-1914 role, the Great Depression, and World War II. Globalization gave way to a maze of national restrictions on currency transactions, as governments sought competitive trade advantages in vain hopes of rescuing their economies from depression.

The Bretton Woods Agreement of 1945 brought some order out of world monetary chaos and inaugurated a period of liberalization. Yet, taking into account the new national participants in world financial markets, the pre-1914 degree of liberalization has not yet been restored, and, more important, transfers of saving from developed to developing economies are still, relative to the size of the world economy, much smaller than at the beginning of this century.

Nostalgia for the gold standard is understandable, but it is misplaced. In the 1920s and 1930s it was disastrous. During World War I, Britain had to sell off its foreign wealth and suspend the gold convertibility of the pound. In 1925, Winston Churchill, chancellor of the Exchequer, bowed to the City and returned sterling to gold at the prewar value, that is, $4.86, prompting John Maynard Keynes to write 'The Economic Consequences of Mr. Churchill'. Because of its wartime inflation of prices and wages, Britain couldn't compete at that exchange rate, and suffered depression and high unemployment from 1925 to 1931, when the coalition government finally gave up and devalued. In 1931–3 the determination of other governments and central banks, including the Hoover administration and the Federal Reserve, to defend their gold parities by high interest rates and austere budgets, aggravated their depressions and provoked bank crises. In Weimar Germany the resulting distress hastened Hitler's advent to power. In America, FDR devalued the dollar in 1933–4; this act was the most effective New Deal policy for recovery from the Great Depression.

The worldwide system of exchange rates agreed at Bretton Woods was a sort of gold standard. Every member of the International Monetary Fund set the gold content of its currency. In practice, conversions of currencies into gold were rare; the US dollar was used instead. The United States Treasury stood ready to exchange gold and dollars at a fixed price ($35 an ounce) – with foreign governments, not with private individuals. Countries' pegs to gold and the dollar were adjustable, and devaluations were frequent. This exchange rate system lasted until 1971, when the Nixon administration abandoned the US commitment to redeem dollars in gold. The dollar was under pressure, and the administration was frustrated because it could not get Germany and Japan to appreciate their currencies against the dollar. The upshot was that since 1973 the exchange rates among the three major currencies – dollar, Deutsche mark, and yen – have floated in free currency markets. Other countries have generally fixed their currencies in terms of one of these three 'hard' currencies or some combination of them.

Western European currencies have typically been pegged to the D-mark, the key currency of the European Monetary System. Now eleven of those currencies are being permanently merged into the euro, which will supplant the D-mark and will float against the dollar and the yen. The new European Central Bank will make monetary policy for all of 'Euroland', the new European Monetary Union. The mighty Bundesbank will be just one of the new bank's branches.

Here is a 'trilemma' of which international economists are quite fond: A nation can maintain no more than two of the following three conditions: (1) a fixed rate of exchange between its currency and other currencies; (2) unregulated convertibility of its currency and foreign currencies; (3) a national monetary policy capable of achieving domestic macroeconomic objectives.

For example, consider a government and central bank that wish to reduce unemployment by raising aggregate demand for the goods and services its economy produces. This typically requires cutting the interest rates facing domestic businesses and households and making its products more competitive in world trade. But this is not possible if the exchange rate is fixed and arbitrages across currencies are unimpeded. The country's central bank will then be unable to reduce interest rates below those available elsewhere in the world, particularly in big centers like New York or Tokyo or Frankfurt or London. Maybe the government can empower its central bank by giving up condition (2) and imposing direct controls over movements of funds across the exchanges. Alternatively, the government could sacrifice condition (1) and let its currency float in the market to a lower level at which activity and employment, especially in export industries, would be greater, while lower local interest rates would also be tenable.

In the wake of World War II, it was apparent that the economies of Europe and Asia were in no position to make their currencies wholly convertible. The articles of the International Monetary Fund adopted at

Bretton Woods did not, and still do not, require that of its members. What they do require is 'current account convertibility', namely, that foreigners be free to convert any of a country's currency they earn in trade. 'Capital account convertibility', which would allow any holder of a currency, resident or non-resident, to buy foreign-currency assets, was put off to the indefinite future. Under the Marshall Plan, 1948–51, the United States encouraged European countries to set up a multilateral clearing system for their currencies, while restricting conversions into dollars. Currency exchange restrictions in Western Europe were not wholly abandoned until the mid-1980s. Today, however, the world financial powers, private and public, are impatiently pushing developing countries and transition economies toward full convertibility.

Likewise, fixed exchange rates, adjustable pegs to hard currencies, are the prevailing exchange rate regime among developing economies, 'emerging' and 'transition' and others. Typically, they are 'managed crawling pegs', which do allow for some flexibility. Markets are allowed to move the exchange rate within a specified band. The entire band is itself moved from day to day by an announced percentage, usually designed to depreciate the currency to compensate for a local inflation trend in excess of the inflation trend in the hard currency's economy. For example, the central parity and the band of Brazil's *real* rise at a monthly rate of 0.7 per cent. However, if under market attack the price of a dollar in terms of *reals* should rise to its upper limit (depreciation of the *real*) then the central bank would have to use its dollar reserves to redeem *reals* just as if it were defending a simple fixed peg.

An attack on a currency is like a run on a bank. A depositor worried about the ability of a bank to redeem deposits will want to ask for her cash before the bank runs out, and any depositor worried about what other depositors will think and do will act the same way even if she thinks the bank is solvent. A country on a fixed exchange rate is like a bank, its holdings of hard currency reserves are like the bank's cash, and the local currency assets outstanding are like the public's deposits in a bank. The same instability and vulnerability apply in both cases. For a domestic banking system, deposit insurance is an effective protection against runs, and a nation's central bank acts as a 'lender of last resort' to provide liquidity to banks under attack. The analogous institutions do not exist on an international scale, to protect currencies against runs.

The recent epidemic of currency crises makes it unmistakably clear that fixed but adjustable exchange rates are a bad idea. The only viable regimes in our increasingly globalized financial world are floating rates, on the one hand, and irretrievably fixed rates, on the other.

Floating rates have since 1973 worked for the Big Three currencies. They have fluctuated, but there have been no crises. From 1995 to 1997, the yen gradually and unobtrusively fell 50 per cent against the dollar, but this decline never rated headlines or evening TV news. (One of the causes was Japan's recession and stagnation, a disaster for Japan itself and for its neighbors – indeed a principal source of their currency crises and economic recessions. But this macroeconomic disaster would have been worse if the yen/dollar rate had been fixed.)

Floating rates would work for most currencies. They would forestall extreme crises. Of course, exchange rates would go up and down, people would speculate on them, and often the fluctuations would be unpleasant for the economies affected. But the trauma of discrete regime change, default of solemn official promises, and the bandwagon momentum these events generate, would be avoided. Foreign lenders would be more careful if they understood that exchange rates were not guaranteed. Events that triggered the Asian crises would have likewise pushed down those currencies had they been floating, but surely not nearly as far as they plunged in the panicky free falls following the collapse of fixed rates. Fixed rates are, after all, a hangover from the pre-globalized Bretton Woods system.

At the other extreme is the alternative of fixing the national currency irretrievably to the dollar or some other hard-currency standard. The trouble with this course is that it surrenders monetary sovereignty. This is what the eleven European countries are doing. They will no longer have their individual monetary policies, or even discretionary fiscal policies. It remains to be seen whether political and economic advantages, comparable to those of the two-hundred-year-old monetary union of the American states, can be quickly manufactured in Europe.

An individual country can tie itself tightly and permanently to a hard currency. Examples are Hong Kong and Argentina, which are effectively dollarized. The idea is to sacrifice every other possible objective of monetary and fiscal policies to the defense of the exchange rate. Indeed the dollar may partly or wholly replace local currency as unit of account and means of payment. This is the essence of a 'currency board' – one well enough endowed with reserves of the hard currency to convince the world of convertibility, and convincingly determined to protect those reserves. For example, if it takes double- or triple-digit interest rates to attract and hold enough reserves, so be it, regardless of macroeconomic consequences. The rule is that local currency outstanding must be covered 100 per cent by the central bank's hard currency reserves. In terms of the trilemma, the country meets condition (1) fixed exchange rate, and (2) convertibility. But it sacrifices (3) monetary sovereignty, and thus forfeits all possibility of controlling its own macroeconomic fate.

In contrast, consider China. Like Hong Kong and Taiwan, China is evidently immune to the 'contagious' currency crises that began in East Asia in 1997. But the reason for the stability of the renminbi is quite different. It is not currency-board austerity or any other capitalist virtue. China allows no 'capital account convertibility', only 'current account convertibility', like European countries in the early days of Bretton Woods. In terms of the trilemma, violating condition (2) enables China to maintain the other two conditions, (1) fixed exchange rate, and (3) monetary sovereignty.

The economic rationale for internationalization of asset markets is movement of productive capital from wealthy developed economies to poorer developing countries. But what matters is the net flows of capital, not the gross volumes of transactions. Despite the limited convertibility of its currency, China is benefiting from a quarter-trillion dollars worth of direct investment in plant, equipment, and technology in China by foreign companies around the world. The emerging economies of East Asia, as well as some in Latin America and Eastern Europe, are also beneficiaries of foreign business investments. But much of their capital inflows have taken the form of loans of hard currencies from banks in financial centers like Tokyo, New York, and Frankfurt to banks in Korea, Thailand, and Indonesia. Many of these were short-term, and crises came when the lenders became distrustful and refused to renew the loans.

Although developing countries have increasingly benefited from inflows of capital, the investments that have propelled their growth have been mainly due to their own internal saving. Capital flows from the world economic core to the periphery, only $150 billion a year in the 1990s, have been less than 15 per cent of their investment and less than 5 per cent of the saving of the developed capitalist economies. These shares are much smaller than comparable figures before 1914, when they were both close to 50 per cent.

The worldwide gross volume of foreign exchange transactions is mind-boggling, 1.3 trillion dollars per business day and growing. Nine-tenths of these transactions are reversed within a week, mostly within a day. Clearly many of these are speculative. The gross volume dwarfs the net capital transfers that carry the economic benefits globalization is advertised to bring.

Most observers, Western and Eastern, public and private, in governments and international institutions, in banks and businesses, in big countries and small, now agree that financial globalization went too far too fast. Some reforms are the responsibilities of the borrowing countries. They need to develop the institutions that make financial markets work in the developed world, banking regulation and supervision, transparency requirements like the US Securities and Exchange Commission, bankruptcy procedures. Since their international reserves are at stake, those governments should limit the hard currency exposures of banks and businesses. They should feel free to slow down inflows of liquid capital, by devices such as extra reserve requirements on new foreign deposits in their banks, used successfully in Chile. They should stress import of capital in the form of direct investment and equity. As argued above, they should let their exchange rates float.

I have proposed a system-wide international measure to slow down flows of 'hot money', without interfering significantly with currency transactions related to trade and productive investment. This is a simple small tax on foreign exchange transactions, levied at an agreed common rate by all countries where such transactions originate in significant amount. The tax, perhaps only 0.1 or 0.2 per cent, means nothing for a round trip of a year or more from one currency to another and back. But for one-week round trips it would be equivalent to a difference between interest rates in the two markets of 10 or 20 per cent per year, a palpable protection of monetary sovereignty. Alas, the lords of finance throughout the world will have none of the 'Tobin Tax'. How would you like to have a tax named after you?

3. Financial globalization: can national currencies survive?*

The largest private bank in a small country fails. Frightened depositors and creditors desert this country, its banks, and its currency, and its central bank's plea for foreign assistance garners little response. Affected creditors in neighboring countries, banks and central banks alike, scramble for internationally liquid assets. Interest rates zoom up everywhere, loans are called or not renewed, economic activity sinks, and unemployment quickly rises to politically hazardous rates. The managers of the world monetary system, central bankers individually and collectively, strive above all to maintain the credibility of the system and confidence in existing currency rates. But the effects of their deflationary policies on business conditions instead destroy confidence. In the end country after country has to abandon its commitments to redeem its currency at the promised price. In country after country, then and only then does economic recovery begin, and it takes many years.

The place is not East Asia in 1997–8 but Europe and North America in 1931. The bank was the Credit Anstalt in Vienna. The monetary system was the gold standard, as revived after a hiatus due to World War I. Central bankers, finance ministers, prime ministers, and presidents put defense of the gold values of their currencies above all else. Weimar Germany maintained the gold content of the mark but rationed its gold reserves. Its deflationary policies in 1931–2 – high interest rates, tax increases, no relief or work for the jobless – paved the way for Adolf Hitler's accession to power in January 1933. In September 1931 Britain was finally forced off gold, after suffering from hard times ever since 1925, when Chancellor Winston Churchill overvalued sterling by returning to gold at the 1914 gold and dollar value of the pound. In the United States, as the recession of 1929–30 became the Great Depression and the banking system collapsed, the Federal Reserve and President Herbert Hoover stubbornly defended the gold value of the dollar. (Hoover actually had some commonsense Keynesian instincts for fiscal and monetary activism until his Treasury

*   This chapter first appeared as the Keynote Address at the *Annual World Bank Conference on Development Economics*, 1998.

warned him that the dollar's gold standard was threatened.) President Franklin Roosevelt devalued the currency in 1933, and recovery began.

I concur with the views of younger scholars that policymakers' *auri sacra fames* (Keynes's and Virgil's term, accursed lust for gold) was responsible for turning a recession into the Great Depression.[1] The international monetary system – the interconnection of national currencies with one another – was then and is now a crucial factor in global economic stability and prosperity. The presumption that currency crises are the fault of the victims is still all too prevalent among the statesmen of world finance and among media pundits. The common view is that good policies and proper institutions will enable a prudent government to keep its currency convertible at an announced parity in gold or in other currencies. The vulnerability of any economy, especially a small country caught in the commodity and financial markets of a big world, is insufficiently appreciated. So is the intrinsic fragility of a fixed exchange rate.

THE END OF THE BRETTON WOODS GOLD–DOLLAR STANDARD

It has been a quarter century since the United States ditched the Bretton Woods system and adjustable pegs were abandoned in favor of floating exchange rates (not always clean floating, to be sure) among the major currencies – dollar, yen and Deutsche Mark (to which other major Western European currencies have been tied most of the time). Floating among the big three currencies presumably will continue as the euro succeeds the Deutsche Mark.

A fixed-rate system had failed again. One reason for the failure was that the United States could not devalue the rate of exchange of the key currency (the dollar) against other currencies without the concurrence of the other governments. The United States wanted Germany and Japan, in particular, to appreciate their currencies (by lowering the price of gold in their currencies), and Germany and Japan thought that adjustment was the responsibility of the United States. A second reason for the failure, which complicated the currency rate conflict, was the peculiar role of gold in the system. Dollars held by foreign governments were convertible into gold at a fixed price. Private dollars were not supposed to be convertible, but they became so de facto because until 1968 the United States and the United Kingdom fed the private gold market to keep the free-market gold price from getting out of line. US balance of payments deficits increased dollar debt in official hands and depleted the US gold reserves available to redeem those dollars. In the ultimate impasse in 1971–3 the United States abandoned its commitment to pay gold for dollars. Unlike Hoover, President Richard Nixon was not willing to sacrifice US prosperity for the gold standard or for fixed currency exchange rates.

I think he was right. I know that among many wise and experienced observers there is nostalgic longing for a return to fixed rates and talk of a new Bretton Woods. The grass is always greener on the other side of the fence! Floating nominal rates are blamed for excessive variability in real exchange rates. The unanticipated appreciation of the dollar against the yen in the early 1980s looms large in the memories of US businesses affected. I suspect, however, that the shocks that have moved exchange rates significantly since 1973 would have brought irresistible pressures on fixed rates, resulting in reserve crises like those of the 1960s and early 1970s.

Instead of being blamed for the volatility of nominal and real exchange rates, floating rates should perhaps be credited for accomplishing economically desirable revaluations without currency crises. A recent example is the 40 per cent decline of the yen against the dollar over two years – a problem never serious enough to be reported on the front pages of US newspapers.

At the opposite extreme, another way to escape currency crises is to adopt permanently and exclusively a common international currency, as is about to occur within the European Union. This approach, of course, has its own problems. Perhaps a worldwide common currency will be adopted sometime in the next century, but not soon.

A VOICE FROM THE PAST

Given my lack of experience and expertise in the World Bank's world, I am unqualified to speak at this conference. But my old friend and onetime colleague Joseph Stiglitz insisted that I do so anyway. To show that I have at least thought about international monetary problems before and to show that today's issues are not altogether new, consider something I wrote in 1972. This passage occurs in a short book on domestic macroeconomic policy called _The New Economics One Decade Older_:

> The most important barrier to flexible monetary policy is the ever-increasing international mobility of liquid capital. The Eurodollar market is unifying the short-term money markets of the major countries on both sides of the Atlantic. European countries have felt keenly, and complained bitterly, that they have lost autonomy in monetary policy. Even the autonomy of the United States Federal Reserve has been diminished. . . . The interest sensitivity of short-term funds can be expected to continue to increase and to pose even greater problems for the international monetary system and for national monetary policies. . . . [A]s substitution elasticities increase . . . the boundless resources of private arbitrageurs

will just erase any rate differentials the national monetary authorities try to create and sustain.

There is no more important item on the agenda of the coming negotiations for international monetary reform. On the one hand, some agreed central coordination of national monetary policies is essential. Otherwise the common international interest rate level, from which feasible national deviations are limited, will be left to anarchy and tug-of-war. On the other hand, there is nowhere near enough economic and political unity among Europe, North America, and Japan to support a single international monetary policy for the whole group. The new international arrangements must protect some national autonomy in monetary policy.

Unless the . . . world acquiesces permanently in [a] fixed-exchange-rate dollar standard . . . we cannot count on a system in which the Federal Reserve makes world monetary policy. Moreover, the Common Market countries will undoubtedly seek greater monetary coordination among themselves, so that Europe will have more muscle in contest with the Federal Reserve.

[It] is clearly desirable to preserve some possibilities of autonomy in national or continental monetary policies and to defend them against the growing internationalization of money markets. Our economies and governments are not sufficiently unified in other respects – goods, labor, and capital markets, taxes and fiscal policies – to live with a single . . . monetary policy. That is where the analogy with the centralization of Federal Reserve policy [in the United States] breaks down. The same forces that unified short-term securities markets throughout the U.S. also produced . . . national markets in goods, labor, and capital . . . [that] can handle regional differences in . . . circumstances in a way that is not possible in today's international economy. And a national government can carry out compensatory fiscal redistributions between regions; there is no comparable international mechanism in prospect.

How can some international monetary autonomy be preserved? Some sand has to be thrown into the well-greased channels of the Eurodollar market. (Pp.84–8)

I went on to advocate increasing exchange risk by making exchange rates more flexible, either through outright floating or widened bands around frequently adjusted parities. Then comes for the first time a proposal for 'an internationally agreed uniform tax, say 1 per cent, on all spot conversions of one currency into another', in order to 'drive a wedge between short-term interest rates in different national markets' (p.89).[2]

My propositions today are similar but applied to a wider universe. Let me summarize them. First, for most countries, fixed exchange rates in their usual form, adjustable pegs, are a bad idea. Developing countries would be well advised to follow the example of the major capitalist countries and let their currencies float like the dollar, yen and Deutsche Mark. It is hard to understand why this did not become normal practice long ago. It would have avoided the worst consequences of recent adjustments in exchange rates. Is the reason that it would relax the discipline for 'sound' policies exerted by fixed rates?

Second, while globalization of financial markets – the liberalization and deregulation of international financial transactions – has made important contributions to the economic progress of developing and emerging economies and can continue to do so, these trends also threaten the monetary sovereignty of those countries. This is especially the case for a country committed to a fixed exchange rate, an adjustable peg that it has promised not to adjust. The logic of financial globalization is to increase the elasticities of substitution between risk-adjusted rates of return on local assets and debts and those in dollar markets until the local central bank has no margin within which it is free to determine domestic interest rates.

Third, once the central bank cannot make monetary policy, a logical next step is 'dollarization' – or 'yenization' or 'euroization' – allowing one of the hard currencies to become the smaller country's means of payment and unit of account. This approach does have some advantages. The trouble is that the big central bank has no reason to consider a satellite's conditions and interests. The same problems will arise in the European monetary union, but in that case the central bank is responsible to all the members of the union.

Fourth, to preserve a local currency with residual monetary sovereignty, some friction in international financial institutions and markets needs to be retained. This is also true in a regime of floating rates, though floating itself is some protection. The new global financial system should be able to contribute to development without rendering central banks impotent or whole currencies obsolete. The governments, banks, and businesses of developing countries should eschew short-term demand debt or short-term debt in hard currencies. Flows of capital to developing countries should preferably take the form of direct fixed investment or equity.

Fifth, developing countries need to build institutions of financial reform and regulation supportive of modern national financial systems and of independent currencies. The International Monetary Fund (IMF) should concentrate on its intended function as a principal source of liquidity for its members. The resources of the IMF and of its members are pitifully small and should be augmented.

ADJUSTABLE PEGS AND BANK RUNS

The trouble with adjustable pegs is that they can be adjusted and therefore invite speculation that they will be. They are no less a potential invitation for speculation than are floating rates. Indeed, a discrete change in an official parity is much more traumatic. It is a loss of face and a blow to pride. It is an administrative decision, that is to say a decision of policy and politics. It necessarily requires responsible officials – finance ministers, chancellors, central bank chairpersons – to go back on their solemn word. Moreover, they or their successors have the unenviable task of choosing a new rate in a climate poisoned by distrust, clouded by uncertainties about the fundamentals, and dominated by unpredictable psychology. It is easy to get it wrong, thereby prolonging and aggravating the crisis. For all these reasons, there is great temptation to stick with an overvalued parity too long.

A central bank managing and defending a currency pegged to an external hard currency, or to a basket of hard currencies, is like a conventional commercial bank. The bank's deposit liabilities are fixed in nominal value and payable in cash on demand or quite soon. They are 'backed' largely by illiquid or imperfectly liquid assets of uncertain ultimate value. The bank's cash reserves – currency and coin and deposits in the central bank – are only a fraction of its cash liabilities. The bank is nevertheless solvent if patient, informed valuations of these assets equal or exceed the liabilities with high probability. *Patient* means that the valuations allow time for the assets to yield their expected values. Premature liquidations by use or sale are costly or impossible, the more so the greater the proportion of its assets the bank must liquidate.

The discrepancy is the basis for the distinction between insolvency and illiquidity, for the belief that 'marking to market' may understate the eventual value of the bank, and for the function assigned to a lender of last resort – namely, to allow the bank time to attract deposits or liquidate assets. The distinction is not absolute. The bank's world is changed by a bout of illiquidity, and by the events that bring it about, in ways that increase the likelihood of insolvency. Help from a lender of last resort may rescue a bank on the brink of insolvency. On the other hand, the lender may find itself keeping alive a crippled bank that will never survive on its own.

Clearly the expectations and risk assessments of depositors and participants in asset markets are crucial. In a benign equilibrium of the bank these estimates are rational and generate patterns of behavior and valuations that keep a basically sound bank liquid. The 'last resort' does not arise, and its lender stays on the sidelines, while its existence supports the equilibrium. But the benign equilibrium is fragile. Every depositor is continuously deciding whether to withdraw cash or not, and her decision depends mainly on what she thinks others are deciding. Adverse events or rumors may tip the scale to runs and panics. Contagion from failing banks nearby can doom intrinsically solvent banks.

Why should a depositor keep funds in a bank if she gains nothing and may lose everything? Bank services are one reason, and nowadays some interest is generally credited. But government deposit insurance, explicit or implicit, is usually essential to keep depositors content. To offset the moral hazard incentive of banks and depositors to seek risky gains while the insurer absorbs the losses, it is necessary to regulate and oversee the balance sheets of insured banks – as the debacle that followed deregulation of the US savings and loan industry in the 1980s dramatically confirmed.

Besides the benign equilibrium, supported by deposit insurance and balance sheet surveillance or not, there is a second, malign equilibrium in which the bank has failed and closed. Depositors have withdrawn all the bank's reserves in cash. Other assets have been sold at losses in a desperate quest for liquidity. Or better, a regulator has closed the bank promptly enough to conserve some assets for eventual settlements with depositors, insurers, and other creditors.

The analogy of a national currency to a bank is clear. The central bank has promised to buy back its own currency with external currency at an announced price, and for that purpose holds reserves of hard currency. In the benign equilibrium of this case, expectations in currency markets around the world support behaviors that validate the expectations and sustain the pegged exchange rate. In the second, pessimistic equilibrium the central bank defaults on its commitment. Like bank depositors worried about what other depositors will do, holders of a pegged currency fear that they will act too late to save their assets. Potential claims on central bank reserves include not only the external liabilities of the central bank and the government but also those of private banks, businesses, and households (domestic and foreign). All the liquid local currency assets they hold can potentially be tendered to the central bank and government to buy up their holdings of hard currency. If those assets are then spent or exchanged for nonliquid assets, they can again fall into hands that will convert them into hard currency.

The benign equilibrium is fragile because estimates of its viability at home and abroad are interdependent, and panicky rushes to convert local into foreign currency can force the central bank to abandon its commitment and let the currency fall – even though economic fundamentals indicate that the currency is worth, if not its original pegged value, much more than its crisis price.

The analogy between the bank-deposit-and-local-currency choice and the domestic-currency-and-foreign-currency choice is imperfect in one respect. Whereas an uninsured bank deposit will not appreciate above its contracted cash value, the local currency's exchange value can rise as well as fall. In practice, however, the exchange rates of developing country currencies often gravitate to the high ends of their bands or of traders' confidence intervals. When currency speculators see only downside risk, they sell – just as depositors run for cash if they see no chance that their bank's condition will improve.

Advocates of fixed rates regard the benign equilibrium as normal and sustainable and the runs as anomalous and avoidable. It is just a matter of adopting and maintaining policies that engender confidence. In the design of so-called bailout packages to reverse attacks on the currency's exchange rate in times of incipient crisis, the first priority is to promise measures that the 'market' will regard as sound. But these measures must overcome the adverse momentum of *sauve qui peut* (get out fast if you can) panic.

Moreover, a suspect currency typically is thought to be overvalued. Perhaps the inflation rate has exceeded the rates of competitors and trading partners. Perhaps export markets are slumping. Perhaps the current account is turning into deficit, reflecting borrowing for domestic consumption rather than productive investment. There may be no credible package of measures that can save the exchange rate or reverse its decline.

An extraordinarily high interest rate is the usual emergency therapy. The idea is to devalue the currency against its own future value, inducing people to hold onto it despite the expected decline in its foreign exchange value. If this works, it raises both the current and the expected market exchange rate. But tomorrow, if the adverse expectation is fulfilled, the rate is again lower. Only when (and if) favorable changes in markets occur can the currency be stabilized without keeping the interest rate extraordinarily high. Meanwhile, the economic damage of that interest rate may be dragging down the exchange rate's prospects. High interest on public debt increases the budget deficit, undermining the recommended therapy of fiscal austerity.

CURRENCY BOARD, MONEY BOARD?

A currency board requires 100 per cent reserves in hard currency against the local currency monetary base. If reserve assets can be bought from the central bank with bank checks, this requirement is no guarantee that the central bank will not run out of reserves. If local currency is a ration coupon for external reserves, bank depositors could obtain these tickets by withdrawing cash from their deposits. Distrust of the currency would then be accompanied by a bank panic. After all, the purpose of a currency board is to freeze the central bank into a permanent commitment to an exchange rate fixed at a particular value, if necessary forcing draconian tactics (most likely astronomical interest rates) to avert defaults on its currency exchange commitment.

Combining a currency board with fractional reserve banking is awkward. If the size of the monetary base is limited to the central bank's holdings of international reserves, the central bank has no way to compensate for increases in the public's demand for local currency at the expense of its willingness to hold local bank deposits. Increased demand could come about for various reasons: some random and innocuous, such as increases in income and consumption spending, some reflecting public concern over the soundness of banks. However caused, the result of shifting a dollar of high-powered money from bank reserves to publicly circulating currency is to substitute one dollar of low-powered money in currency form for, say, five dollars of low-powered money in bank deposit form (assuming a reserve ratio of one-fifth).

Those of us with long memories recall the bank runs in the United States in the early 1930s, triggered by bank failures and, in turn, the cause of further failures. The unwillingness or inability of the Federal Reserve to respond with open market purchases to expand the monetary base was disastrous, dooming both the economy and the banking system. At the time Federal Reserve monetary base liabilities were not constrained by a currency-board-type 100 per cent gold reserve requirement, although they were supposed to be backed by some combination of gold, Treasury bonds, and commercial paper eligible for rediscount. The point here is that a currency board makes it impossible for the central bank to perform its normal domestic functions – either that of macroeconomic stabilizer or of lender of last resort.

A 100 per cent reserve requirement on bank deposits is a logical extension of the currency board idea to a money board system. It would allow the system, originally used in British colonies dependent mainly on paper money, to catch up with the rise of bank deposits as the main medium of exchange.

A 100 per cent reserve banking system would tighten the country's commitment to its exchange parity, but at heavy cost. It would deprive the economy of the intermediary functions performed by fractional reserve banks. Presumably some non-bank intermediaries would take their place. They would seek liabilities to the public as close to bank deposits as the authorities permit. These would require some regulation, although the availability of fully backed deposits in narrow banks would relieve the government of moral compulsion to guarantee the liabilities of other intermediaries.

A currency board, or a more comprehensive money board, sacrifices real macroeconomic performance in all its significant dimensions – employment, production, income, growth, trade, saving and investment – to the strength of the currency and indirectly to the prevention of inflation. When the successes of the device are touted, it is in these narrow terms. The currency board is an extreme form of the fixed exchange rate as a 'real anchor', a tactic of national self-discipline popular in recent years. However, the true test of successful policy is not conquering inflation with an open-ended sacrifice of prosperity but conquering inflation while achieving full employment and reasonable growth in economic well-being. Argentina stabilized prices by tying its currency to the dollar, but its unemployment rate is stuck in the double digits.

In any case, it is by no means certain that a currency board or any similar fixed exchange rate commitment will work. Once again, there is a bad outcome as well as a good equilibrium. If the initial stock of external reserves is small, the cost in economic activity of cutting the stock of local currency may be devastating, and it may set off a scramble for hard currency. Those who get their hands on local currency will buy up the central bank's hard currency and force further deflation on banks and the economy. These unstable dynamics will force the country to cut itself loose from the currency board.

A successful commitment to a fixed exchange rate requires an ample initial stock of unborrowed reserves, as well as policies that reinforce the virtuous circle of the good equilibrium, as in Hong Kong (China) and Taiwan (China). In less auspicious circumstances the real anchor strategy has contributed to overvaluation of the currency. This can happen when the small country's inflation exceeds expectations or when the anchor country's inflation declines.

WHY NOT THE DOLLAR?

The currency board arrangement is a way, albeit somewhat technically flawed, of surrendering independent monetary policy and acknowledging subordination. At that point, why not go all the way, drop the local money, and adopt the hard currency as a medium of exchange and unit of account? Argentina is well on its way to doing this. Federal Reserve policymakers, however, are not going to weigh macroeconomic problems in Patagonia even as much as those in Idaho. But this is the destination to which financial globalization is taking developing countries, whether the IMF, the US Treasury, and the other lords of international finance acknowledge it or not.

In a dollarized regime some of the functions central banks now play might be taken over by private banks. They would accept deposits in dollars, as many do already. The acceptance in New York of checks in dollars drawn on Indonesian or Korean banks might be subject to a discount reflecting the reputation of the bank and its assets, like the discounts on bank notes issued by wildcat banks in the American West in the 19th century. Those discounts could take the place of an exchange rate. Of course, in an integrated global financial system US-chartered banks would be competing in Indonesia and the Republic of Korea for deposits and loans.

The informal use everywhere of dollar bills for hand-to-hand currency and 'under the mattress' hoarding is one thing. Adoption of the dollar as legal tender, in place of or in addition to a country's national currency, is quite another. This move would best be negotiated between governments, so that the handling of checks between banks in the smaller country and the United States could be systematized. Similar problems have been painstakingly resolved in the European Union. Effective internationalization is not unmitigated laissez-faire.

Dollarization deprives the government of the small country not only of monetary sovereignty but also of seigniorage. Given the costs of borrowing in dollars, inclusive of country risk premium, this could be a substantial fiscal loss.

IN PRAISE OF DIRTY FLOATING

Surely the most important lesson of currency crises is the most obvious. Countries should not peg their exchange rates. They should let them float. They should not even confine rates to a broad band, with or without a moving central parity. If an exchange rate hits the bottom of the band, it is pegged and invites speculative attack. Just let it float.

I am not a purist. I think dirty floating is all right. Interventions are sometimes called for and need not be transparent. For occasional dirty floating – defensive or offensive – hard currency reserves are needed. The central bank must husband them in the national interest, whether the exchange rate is fixed or floating. In either case the government needs to limit private external financial transactions that may force the country to lose reserves or to suffer unwelcome currency depreciation.

GLOBALIZATION AND FINANCIAL REFORM

Developing economies, especially the East Asian tigers, have made great strides in liberalizing and globalizing their financial systems, markets, and institutions. Local non-financial businesses borrow, lend, and sell shares in major international markets. The balance sheets of banks and other financial institutions contain assets and liabilities in various currencies. Gross volumes of currency transactions involving these economies have multiplied, and net flows of private capital into these economies have greatly increased. No doubt these developments reflect liberalizations that have opened these economies to foreign investment and made them increasingly attractive.

At the same time, some aspects of financial globalization are perilous to the health of central banks and economies, as recent currency crises show. This is especially clear in fixed exchange rate or adjustable peg regimes. When private banks and businesses can borrow in whatever amounts, maturities, and currencies they choose, they create future claims on their country's reserves. This may force on the central bank and the government monetary and fiscal policies that sacrifice the country's prosperity and growth in order to protect the reserves on which these debts are potential claims. They might indeed threaten to exhaust the nation's reserves.

Integration and perfection of financial markets will bring money market interest rates in different financial centers closer and closer together. In 1997, US, Japanese and European banks saw loans to Korean banks as great opportunities because the interest rates were higher than those they could earn at home. At the same time, Korean banks seized the chance to borrow at what they regarded as low rates. Arbitrage was chipping away at the risk premium implicit in the rate differentials. The longer the peg of the Korean won survived, the closer the Korean short rate (whether on won or dollar liabilities) would come to New York or Tokyo rates. As net demands across markets become more elastic with respect to interest rate differentials, the less autonomy the central bank of the smaller country will have over its interest rates and monetary policies. The smaller country loses monetary sovereignty and becomes in effect a monetary province of the large country to whose currency its own is pegged.

Short-term private bank debts in hard currencies were fatal to the Indonesian and Korean currencies in the last months of 1997. These debts, though they seemed to the foreign lenders and domestic borrowers directly involved to be straightforward business deals, visited that were severe negative externalities on their fellow citizens, bringing about currency crises devastating to entire economies.

The central bank, committed to honor the peg and to maintain the country's terms of trade, has to protect its reserves. It cannot be indifferent to the claims on those reserves negotiated by private parties, domestic and foreign, who ignore the social risks. An obvious precaution is to limit even to zero the net indebtedness (particularly the short-term debt) in hard currency permitted any private bank. The device used in Chile and Colombia, an extra reserve requirement, is evidently successful. It is more important to slow down incoming funds than outgoing money and to install such hurdles permanently rather than just in emergencies.

These grains of sand in the wheels are, to be sure, departures from the goal of complete integration, with universally free asset markets blind to currency denominations, geographic locations, political jurisdictions, and nationalities of transactors. But it is hard to see how governments outside the major industrial capitalist democracies can maintain monetary sovereignty without some regulations to protect their international reserves.

It is worth considering why China is evidently immune to the 'Asian flu'. It is not because China has a currency board, or, like Taiwan (China) and Hong Kong (China), immense nest eggs of hard currency reserves. Rather, it is because China restricts the convertibility of its currency. Only foreigners who have earned renminbi in commercial transactions are guaranteed the right to convert them into foreign currencies. Free capital account convertibility, the essence of financial globalization, does not exist. As a result, China has ample monetary sovereignty. Restricted convertibility has not deprived China of massive infusions of foreign capital and technology.

In the 'bailout' packages for East Asian economies further cross-border financial liberalization was one of the conditions imposed by the IMF and the US Treasury for official loans. This was a surprising requirement, given the evident facts that excessive private external short-term debt was, if not a cause of the crisis, a serious aggravation of it, and that banking and financial institutions seemed to need more regulations in several respects as well as fewer in other respects.

US experience suggests the importance of distinguishing among several kinds of public regulations of financial institutions and markets. First are requirements designed to make markets work better, by outlawing fraud and self-dealing and by requiring depositories, investment banks, and sellers of financial instruments to inform the public clearly and completely exactly what it is they are selling. Second are limitations on balance sheets of intermediaries, in cases where the public cannot be sufficiently protected by information alone or where the state has an implicit or explicit responsibility to compensate losers. Third are protections of competition against concentration and collusion in restraint of trade. Fourth are regulations like reserve requirements and capital ratios, which are essential to make government policies workable. Fifth are orderly legal procedures for handling bankruptcies and defaults. (A useful precedent for handling the rash of insolvencies now afflicting some East Asian economies is the US Depression-era Reconstruction Finance Corporation. For example, this corporation put public money into defunct companies by investing in their preferred stock. Preferred stock was also offered to depositors in failed banks up to the amount of their lost deposits.)

On the other hand, US history is also full of insalubrious regulations designed to protect vested interests against competition – forbidding entry into particular markets, setting prices and interest rates, distorting market outcomes by taxes and subsidies. Presumably we want developing countries to follow our good examples and not our bad. Let us encourage them to build good national financial systems, not just to open their doors ever wider.

Some critics of the victims of the currency crises and of the bailouts extended to them assert that if governments and international agencies would just get out of the way, free markets would reach ideal solutions to all the problems. We economists should be cautious in applying 'invisible hand' propositions – the theorems of optimality of competitive equilibrium that we love so much – to money and finance, especially international money and finance. Those theorems apply strictly to a single closed real economy, without money, presumably one where incredibly efficient multilateral barter determines relative prices and allocates resources over future times and states of nature.

Fiat money does not figure in production or utility functions, so why it has a particular value or any value at all is one of those puzzles that economic theorists pose for themselves. Even more mysterious are the relative values (exchange rates) of various fiat moneys, none of which has intrinsic value. Since these are creatures of governments, it is not surprising that some government regulations are necessary to make them work. I certainly am not saying that we can dispense with governments or money. Quite the opposite. We do not in fact have moneyless efficient multilateral barter. I am simply warning against relying on a priori ideological shortcuts instead of pragmatic architecture.

WE NEED LENDERS OF LAST RESORT

Moral hazard has become almost as fashionable an expression as *transparency*. Many pundits have discovered that moral hazard is intrinsic in 'bailouts', the prejudicial word for lender of last resort operations, and they are generally quite indignant about it. Among economists and financiers looking for better ways of handling future debt crises, minimization of moral hazard seems to be the primary goal. I think this is a misplaced priority. In liquidity crises that necessitate emergency loans, lenders and borrowers may be spared losses of principal, but they hardly escape unscathed. They are not likely to find the experience one they would wish to repeat. More important, the social costs of unmitigated currency collapse extend far beyond the parties to financial deals, to ordinary people who lose jobs, savings, and income. It is worth putting up with some moral hazard in order to limit these third-party effects.

The IMF needs to take a lender of last resort responsibility more seriously. It was founded to tide members over during temporary liquidity crises, not to shape the permanent economic structures of economies and guide their long-run development strategies. For its fire-department function, the IMF needs more money, not less, and more than is currently under debate. Aggregate quotas of $150 billion? That is peanuts! Within larger quotas, members should have bigger unconditional drawing rights.

A PLEA FOR HUMILITY

A final remark. One of the more unseemly by-products of the East Asian crisis is the triumphalism of US commentaries on the events. The currency troubles have been interpreted as demonstrating the hollowness of the 'Asian model' of capitalism. Not many years ago many Americans admired and feared the performance of Japan and the smaller East Asian economies. We wondered whether their model of capitalism, in particular of corporate governance and employment, was better than ours – and we hated having to consider that possibility. Some silly popular economics books exploited these worries. Then the Japanese slump of the 1990s and now the come-uppance of the miraculous East Asian tigers, in contrast to American and British prosperity, have given us new confidence in the 'Anglo-American model'. Some spokespeople for our kind of capitalism have not resisted the temptations of triumphalism – even though the over-zealous reach of our practitioners of global finance might bear some responsibility for the crisis.

NOTES

1. Keynes's essay of that title was published in his *Essays in Persuasion* (New York: Norton Library, 1963, pp.181–5).
2. The 1 per cent tax I suggested then was much too high. A practical tax would be one- or two-tenths of 1 per cent.

REFERENCE

Tobin, James (1972), *The New Economics One Decade Older*, Princeton, NJ: Princeton University Press.

4. Foreword to *Global Capital Flows**

The fantastic revolution in financial markets of recent decades is still gaining momentum. Thanks to technological miracles of communication and computation, the scope and volume of financial activities rapidly multiply, greatly surpassing the growth of other industries. Advances in mathematical sophistication and statistical technique, combined with powerful entrepreneurial response to new opportunities, have kept pace with the new hardware. The number and range of financial instruments and markets have ballooned.

These developments are encouraged by the dominant trends in political ideology and economic policy throughout the world – in leading capitalist democracies and in former communist countries, in the Third World and in the First. Prevailing doctrines foster deregulation and privatization; they downsize governments and exalt free markets; they stress international trade and investment as against economic nationalism and protectionism.

Not surprisingly, the approach to free worldwide markets has been more rapid and more thorough in the financial sphere than in the production of goods and services. Likewise the expansion of financial activity has dwarfed the growth of output and trade in 'real' economic activity. Even in the emerging economies enjoying spectacular real growth, the 'paper economy' has zoomed even faster. In Russia and other former Soviet republics, finance has been virtually the sole growth sector. Indeed in transition economies financial markets are welcomed as the hallmarks of capitalism. They are the easiest institutions to import, and they are the avenues to fabulous wealth for the privileged elites who understand them.

In the advanced capitalist democracies, too, financial ebullience contrasts with disappointing real performance. Productivity growth has yet to recover from a slowdown that began in the early 1970s. In addition, Western Europe and Japan have been suffering macroeconomic stagnation since the early 1980s. Even in these countries, with well-established monetary and financial institutions, paper-economy enterprises have been the sources of new concentrations of wealth, attracting the energies and abilities of the best young minds.

---

* This chapter first appeared as 'Foreword' to Stephany Griffith-Jones, *Global Capital Flows: Should they be Regulated?*, Macmillan Press, 1998, pp.xi–xiii.

Globalization of free markets has been much more rapid in finance than in trade. Barriers to cross-border transactions in capital assets have been falling away much faster than national obstacles to movements of goods and services. Current financial orthodoxy is pressed on developing and transitional economies by international lenders: the International Monetary Fund, the World Bank, and the European Development Bank; by the United States, the European Union and other sources of inter-governmental credit; and by private investors and lenders worldwide. Economists from First World countries, offering advice to fledgling capitalist regimes, deliver the same messages: welcome foreign banks and financiers. Integrate your financial markets, old and new, with those abroad. Make your currency freely convertible into dollars both by foreigners and by residents. Follow resolute anti-inflationary monetary and fiscal policies. These, they are told, are the first requisites of successful reform.

Likewise, in the First World itself, countries of the European Union are among under the Treaty of Maastricht to a single currency, with integrated and largely deregulated asset markets and financial institutions. Not only are microeconomic financial regulations being minimized, but governmental macroeconomic policies are being virtually abandoned. The member governments will, of course, have no monetary polices. Their fiscal outcomes will also be strictly circumscribed, by the rules of the Union and by private bond markets, which will punish members who 'misbehave' in deficit finance and inflation. The Union itself will have too small a budget to have a fiscal policy. As for monetary policy, the mandate of the Union central bank will be to stabilize the price level, evidently regardless of outcomes in unemployment and production.

The orthodox prescriptions have not, at least not yet, generated the prosperity and growth that are supposed to be the glories of free markets. The problems of Europe, and specifically the difficulties of recent years in the European Monetary System, are not reassuring. The Mexican crisis of 1994 and its economic aftermath appears to be a case where the government followed orthodox precepts and its economy was severely punished for crimes it had not committed.

In this book Stephany Griffith-Jones reviews the breathtaking recent history of financial deregulation, liberalization, and globalization. She sees considerable merit in these trends, at the same time that they can and sometimes do generate volatility and instability that inflict real costs on whole economies. She earnestly seeks some feasible compromises.

A great advantage of financial liberalization is the creation or perfection of markets where buyers and sellers can make transactions of mutual benefit. An important feature of the invention of new instruments and contracts is that the markets where they are traded achieve welfare-increasing reallocations of risks. The range of possible losses that can be insured is enlarged.

Sometimes events that bring losses to A bring gains to B, so A and B welcome the chance to do business. But typically markets are not naturally balanced, and 'risk management' requires the participation of speculators, who assume part of the risk. They perform important functions. At the same time, their self-generated expectations, enthusiasms and fears can impact excess volatility to asset prices.

Some of the risks most important to ordinary individuals and families are still not covered by private markets: inflation, unemployment, disability, obsolescence of skill. Insurance of many individual risks is rife with moral hazard, especially when there is a residual public commitment, even if only implicit, to victims of misfortune.

Enthusiasm for free financial markets boast that they make assets liquid to all holders, even when they are intrinsically illiquid. A creditor can sell off his loan to a farmer or a businessman or a government long before it is due. A share-owner can liquidate her equity in a joint stock company, though the shares are titles to durable machines and buildings of no use or value outside the company. Facilitation of such liquidations is a public service. However, it is feasible only if prices are not guaranteed.

With flexible prices, these markets are necessarily speculative. Their volatility and the associated risks must be weighed against the liquidity they provide. After all, the wealth of nations, in the sense of Adam Smith, is intrinsically quite illiquid. Whatever illusions financial markets may create for individuals, nations cannot consume all their wealth at once.

The traditional crises of financial markets generally arise from liquidity promised at fixed prices. This is the business of banks and other depositories, borrowing short and riskless while lending long and risky. The contrast is the reason for regulating their balance sheets. The folly of combining deregulation with contingent guarantees at taxpayers' expense was demonstrated by the debacles of the United States Savings and Loan industry in the 1980s, and by the bankrupt conditions of giant Japanese banks in the 1990s.

Governments must be chary of extending guarantees to owners of mutual funds, pension claims, and other assets of uncertain value. Whenever this is done, institutions' portfolios must be regulated. In the absence of government guarantees, protections of ultimate investors are still essential, but should be informational. Government must insist that investors be fully informed of the risks they are assuming. The United States Securities and Exchange Commission is a good example of informational regulation. It is hard to understand why free market ideologues should oppose measures of this kind, which increase the economic efficiency of these markets. Unfortunately in emerging and transition economies, enactment of such regulations lags far behind the introduction of the markets.

The volatility of liquid flexible-price asset markets stems in part from the Keynesian 'beauty contest' game played by herds of speculators. High liquidity also facilitates arbitrage between assets which are close substitutes, diminishing the costs of moving from one to another, as across stock markets and currency markets. To limit these unwelcome effects, Keynes suggested transactions taxes, which are incentives for longer holding periods. A similar motivated measure is a capital gains tax rate inversely related to holding period.

I have advocated, beginning at the demise of Bretton Woods in 1971, a small tax on foreign exchange transactions, a bit of sand in the wheels of the over-efficient machines of currency deals. I am gratified that the author of this book likes the 'Tobin tax'.

The thin markets in bills, bonds and currencies in less developed economies are particularly vulnerable to swings of speculative fashion. It takes big changes of price to bring forth 'fundamentalists' to buck the speculative tides and arrest or reverse such swings. Meanwhile real production and trade may be devastated, as occurred in Mexico. Millions of third parties, innocent bystanders, lose jobs, business and savings.

Those who rush emerging and transition economies into premature currency convertibility and free trade in financial instruments are not doing those countries a favour. After all, during 1947–72, the halcyon quarter century of economic growth, world trade, and international real investment, some major capitalist democracies maintained controls on currency transactions and capital movements. These were not fully dismantled until the 1980s. Experience has not, not yet anyway, vindicated current orthodox confidence that free global financial markets are the keys to stable worldwide prosperity.

Stephany Griffith-Jones expounds these themes with clarity and conviction, firmly grounded in her thorough knowledge of the theory and practice of the economics of finance.

5. Prologue to *The Tobin Tax: Coping with Financial Volatility**

The publication of this book and the holding of the conference that preceded it testify to an active interest in my proposal for an international tax on foreign exchange transactions – the so-called Tobin tax. Bob Haq, once a student of mine, Inge Kaul, Isabelle Grunberg and their colleagues deserve great credit for their initiative in organizing this project – they assembled leading experts in international economics, development, global finance and world politics. They have certainly earned my gratitude. I appreciate immensely the serious consideration the authors of these excellent papers have given the proposal. Their research and analysis have certainly advanced understanding, mine in particular, of the issues raised by the proposal, while pointing out the need for further study.

THE PROPOSAL AND ITS COOL RECEPTION, 1972–95

I dropped the idea of a currency transactions tax into the pool almost a quarter of a century ago – in my Janeway Lectures at Princeton in 1972 (published in Tobin, 1974). The tax was on my list of measures to enhance the efficacy of macroeconomic policy. In 1977, I was emboldened to devote my presidential address to the Eastern Economic Association entirely to it (Tobin, 1978). It did not make much of a ripple. In fact, one might say that it sank like a rock. The community of professional economists simply ignored it. The interest that occasionally arose came from journalists and financial pundits. It was usually triggered by currency crises and died out when the crisis passed from the headlines.

The idea was anathema to central bankers. The most recent currency crises led reporters to ask Ottmar Issing, the economic brain of the Bundesbank, about the Tobin tax. He replied with some asperity, 'Oh, that again. It's the Loch Ness Monster, popping up once more!' When I next encountered Issing, whom I like and respect, I said, 'Well here I am, the Monster still.'

*   This chapter first appeared as 'Prologue' to Mahbub ul Haq, Inge Kaul and Isabelle Grunberg (eds), *The Tobin Tax: Coping with Financial Volatility*, Oxford University Press, 1996, pp.ix–xviii.

Another source of recent and current interest in the proposal (for example, shown by President Mitterrand at the World Social Summit in Copenhagen in 1994) is its potential as a generator of revenue – revenue that could be dedicated to multilateral purposes, given the probable necessity of having a tax that is implemented internationally. I had suggested this use in Tobin (1978) as a by-product of the proposed tax, not as its principal purpose.

Some of the interest in the tax at the Social Summit and on the fringes of the 1995 Halifax G-7 meeting arose from motivations in a sense similar to my own – to improve the macroeconomic performance of economies trapped by external financial pressures. These sympathizers, though their interest and support were welcome, often seemed to expect more from the Tobin tax than it could deliver.

As for economists, my friend John Williamson, himself a skeptic, remarked at the conference that only now was the idea emerging from the dismissive footnotes where it had long been consigned. I was naturally disappointed by the proposal's summary rejection. Usually, those of my professional colleagues who took any notice of it at all rejected it on the same general grounds that incline economists to dismiss out of hand any interferences with market competition, including, of course, tariffs and other barriers to international trade in goods and services. They seemed to presume that the same reasoning extends to trade in financial assets. Those who did make specific objections said the tax would damage the liquidity of currency markets. They said it would move the world's currency markets to tax-free jurisdictions, like Indonesia or the Cayman Islands. They said it wouldn't keep exchange rates from fluctuating; it wouldn't save overvalued currencies from speculative attacks and devaluations. And they said these things as if I had overlooked them.

Most disappointing and surprising, critics seemed to miss what I regarded as the essential property of the transactions tax – the beauty part – that this simple, one-parameter tax would automatically penalize short-horizon round trips, while negligibly affecting the incentives for commodity trade and long-term capital investments. A 0.2 per cent tax on a round trip to another currency costs 48 per cent a year if transacted every business day, 10 per cent if every week, 2.4 per cent if every month. But it is a trivial charge on commodity trade or long-term foreign investments. I am glad to see that this essential feature was emphasized by Eichengreen and Wyplosz, Frankel and other authors here.

An important general trend in the practical economics of regulation – in particular, the handling of environmental externalities and the safety of workers and products – has been the substitution of taxes and other quasi-price incentives and disincentives for arbitrary and absolute quantitative constraints, whether prohibitions or quotas. The transactions tax is proposed in this spirit. It handles, with built-in flexibility, problems that were formerly tackled by rigid quantitative exchange controls or financial regulations. On this score, it deserves the sympathy of modern economists.

RECOGNIZING THE PROBLEMS OF FRICTIONLESS MARKETS

The tax especially deserves their sympathy in the light of recent changes in the climate of opinion regarding the desirability of completely unfettered mobility of financial capital across currencies. Throughout the Bretton Woods era and for a decade afterwards, official restrictions were common, even among industrial countries with sophisticated domestic financial institutions and markets. In retrospect, those years look pretty good compared with the volatilities and crises of the past 10 years (see the papers by Eichengreen and Wyplosz, and by Felix and Sau). The 'Bretton Woods Commission' chaired by Paul Volcker recently expressed anxiety about world monetary turmoil.

At the annual meetings of the American Economic Association in San Francisco in January 1996, worries about excessive volatility were the main concerns of participants in a session on exchange rates, and the Tobin tax was seen as a potentially useful measure if enforcement problems could be solved (IMF, 1996). Stanley Fischer, First Deputy Managing Director of the IMF and thus the Fund's chief economist, agreed. He observed that exchange rate systems would still need to allow flexibility. I certainly agree with that. I have never believed that the transactions tax could make an adjustable peg system like Bretton Woods viable; the masses of private funds that can move across currencies overwhelm the funds available to central banks to defend parities.

Before 1995, the Managing Director of the IMF was promoting the idea of amending the Articles of Agreement to require complete convertibility of all members' currencies – not just of current account transactions but of all transactions, not just for foreigners but for residents too. The Mexican crisis may have convinced the IMF that there are times when some kind of sand in the wheels may be desirable. In my opinion, this, along with Fischer's willingness to consider a Tobin tax, is a fortunate change of heart. The IMF is in a good position to develop ways in which a transactions tax could work.

OBJECTIVES: REDUCING SHORT-TERM SPECULATION AND INCREASING NATIONAL POLICY AUTONOMY

My main objectives for the tax are two. The first is to make exchange rates reflect to a larger degree long-run fundamentals relative to short-range expectations and risks. While I always recognized that 'fundamentalists' would be taxed too, I thought that they were likely to have longer horizons than 'Keynes-beauty-contest' speculators and therefore would be less discouraged by the tax. Consequently, I thought the tax would strengthen the weight of regressive expectations relative to extrapolative expectations. Volatility – in particular detours from fundamentals (of which Eichengreen and Wyplosz provide several examples) – would be diminished. I am glad to see this commonsense conjecture confirmed by theoretical models (see Frankel) and empirical evidence.

Evidently, 80 per cent of foreign exchange transactions involve round trips of seven days or less. Most occur within one day. An undergraduate student of mine, upon graduating, got a job in the Chicago mercantile exchange and became assistant and apprentice to an active trader who had been an economics professor. After a few weeks the young man made bold to ask his mentor about the long-run calculations that must – necessarily he thought – govern his trades. The reply was 'Sonny, my long-run is the next ten minutes.'

My second objective is to preserve and promote autonomy of national macroeconomic and monetary policies. I realize that here, as is often the case, I am opposed by a powerful tide. A widespread orthodoxy holds that financial markets know best, that the discipline they exert on central banks and governments is salubrious. Adverse capital movements should be taken as a correct judgment that internal fiscal and monetary policies are unsound and need to be changed. The example of Mexico, which is suffering cruel and painful punishments for crimes of fiscal and monetary policy it did not commit, should suffice to raise doubts about the 'markets-always-know-best' proposition. The conference papers, that by Eichengreen and Wyplosz in particular, cite other cases.

WILL THE TAX WORK IN FIXED- AND FLOATING-RATE REGIMES?

My articles of the 1970s were written in the aftermath of the demise of Bretton Woods. By 1978, there was already considerable discontent with the floating-rate regime that had replaced Bretton Woods and considerable nostalgia for fixed rates. I thought that this debate was misplaced. For one thing, the Bretton Woods system could not be restored. In the circumstances, floating rates were an improvement, certainly among the G-3 currencies – the dollar, yen and Deutsche Mark. At the same time, floating rates were not going to restore domestic monetary and macroeconomic policy autonomy – contrary to the more enthusiastic claim.s of its proponents, notably Milton Friedman.

The reasons were the increasing international mobility of massive amounts of financial capital, abetted by deregulation and by revolutions in the technologies of communication and computation. I thought that international interest rate arbitrage among money markets would be increasingly efficient and increasingly beyond the capacities of national central banks and governments – individually and in concert – to control. Yet sometimes the exchange rates brought about by these financial movements, or the interest rates necessary to prevent them, would be damaging to the affected countries. An important contribution of the Eichengreen and Wyplosz paper, and the Felix and Sau paper, is that they document the relationship of intercurrency interest rate differentials to various forms of sand in the wheels – exchange controls, transactions taxes and deposit requirements.

I still do not favor restoring Bretton Woods. Adjustable pegs are not feasible. When they have to be changed, one-way speculation against a misaligned currency is bound to prevail. Devaluation is inevitable, but the process is politically and economically traumatic. Floating rates among the Deutsche Mark, the yen and the dollar allow economies differing in cyclical phase and in appropriate macroeconomic policies to coexist much more painlessly than pegged rates could.

The transactions tax could be helpful in either regime – fixed or floating, or in hybrids like floating bands. The numerical tax costs cited above are margins by which money market interest rates in two currencies can differ without provoking movements of funds. They provide the two central banks with some freedom to maneuver. The tax would not be necessary or possible within a single-currency area, whether the European Union or the whole world.

WILL FINANCIAL ACTIVITY MIGRATE TO THE CAYMAN ISLANDS?

There are two issues on which I have been quite uncertain and inconstant. One is the danger that the tax can be evaded by moving transactions to tax-free jurisdictions. The other is evasion by substituting untaxed transactions.

On the whole, I found the papers reassuring. The studies in this volume are particularly informative on these points.

Regarding the shifting of transactions to tax-free jurisdictions, Kenen's devices seem to be feasible protections. One is to consider transfers of funds to or from such locations as taxable transactions – at penalty rates. The other is to tax at the site where the deal is made rather than at the site where the transaction occurs.

Anyway, I suspect that the danger of pushing transactions to the Cayman Islands is overblown. The already existing attractions of low-cost sites for financial dealings do not seem great enough to drive activity away from London, New York and Tokyo. I doubt that the transactions tax would move them, either. Perhaps agreement on the tax among the G-7 countries and a few other financial centers – the sites of big bank foreign exchange dealers – would suffice.

If not, the administration of a transactions tax could be assigned to the IMF, as I suggested in a recent paper. Each IMF member would be required, as a condition of membership and of borrowing privileges, to levy a tax in compliance with IMF specifications. The carrot would be that most members, all but the jurisdictions of the major financial centers, would keep for themselves the taxes they collected. Implementing this measure would require amending the Fund's Articles of Agreement. In any case, the IMF or the Bank for International Settlements (BIS), or the two together, would be the logical administrators of other details of the transactions tax: the rate of taxation, the definition of taxable transactions and the exemption of some currencies from the tax.

MUST ALL DERIVATIVES AND NON-CASH ASSET EXCHANGES BE TAXED?

Defining those currency transactions that would be subject to a Tobin tax presents some difficulties. I first thought that the tax could be confined to spot transactions. I thought that derivatives need not be taxed, except at the time and to the extent that they are settled by spot transactions in currencies. The purpose of the levy, after all, is to tax transactions that affect the demand for and supply of currencies and thus the spot exchange rate. If you and I bet on the baseball World Series, the bet is a derivative of the game and does not affect the game's outcome. (When it did, as in the Black Sox scandal of 1919, there was hell to pay.) The analogy applies to future contracts and options, which are settled entirely by payments in the currency in which the value of the contract is expressed.

Thanks to Peter Kenen, I see that forwards and swaps are so much like spots that they also must be subject to the tax. For simplicity, the spot contents of such contracts could be taxed all at once.

Peter Garber points out that transactions could be settled in Treasury bills or in agreed mutual exchanges of other assets instead of in bank deposits. He warns that if the definition is broadened to extend the reach of the tax, this process could be never-ending. I am not as worried about this possibility as he is. Widening the range to cover the loophole of mutual deliveries of Treasury bills should not be too difficult. Beyond that, I am consoled by the likelihood that these exchanges can be transformed into exchanges of liquid means of payment only at costs that would probably be no less than the tax itself. If Professor Garber would like to trade his home in Providence for an Oxford don's abode for an academic year, I wouldn't cry over the loss of tax revenue that would have been collected, had the equivalent trade involved two opposite dollar–sterling conversions. I don't think such barters would become routine speculations or hedges. What is important is to tax transactions that make the exchange rates for trade in goods and services volatile and transactions that perfect the arbitrage between the interest rates relevant to monetary policies. The objective is not to maximize revenue.

SHOULD WE TAX ONLY CUSTOMER-ORIGINATED TRANSACTIONS?

Most currency transactions are made between banks and dealers. Three or four such transactions occur for every one transaction initiated by an outsider. Generally, banks and dealers are engaging in these secondary transactions in order to maintain balanced positions. If so, those transactions are not affecting exchange rates. The margins in such deals are very small, so that there is little room for a tax.

Retail transactions with customers, both non-financial individuals and businesses and other financial institutions, are a different matter. They move exchange rates, and the margins are much bigger. They could be taxed, while leaving the secondary transactions tax-free. Recognized bankers and dealers could instead be taxed on the changes in their daily net positions in currencies.

REVENUES WILL BE LOWER THAN EXPECTED

In Tobin (1978), I recognized that a universal transactions tax would raise substantial revenues, and I observed that it would be appropriate to devote the proceeds of an international tax to international purposes. My specific suggestion was to augment the resources of the World Bank, but it was only an example. Raising revenue has never been my main motivation.

In recent years, the burdens on the United Nations and other international organizations have multiplied, while fiscal and political circumstances have caused national governments to curtail their financial support. As a result, the Tobin tax has been seen as a possible source of funds for international purposes. For some advocates of the tax, this is the principal motivation.

The volume of foreign exchange transactions worldwide reached $1300 billion a day in 1995 – $312 trillion in a year of 240 business days. With this volume, it seems at first that even a small tax would yield mammoth revenues, for example $312 billion a year from every 0.1 per cent of tax. I have learned from the conference papers to expect much more modest yields, for several reasons.

First, the tax rate must be lower than I originally thought. It should not exceed 0.25 per cent and perhaps should be as low as 0.1 per cent. Otherwise, the tax would swamp the normal commission charged.

Second, allowance must be made a for tax-induced reduction in the volume of transactions. After all, the primary purposes of the tax, in my mind, depend on just such shrinkage. As Frankel and other authors suggest, the present bank-centered organization of the market, which entails three to eight interbank transactions for every customer–bank transaction, might give way to arrangements that entail fewer taxed transactions. A market organized like securities markets would enable non-bank transactors to make deals directly with each other.

Third, if my suggestion that banks and dealers be taxed only on changes in their end-of-day open positions were adopted, only 30 per cent of the gross volume of transactions cited above would be taxable, plus the unknown volume of taxable open positions. This is roughly the same number as would be taxable if an organized market replaced the present institutional arrangements. The revenue yield would be $94 billion a year for a 0.1 per cent one-way tax, and perhaps as little as half of that because of the tax-induced reduction of transactions volume.

Fourth, the actual collection of the tax could be the job of the tax authorities of member nations. In order to obtain their agreement and cooperation, it would be desirable to let the various jurisdictions retain shares of the collected revenues. For small countries, the shares could be 100 per cent – the purpose of requiring them to levy the tax is not to gather revenue but to prevent them from setting up tax-free facilities, while undermining the tax base of the major market centers. These centers could be expected to dedicate larger shares to international purposes.

Clearly, there are difficult political problems in any international agreement under which sovereign nations levy a tax tailored to international specifications and turn over part or all of the revenues collected. It might sweeten the pill if each nation were allowed to retain at least 50 per cent of the proceeds and to choose – among internationally agreed alternatives – where the tax revenues would go.

Several of the papers argue that the currency transactions tax is not the only possible source of revenue dedicated to international purposes, or necessarily the most appropriate source. I agree that a range of alternatives should be considered. A carbon tax, for example, makes a great deal of sense. I do believe that a well-functioning international monetary and payments system is a public good to which national members could legitimately be expected to contribute.

In summary, the authors of the papers differ in their verdicts on the Tobin tax; many of them are still uncertain. I am neither surprised nor dismayed. I am just pleased that the proposal is finally being seriously evaluated.

REFERENCES

IMF (International Monetary Fund) (1996), 'International Issues Prominent at AEA Meeting', *IMF Survey*, January 22, 32.

Tobin, James (1974), 'The New Economics One Decade Older', *The Eliot Janeway Lectures on Historical Economics in Honour of Joseph Schumpeter, 1972*, Princeton: Princeton University Press.

— (1978), 'A Proposal for International Monetary Reform', *Eastern Economic Journal*, 4 (July–October), 153–9.

6.   Remarks at a round table on Tobin Tax

I begin by reviewing the developments in international financial markets and Institutions that led me to propose a tax on currency exchange transactions in 1972 and to elaborate the proposal in my 1978 presidential address to the Eastern Economics Association, titled 'A Proposal for International Monetary Reform'. This has come to be known as the Tobin Tax. It's no fun having your name attached to a tax these days.

At the time the debate on reform focused on alternative exchange rate regimes, fixed versus floating with variations. A transactions tax was a very different approach. Developments in the near 25 years since have confirmed my concerns.

Capital movements across exchanges, especially gross transactions, have grown rapidly in size and in importance in determining exchange rates, relative to trade in goods and services. Short-term asset transactions have exploded in volume, absolutely and relative to long-term international investments. Thanks to the current revolution in electronics and the technologies of communication and computation, the cost of making transactions has gone down. Internationally, mobile private funds greatly exceed the reserves that central banks and governments hold or can mobilize, individually or collectively.

At the same time, national governmental controls over capital transactions and currency exchanges have gradually been abolished. Even so, even in developed countries, such as France and Italy, some regulations lasted well into the 1980s. But now the tide of deregulation and financial globalization is sweeping the world of LDCs and poor countries, such as Mexico. Originally, the IMF did not require or expect full convertibility of currencies, and restrictions on resident convertibility were common. The IMF sought mainly to make exporters' earnings convertible. Throughout the golden age of the world economy 1947–72, production and trade and international investments flourished despite the prevalence of national exchange controls.

The Bretton Woods system of fixed but adjustable exchange rates – a modified gold standard under which dollars were de facto as good as gold for most central banks – collapsed finally in 1971–3. The dollar was overvalued but could not be depreciated against other currencies, and gold was leaking into private hoards.

Now clearly the adjustable peg system is not viable, because central banks do not have the ammunition to defend the pegs against speculative attacks. For example, within the European Monetary System (EMS), a regional Bretton Woods pivoted on the Deutsche Mark, a member whose currency is under attack must either devalue or defend its parity with high interest rates, at the expense of its internal prosperity, or do both. Mexico was victim of a similar problem.

One solution would be non-adjustable pegs, common currency, as planned for the EU. I doubt this can or will happen soon (except possibly for a core minority of members), and in any case it is not a possibility for the whole world for decades.

The solution actually adopted in 1973 is market floating exchange rates, among the three major currencies and others. This has worked pretty well, notwithstanding nostalgia for Bretton Woods (BW) and gold. But contrary to some claims and expectations countries are not, cannot be, indifferent to exchange rates. Their unexpected changes can do bad things to domestic economies (the USA in the early 1980s, Japan in the last two years). Central banks do not always have power to follow their own desired domestic policies if interest rate arbitrage is too strong.

Like other asset markets, exchange markets are moved by short-term speculators worrying, as Keynes described stock markets, about what other speculators are doing and will do, and overreacting to identifiable current events on which market participants conventionally focus. This is an acute problem in currency markets where most transactions are very short-run, reversed within a week. The problem is not just volatility but deviations from long-run fundamental values. Keynes had toyed with the idea of a stock market transactions tax.

The transactions tax is well designed to deal with these problems – I thought and I think. Most people think its effect is just to deter transactions. They miss the beauty of the tax: it is selectively deterrent. For trade and real investment, which involve long-time round trips, the tax is too small to matter. We are talking about a tax rate for a round trip between 0.1 and 0.5 per cent. It is trivial for a one-year stay in a foreign currency. But if you do it weekly, 50 times a year, the taxes of 0.2 per cent for a round trip add up to 10 per cent to be deducted from your annual rate of return. That wedge means that the market impact of fundamentalists is enhanced, as are central banks' freedom to maneuver. Those are the main objectives.

Of course the tax will not deter all transactions, and should not. A nontrivial amount of revenue would be collected, maybe as much as $100bn a year. In the 1970s, I suggested that such revenue be devoted to international purposes, and I mentioned the World Bank. An international tax should be devoted to an international purpose. Of course, the tax would be levied by national states, which would keep some of the proceeds. Of course, the tax rates and terms would have to be the same in the different jurisdictions. All this would have to be negotiated and agreed by treaty.

How universal would the coverage of such an agreement have to be? Precisely what transactions would need to be subject to tax? These questions bear on the feasibility of the proposal. I know they will be discussed by subsequent panelists, so I will defer comment until later.

I have sometimes referred to the tax as throwing a little sand in the wheels of an excessively lubricated vehicle, the currency exchange market. Sand formerly came from national quantitative regulations. The world economy did quite well in spite of, maybe because of, those frictions. But they are gone now. The tax is preferable because it is a market-based solution – not bureaucratic or nationalistic.

I have to admit that this proposal has been mostly ignored – at most cited in dismissive footnotes – in the quarter-century since I first advanced it. I threw it into the pool, and it sank. It has resurfaced occasionally during currency crises. The chief economist of the Bundesbank, when reporters asked him about the Tobin Tax during one such crisis, said, 'Oh, Oh! the Loch Ness monster again!' We're still friends.

The surge of interest in the last five years comes less from economists than from persons interested in international political economy, who see the need for new and assured sources of funds for the UN or other international institutions, squeezed between the booming demands for their services and the stinginess of member nations, most notably, of course, the USA. I sympathize. At the same time I remind them and you that collecting revenue was, in my mind, not the principal purpose, and also that the Tobin Tax is not the only way of collecting revenue in an agreed international way for international purposes.

I do want to express my appreciation to UNDP, where Mahbub ul Haq and Inge Kaul, here today, organized the first serious conference on the Tobin Tax. Two of today's panelists, Garber and Kenen, contributed important papers – and arranged for publication of the proceedings. Unfortunately, these activities aroused the anger of Senators Dole and Helms, who apparently thought, or pretended to think, that the idea was for the UN to levy taxes on their constituents without votes of Congress.

7.   Why we need sand in the market's gears*

For the peoples of Southeast Asia, the worst is yet to come. The bailouts of South Korea, Thailand and Indonesia will be more painful to more people for more months than the currency crises themselves. The International Monetary Fund (IMF) and the US Treasury are making new financial aid for these countries conditional on their acceptance of economic austerity measures. South Korea, for example, is expected to boost interest rates, raise taxes, reduce government spending and lower economic growth from 6 per cent to 2.5 per cent.

South Korea and other Asian countries – like Mexico in 1994–5 – are being punished for offenses they did not commit. They have inflation and government budgets under control. They are not sinners, but victims of a flawed international exchange rate system that, under US leadership, gives the mobility of capital priority over all other considerations. It is simply too easy for banks, governments, businesses and speculators to buy and sell huge blocks of a country's currency in panicky moments. Such flows of capital can throw a country literally overnight into a crisis.

The lesson of the Asian meltdown ought to be that the leaders of the global economy need to find ways to make the currency exchange system less volatile, so as to protect innocent bystanders from sudden economic crashes that destroy jobs and income. A global tax on currency transactions is one possible solution.

Under the present system, the main priority of the United States and the IMF is to restore and preserve the credibility of national currencies in the eyes of foreign leaders. The main beneficiaries of bailout funds – which make good these nations' debts – are big banks, investment houses and speculators who deposited or lent dollars and yen in Southeast Asia. They will be repaid in full, on time and at the high interest rates that attracted them in the first place. Those rates were high to reflect the higher risks of lending to banks in Asia. But since the IMF bailout program is now making sure that lenders are repaid, there really wasn't any risk.

---

*   This chapter first appeared as an article in *The Washington Post*, Sunday, 21 December 1997, p.C3.

Notably absent from the bailout programs are measures to distribute the burden more equitably between Asian borrowers and foreign lenders. Negotiations to consolidate debts, moderate their terms and stretch repayments over longer periods have been common features of the settlement of international debts in the past, such as in the resolution of the Latin American debt crisis in the 1980s.

Here is the step-by-step breakdown of how capital mobility leads to crisis:

The peg: a country pegs its currency to a 'hard' currency – the dollar, yen, Deutsche Mark or a mixture of them. (These currencies are accepted the world over.) Countries adopt a peg as a way of promoting international confidence in their own currency. Its central bank promises to buy or sell its own currency in foreign exchange markets for hard currency at pegged values. To meet this commitment, the central bank holds reserves of hard currency. Usually the commitment is to a range rather than a precise value, and often the peg crawls down at an announced pace.

Overvaluation: if a country's exchange rate is pegged too high, its exports are costly to foreigners, while imports seem cheap to residents. An alarming trade deficit then arises. Speculators begin to suspect the peg won't hold, that is, that the central bank won't have enough reserves to fulfill its promise to convert on demand its own currency into hard currencies at the pegged rate.

What can make a pegged currency overvalued? A government's inflationary monetary and fiscal policies are often culprits, but external events can afflict the currencies of even prudent governments. Before the Southeast Asian crises, the IMF regarded South Korea and Thailand as models of capitalism. The IMF's 1997 Annual Report praised 'Korea's continued impressive macroeconomic performance' and 'enviable fiscal record', likewise 'Thailand's remarkable economic performance and . . . consistent record of sound macroeconomic policies.'

Japan was a big source of trouble for the Southeast Asian economies in recent years. Because of Japan's economic weakness, the dollar has appreciated 56 per cent against the yen over the past two-and-a-half years. Because Southeast Asian countries had pegged to the dollar, their currencies also rose against the yen, damaging their industries' competitive position in Japan, the region's largest market. To make things worse, Japan's imports were also down because of the country's prolonged depression.

The panic: in free global markets, vast amounts of private money move anywhere at the speed of light. Speculative movements can quickly clean out a central bank's currency reserves once its ability to defend its peg becomes suspect. As in a run on a bank, a herd mentality takes over, forcing the country to abandon the peg and let its currency fall, trying to conserve the remnants of its reserves.

The bailout: suddenly, IMF and US officials judge South Korea, Indonesia and Thailand very harshly. They attribute the plight of South Korea, for example, to the same corporate-state institutions that brought the nation from Third-World destitution in 1960 to First-World opulence today. They prescribe heavy doses of free-market liberalization and globalization. It is hard to escape the conclusion that the countries' currency distress is serving as an opportunity for an unrelated agenda – such as the obtaining of trade concessions for US corporations and expansion of foreign investment possibilities. This is certainly an increasingly popular interpretation among South Koreans.

What can be done to make the world system of exchange rates and financial markets less prone to these sorts of crises?

First of all, let the currency – won or baht or ringgit – depreciate and 'float' in the market to its own level. Don't invite another crisis by pegging again. Floating is a preferable permanent policy. After all, the big three currencies – dollar, yen and Deutsche Mark – have not been pegged to one another since 1971. The advantage of floating is illustrated by the recent appreciation of the dollar and depreciation of the yen – no crisis, no headlines, no bailouts.

Second, as the IMF points out, local banks' short-term debts in dollars and yen contributed to the crisis. Private banks must not be allowed to have debtor positions in foreign currencies that threaten national reserves. Emerging economies have been too ready to imitate the facades of Western financial markets – without the prudential regulations and legal frameworks that make them work.

The fundamental question is: how open should these countries be to international financial transactions, currency conversions, bank deposits and withdrawals, security purchases and sales? The position of the IMF and the US Treasury is that more freedom to make international transactions and to allow banks and other financial firms (wherever they are based or chartered) to function everywhere is always good.

But one conceivable outcome of such a policy is that dollars become the effective unit of account and medium of exchange, whether pegged or floating with the local currency. The country then loses its monetary sovereignty. If the dollar becomes the effective currency of South Korea, then the country's interest rates will essentially be set in New York. The drawbacks are that the Federal Reserve and the US Congress don't have to worry about workers and businesses in Seoul (or Bangkok or Kuala Lumpur), and that America is resented for both its dominance and its indifference.

One way to make the international exchange system more stable would be to establish a tax on currency transactions, a measure I first proposed in 1971. The tax would need to be the same wherever a transaction takes place, so it would have to be agreed upon internationally. It might be administered by the IMF, with the funds retained by the national jurisdictions collecting the tax. The nations involved might also agree to devote some of the proceeds to international purposes. Because this tax would be the same whether funds are moving on a round trip of hours or years, it would be a significant deterrent to short-horizon speculation but a negligible factor in commodity trade and long-run investment. It would diminish unproductive volatility in exchange rates. The 'Tobin tax' could not be expected to protect overvalued exchange rates. But it could moderate their declines and buy time for adjustments.

Events like those in Southeast Asia call into question the claims that liberalization and globalization of financial markets are the path to prosperity and progress. As long as the world is divided into sovereign nation-states, some sand in the wheels of international financial transactions is likely to be beneficial.

8. They are misusing my name*

James Tobin, Nobel Prize winner for economics, is interviewed about the unexpected resurrection of his speculative tax, his troubled relationship with the opponents of globalization and the mistakes of the European Central Bank.

Spiegel: Mr Tobin, here you sit, calm and unruffled, on the lake, while the critics of globalization in Europe are practising revolution under your name. Isn't that enough to tear you away from your garden bench?

Tobin: Certainly not. I have nothing in common with practitioners of revolution against 'globalization'.

Spiegel: The protest organization Attac had originally named itself after you; opponents of globalization are rallying for a Tobin tax. Doesn't it please you that now, 30 years after you proposed a speculation tax on currency transactions, your idea is finally finding supporters?

Tobin: I appreciate attention to my proposal, but much of the praise comes from the wrong side. Look, I am an economist and, like most economists, an advocate of free trade. Moreover, I support the International Monetary Fund, the World Bank and the World Trade Organization – everything that these movements are attacking. They're misusing my name.

Spiegel: This movement seeks the introduction of a tax on currency transactions. The objective is to get some control over capital markets and with the additional revenues to strengthen development assistance for the third world. Doesn't that sound like your proposal?

Tobin: I did suggest that revenues from the tax might go into the World Bank. The turnover tax on foreign exchange trading was intended to limit exchange rate fluctuations. The idea is very simple: on every exchange of one currency for another a small tax would become due, let's say one-half of a percent of the transaction. That would scare speculators away. For there are many investors who put their money into currencies for the very short term. If this money is suddenly withdrawn, the countries have to raise interest rates drastically so that the currency remains attractive. High interest rates often are disastrous for the domestic economy, as was

---

*   This chapter first appeared as an interview in *Der Spiegel*, 3 September 2001.

demonstrated by the crises in Mexico, Southeast Asia and Russia during the 1990s. My tax would restore some room for maneuver to small countries' central banks as against the tyranny of the financial markets.

Spiegel: Scaring away the speculators, breaking the tyranny of the financial markets – isn't that the language of the people who oppose globalization?

Tobin: Mostly, I think, they are interested in the revenues from the tax, with which they want to finance their projects for world improvement. But raising money is not my major objective. I wanted to slow down currency transactions. Revenues would only be a by-product.

Spiegel: What's wrong with using this by-product for good purposes?

Tobin: Nothing. I would be happy if the revenues found their way to the poor people of the world. However, the participating governments at the time would have to make those decisions on that.

Spiegel: Do you feel that you've been misused by the opponents of globalization?

Tobin: I feel that I am being misunderstood and that my name has been wrongly coopted for other people's priorities. The Tobin tax offers no platform for the reforms that these people are seeking. But what can I do?

Spiegel: Don't you at least credit your fans with a good purpose?

Tobin: Their intentions are good, I assume, but the proposals are badly thought out. But maybe I just don't understand it correctly.

Spiegel: What impelled you to develop the Tobin tax in 1972?

Tobin: First, I am a follower of Keynes who, in his famous Chapter 12 of his *General Theory* on the stock crash of 1929, had suggested a turnover tax to marry investors more durably to their assets. In 1971, I applied this tax to the foreign exchange markets. The United States departed from the Bretton Woods system of fixed exchange rates. At the same time, electronic transactions promised to bring an enormous increase in the speed and the number of transactions. I wanted to slow this process down so that there wouldn't be so much speculation and so much volatility in the exchange rates. Now that anyone can make financial deals at any time on his home PC, problems I foresaw have grown by multiples.

Spiegel: Last week the French Prime Minister, Lionel Jospin, spoke out in favor of the Tobin tax – the first head of government to do so; on the international scene more than 300 parliamentarians have by now come to support the idea. Its implementation, however, would have to be carried out at the same time throughout the world in order to avoid loopholes and tax oases. Who should organize that? An international Tobin tax authority?

Tobin: The International Monetary Fund (IMF) could do that. It has experience with the global currency system. Almost every country in the world is a member of it.

Spiegel:　The IMF, of all things? It is viewed as a handmaiden of global capitalism that ought to be abolished – and not just by the opponents of globalization.

Tobin:　On the contrary, I think the IMF must be strengthened and enlarged. Certainly it's made many mistakes – no question about that – but it, like the World Bank, has far too few resources at its disposal to help the member countries, especially the poor and less developed economies. The World Bank and the IMF are not part of a conspiracy called globalization.

Spiegel:　Does that also hold true for the World Trade Organization (WTO)?

Tobin:　Certainly. Its predecessor, the GATT, did much good in expanding world trade.

Spiegel:　Not everybody believes that. In 1999, the WTO meeting in Seattle failed as a result of pressure from tens of thousands of opponents of globalization.

Tobin:　WTO may need more power – vis-à-vis the United States, among others. The WTO ought, for example, to be in a position to prohibit the industrialized countries from setting up all sorts of trade barriers to exclude imports from developing countries.

Spiegel:　The fact is that the industrialized countries flood the markets of the Third World with their goods and use those countries as a source of cheap labor.

Tobin:　I think this whole idea that the IMF, the World Bank and the World Trade Organization are the enemies of the developing countries is misconceived. The problems of globalization will not be solved by trying to prevent it from going forward. All countries, along with their inhabitants, profit from the free exchange of goods and capital.

Spiegel:　Then why has world poverty increased?

Tobin:　It hasn't done that at all. Take South Korea, for example, which in 1960 was a bitterly poor country. Now it belongs with the great industrial nations of the world. The same applies to many other 'Tiger' states, despite the Southeast Asia crisis three years ago. These countries are still more prosperous than they were three decades ago. And they have become that way through trade and foreign capital.

Spiegel:　Individual countries may profit but in global terms the rich are getting richer and the poor poorer. Would you deny that?

Tobin:　Poverty can have many causes. Most of them lie in the countries themselves. They will not improve their situation through some measures the opponents of globalization recommend, such as the worldwide implementation of the workplace standards of the Western nations. Their proposals reduce the competitiveness of poor country imports into the rich markets.

Spiegel: You accuse Attac of being a bad advocate for poor countries?

Tobin: I really don't know details of Attac proposals. The demonstrations you were speaking about were pretty incoherent, but I don' know that they reflect Attac. In general, there are well-meant positions, badly thought through. I just don't want them associated with Tobin.

Spiegel: Have you ever talked to Attac?

Tobin: The chairman of Attac, Bernard Cassen, once called me up and invited me to Paris. The idea was for me to appear there before a few thousand of his cheering followers.

Spiegel: What did you say to him.

Tobin: I regretted, for family reasons and because I did not want to be identified with Attac's objectives. He had not informed me about them. I had no part in their formulation. I haven't heard anything more from him since that time.

Spiegel: How do you explain the fact that your tax idea has many supporters among political activists but is criticized by economic experts?

Tobin: They don't all do that. For the most part, economists simply ignore my proposal. There is a series of books and papers on the Tobin tax, some supportive, some critical, some in between.

Spiegel: Professor Rudi Dornbusch of the Massachusetts Institute of Technology is critical; Robert Mundell, a Nobel Prize winner in economics like yourself, thinks your tax a 'dumb' idea.

Tobin: I hope they are referring to Attac and similar movements, not to my tax per se. But I can believe that Dornbusch and Mundell are against it.

Spiegel: George Soros, for example, none other than the most famous speculator in the world, praises your tax for defending against speculators. Is this, once again, praise from the wrong quarter?

Tobin: George Soros has spoken and written favorably about my proposal. He certainly knows what he's talking about. He has earned a great deal of money in the financial markets. That, in itself, is no sin. Moreover, he has very unorthodox ideas about the world currency system. The finance ministers of the world have more reason to fear him and heed him than me because Soros has the means to carry out his plans.

Spiegel: Do you believe that your Tobin tax will be implemented some day?

Tobin: Not a chance, I am afraid. The decisive people on the international financial scene are opposed to it.

Spiegel: The European finance ministers are going to discuss the Tobin tax in Liège at the end of September.

Tobin: That is likely to be pure show, I doubt they're thinking seriously about it. They don't want to burden their finances with yet another tax. The most important finance ministers in the world are opposed to the Tobin tax, including the US Secretary of the Treasury, whether Clinton's or Bush's.

Spiegel: Why don't we protect the currency markets by simply returning to the old system of fixed exchange rates in which the central banks of the participating countries maintain stable rates?

Tobin: This was tried and failed. Speculators like Soros could outmaneuver the central banks. Look at Argentina, which has tied its peso directly to the US dollar. What's happening there is a disaster, an absolute disaster. Irretrievable exchange rate commitments are an invitation to adverse speculation. The dealers bet on whether the central banks are willing and able to defend the established rates. The system of fixed rates has gone out of fashion, and that is a good thing.

Spiegel: In Europe the concept of target zones is discussed again and again. According to that scheme the currencies of the United States, Japan and the European central bank would have no established rates but broad ranges in which they could reside.

Tobin: That does not really solve that problem. After all, when a currency bumps up against the border of the zone we're right back in the same miserable situation as with fixed exchange rates. Then the rate has to be defended and a lot of currencies are wasted for support purchases. And if the International Monetary Fund also becomes involved the countries may face strict and expensive conditions and penalties. By now even the IMF has given up the idea of firm exchange rates. And that's a good thing. The IMF support of Argentina is an exception to this policy, and a lesson for the future.

Spiegel: Why not avoid currency crises by doing away with currencies? Wouldn't currency unions on the model of the Euro make sense in Asia and America as well?

Tobin: As I see it, the Euro is not exactly the big success that would be a model for other regions of the world.

Spiegel: The Euro is catching up to the dollar pretty well . . .

Tobin: I am not referring to the value of the Euro. What Euroland is suffering from is that, in macroeconomic terms, Europe is not in good condition. The fault for this lies with the European central bank which has not pursued a policy like that of the American central bank – the Fed.

Spiegel: And what might that policy be?

Tobin: Wim Duisenberg, the president of the European central bank, told me once that he has nothing to do with real economics, with growth and employment. His job is to keep prices stable, that is, to fight inflation. If that's all that European monetary policy has to offer then it's not surprising that the economy in Europe is weak.

Spiegel: How did Duisenberg justify his attitude?

Tobin: He has a very ideological view. For him price stability is a kind of religion, as it used to be in the United States amongst the 'monetarists'. Happily, the head of the American central bank, Alan Greenspan, was not one of them. The Fed does not limit itself to keeping prices stable. Greenspan has always said that the Fed tried its best to achieve both – price stability and growth.

Spiegel: Was that a marvellous feat, considering that it occurred during the longest economic boom in American history?

Tobin: The boom was not just historical accident. Greenspan had a lot to do with it, as did the Clinton administration. There's no doubt that Greenspan was lucky, but he was also courageous. In 1994, it was holy writ in the central bank that inflation becomes a threat when the unemployment rate sinks below 6 per cent. When we reached this point at that time and inflation continued to behave itself, Greenspan resisted pressure and did not intervene with tight money. We hit 4 per cent unemployment and nevertheless no inflation – only because Greenspan dared to take a stand against the traditional teachings. Duisenberg would never dare to do such a thing.

Spiegel: Mr Tobin, we thank you for this conversation.

9. An idea that gained currency but lost clarity*

More than 30 years after I first explored the idea of a levy on cross-border currency speculation, the 'Tobin tax' is gaining popularity. In Europe, France's Lionel Jospin and Germany's Gerhard Schröder have both expressed enthusiasm, so, too, have various critics of globalization. Of course, there are no such transactions within the eurozone. But it may be time to recall the origins of the proposal and the uses to which, I believe, it should properly be put.

In 1971, I gave the Janeway lectures at Princeton. My subject was macro-economic policy, in which my long-time academic interest had been deepened by service on President J.F. Kennedy's Council of Economic Advisers 10 years earlier. The early 1970s were troubled times for the US dollar and currency markets were becoming crucial for policy-makers everywhere. In my lectures, I found myself giving much more attention to foreign payments balances and exchange rates than had seemed necessary in America in 1961.

The Bretton Woods system of exchange rates had collapsed after the US withdrawal. As financiers and economists surveyed the wreckage, they mainly debated whether to restore fixed exchange rates or settle for market-floating rates. I though the difference was exaggerated, because fixed rates were not really fixed. They were 'adjustable pegs', vulnerable to change when central banks lost reserves because of trade deficits or speculative runs. The International Monetary Fund still allowed exchange controls of capital outflows but these defences were crumbling. Private claims on central banks' reserves were multiplying much faster than these reserves and IMF resources. Advances in communications and calculations were making worldwide financial transactions fast and easy for anyone anywhere at any time. And in 1971 all this was just beginning.

Why not a single world currency, unadjustable pegs, world currency union for ever, the euro writ large? Very desirable, I thought, but not feasible, then or now, given the heterogeneity of nations. We cannot even yet be sure of the euro. Argentina today is a frightening object lesson.

---

* This chapter first appeared as an article in the *Financial Times*, Tuesday, 11 September 2001.

In 1971, I thought the issue of international monetary reform was not a question of fixed versus floating rates but of how to impart reasonable stability to market exchange rates. I remembered Keynes's interest, after the 1929 stock crash, in a turnover tax to 'marry' investors to their assets. He was thinking of US speculators; his countrymen, he thought, were sufficiently sobered by the London Stock Exchange's own turnover charge.

My principle objective has been to preserve some measure of national monetary autonomy. Market arbitrage and speculation tend to keep money-market interest rates (risk-adjusted) the same in every currency throughout the world, preventing a central bank from adjusting its monetary policy to its local economy. But if such arbitrage and speculation require repeated taxed transactions, one nation's interest rate can differ from those in New York or Tokyo.

A tax of 0.05 per cent is negligible, for a one-time transfer but, if paid once a week, it cuts 2.5 percentage points off the annual rate of return and much more off the yield of day trading. The buffer, 2.5 percentage points in the example, provides the central bank with some room to move its own short-term interest rate.

Briefly described in the Janeway lectures, then elaborated in 1978, my proposal was mainly ignored for many years but was the subject of a scholarly symposium at the United Nations Development Programme in 1995. Still ignored in the US, the Tobin tax is in Europe now the focus of reform and protest movements. I have had nothing to do with them and am not informed of their platforms.

This disavowal does not mean I disavow my own proposal. I certainly do not. I cannot control the use of the words 'Tobin tax'. While I assume that most advocates mean well, I deplore the tactics of some extremists.

I am, like most economists, in favour of free trade and I welcome developmental capital investment in poor countries, both private and public. I regard the World Bank and the IMF as essential institutions; while critical of some of their policies and actions, I favour expanding their resources and functions. Ideally, the IMF could be the instrument for administering the transactions tax.

I do understand that a transaction tax impairs liquidity and that the tax would have to be paid on the stabilizing transactions of fundamentalists as well as the destabilizing transactions of speculators. The virtue of the tax is that it hits the most frequent transactors hardest. (The foreign exchange market does involve frequent technical trades among banker-dealers. They should not be taxed on each transfer but on net changes in positions over a period of time, maybe a week.)

To ward off tax havens, the tax would have to be levied in most nations where currency exchanges are significant banking business. A further defence would be for jurisdictions with the tax to define as taxable any transfer of funds to non-tax jurisdictions, even within the same bank.

Contrary to suspicions raised by Senators Jesse Helms and Bob Dole in election year 1996, I was not advocating UN taxes. I would expect each national government to levy and collect the agreed tax by its regular procedures and to decide for itself what to do with the revenues, which might provide inducements to participate. From the beginning I suggested that revenues from multinational taxes might appropriately be used for international purposes, such as World Bank activities. But this was never my primary purpose; indeed I aimed to diminish the volume of taxable transactions. But revenue may be the Tobin tax's principal attraction for its enthusiasts, along with the mistaken notion that it somehow would be a blow against the alleged evils of globalization.

PART II

Currency Crises and Bailouts

10. The IMF's misplaced priorities: flawed fund*

They did it in the 1930s, and now they're threatening to do it again. 'They' are the lords of world finance – international bankers, central bankers, finance ministers, and, since 1945, the International Monetary Fund. Faced with currency crises that endanger both financial systems and whole economies, they invariably give priority to finance. Their standard remedies, fiscal stringency and punitive interest rates, are devastating to economic life. They destroy jobs and bankrupt enterprises. But their authors assure the world that restoring the confidence of lenders and investors worldwide in the soundness of governments' financial policies is essential for prosperity and growth. Prime ministers and presidents have to go along.

The trouble is that the resulting recessions themselves undermine the credit-worthiness of businesses and governments. During the 1930s, financial soundness meant sticking stubbornly to the established gold values of currencies. The attempt led to the Great Depression, and the gold standard ultimately collapsed anyway. The recent IMF bailout packages for Thailand, Indonesia, and South Korea, true to form, demand austere fiscal and monetary policies along with drastic structural reforms. But the announcement of these packages did not inspire the hoped-for confidence in financial markets. The runs on the countries' reserves continued, and their currencies and stock markets continued to slide. This episode will not end in world depression, but it will doom Asian tigers, accustomed to 6 to 8 per cent growth, to severe slowdowns.

In the 1930s, Weimar Germany's Chancellor Bruening ignored his country's 20 per cent unemployment rate and succeeded only in paving the way for Hitler's accession. Britain, having endured depression since returning to the gold standard in 1925, was finally forced off in September 1931 to the immediate benefit of its economy. In 1932, as the depression worsened, the Hoover administration and the Federal Reserve were desperately defending the gold value of the dollar. Roosevelt let the dollar depreciate in 1933, and recovery began at last.

---

*   This chapter first appeared as an article, written with Gustav Ranis, in *New Republic*, 9 March 1998, pp.16–17.

An important purpose of the IMF was to tide countries over during temporary shortages of international liquidity, giving them time to make adjustments to their policies and exchange rates. The architects of the IMF, unlike their latter-day successors, did not presume that currency difficulties were the victims' fault.

Originally, the IMF reestablished a sort of gold standard. Each member made its currency convertible into dollars at a fixed rate, and the dollar was convertible into gold. This system lasted until 1971, when the United States ceased to guarantee conversion of dollars into gold. Since 1973, exchange rates among the dollar, the mark, and the yen have floated freely with no official parities, though central banks occasionally buy or sell in the currency markets. This system has the great virtue that exchange rates can adjust without precipitating financial and political crises. For example, there was no crisis from 1995 to 1997 when the yen gradually lost about 40 per cent of its dollar value.

Other countries generally adhere to semifixed exchange rates. They promise to keep their currencies within a band relative to one of the three 'hard' currencies or to a mixture of them. The band itself usually is nudged up or down in response to persistent market trends. Crises occur when a currency's dollar value gets stuck at the lower limit of the band and speculators become sure it will fall further. They sell, and the hapless central bank has to buy, using up its reserves. A pretty obvious lesson of the recent crises is that most countries would do better to abandon fixed or semifixed exchange rates in favor of freely floating rates.

The IMF's Asian packages are based on its experiences with Latin America, in particular with Mexico in 1994. Mexico had appeared to be in fair shape by IMF standards. Its budget was close to being balanced; its inflation was single-digit; wages were stabilized with the help of a pact with organized labor; and Mexico was deregulating its economy and opening itself further to foreign trade and investment. Nevertheless, from 1993 to 1994, Mexico allowed the peso to become overvalued. Dollars poured into Mexican financial markets, bidding up the peso on the way. At the same time, commodity prices were rising faster than they were in the United States. Consequently, Mexico ran a trade deficit that was financing a consumption binge rather than productive investment. The government itself was borrowing dollars short term, but the inevitable lowering of the exchange-rate band was too little and too late. Lenders took flight.

At that point, the IMF and the USA arranged a $50 billion bailout. The familiar prescription was to float the peso, tighten the budget, restrain the money supply, and raise interest rates. Mexico's real GDP fell 6 per cent in 1995, but growth resumed the following year. The 20 per cent fall in the peso's real value in dollars sufficed to restore trade balance, and the accompanying bulge in inflation subsided. Mexico repaid its bailout loans.

In 1997, the IMF and the US Treasury responded to Asia's currency crises in the same way that central banks and governments had responded to the gold crises of the 1930s. They diagnosed Asia as a victim of the 'Latin American disease' and prescribed the usual medicine. Yet, prior to 1997, the Asian tigers appeared to be model economies by IMF criteria. They were generally running budget surpluses, and money growth was moderate. Inflation rates were low, and saving rates high. Some countries, notably South Korea, had incurred large volumes of mostly short-term foreign debt. Unlike Mexico's dollar-guaranteed debts, these were almost all private debts. As the IMF noted, these countries were running trade deficits. But, unlike Mexico, they were not importing for consumption. It is quite legitimate for developing economies to borrow abroad for investments at home, though some of South Korea's recent investments apparently were ill-advised prestige projects in heavy industry, land, and real estate. The key problem was misallocation of private credit, not governmental profligacy.

The heavy private indebtedness of Asian countries clearly aggravated their situation. Once the central bank commits itself to sell hard currency for local currency on demand, its international reserves become hostage to repayment of private foreign debts. Commitment to a fixed exchange rate relieves local borrowers and foreign creditors of risk. The borrowers do take some risk only if the central bank lets the price of foreign currency rise as debtors bid for it in order to repay loans.

The IMF–US package has been criticized for bailing out South Korean banks and industries indiscriminately. Some deserve to be rescued by public funds or mergers. Owners of others should be permitted to take a bath. The worst injustices and worst precedents occur when foreign lenders are guaranteed to get all their money back; having made risky investments in search of profits, they should not be immune to losses. Converting all debts into government liabilities, as some foreign banks have demanded of South Korea in return for lengthening maturities, is another bad precedent. However, some degree of 'moral hazard' is inevitable in any system of insurance. That is not a reason for abolishing 'lenders of last resort' within nations or between nations. It is a reason for designing bailouts with care.

The IMF–US explanation of the currency crises emphasizes long-standing fundamental defects of economic structure – anti-competitive and corrupt alliances among oligopolistic businessmen, bankers and politicians. However objectionable this 'crony capitalism' may be, it is nothing new. It could hardly have been the main cause of the 1997 financial crisis.

A more likely cause is that Japan's prolonged recession weakened the major export markets of its neighbors. Their trade deficits are counterparts of Japan's surpluses. Yen depreciation, along with China's devaluation in 1994, further contributed to overvaluation of Asian currencies, especially those tied too inflexibly to the dollar. Once foreign lenders suspected that these countries' exchange rates were not sustainable, they dumped them. Adding insult to injury, Japanese banks were among the first to pull out. The creditors' panic, accentuated by the dismal prospects of economies under IMF surveillance, depressed exchange rates much further than necessary to correct their basic overvaluations.

The spectacular growth of the Asian tigers in recent decades was not a mirage. It was based on combining an educated labor force, high saving and rapid capital accumulation, modern technology, and resourceful entrepreneurship – fundamentals which still bode well for the future, and in which, incidentally, East Asia surpasses Latin America.

The Asian tigers do need structural reforms: continuous full disclosure of the size of central-bank reserves and of bank balance sheets and non-performing loans; orderly bankruptcy procedures; substitution of objective risk analyses and arm's-length credit allocations for political favoritism and for government guarantees of private loans; and adequacy of bank capital by international standards. Most importantly, local banks must be forbidden to be net debtors in hard currency.

But these problems do not justify forcing these economies into deep recession, which is bound to be especially painful for the poor, dependent as they are on maintenance of public-health and education expenditures, plus other safety nets. Nor will such a prescription restore the confidence of investors, foreign or domestic.

Finally, the IMF–US doctors insist that these Asian governments open their doors wider to international financial transactions. This is a particularly inopportune time to urge further globalization. Encouraging inflows when exchange rates and local asset values are so depressed creates the image and the reality of arranging bargain-basement deals for foreigners, thus undermining the faith of many residents of these nations in the intentions of the international lenders, public and private. Anyway, entry of foreign capital should not be further eased before domestic banking and financial reforms are in place. That would only attract inflows of nervous funds ready to move out when interest-rate differentials and/or devaluation expectations change, funds of the type that contributed so heavily to the present crisis. To avoid attracting hot money, a Chile-type tax or special deposit could be required of inflows. In the longer run, an internationally negotiated tax on currency transactions might deserve consideration.

Some critics of the IMF's bailouts want to abolish the IMF. Free-market ideologues have faith that completely liberalized international financial markets will handle all shocks optimally, if only governments and international institutions will stay out of the way. No convincing evidence or logic supports this faith. Currencies are not market institutions, and cannot be. Critics from the opposite side regard the IMF as an instrument serving multinational capitalism at the expense of ordinary people throughout the world. We believe that the world needs an IMF, just as nations need central banks, and that the IMF needs loans of hard currencies from its major members. The lesson of current events is that the IMF should stick to its original mission, saving its members from disasters due to short-term illiquidity. The World Bank and other international lenders are better suited to handle long-run structural and developmental issues.

11. Tighten belt? No, spend cash*

LESSON NO. 1

Fixed but adjustable exchange rates are a bad idea for almost all national currencies.

The only viable regimes in our increasingly globalized financial world are either floating exchange rates or irretrievably fixed rates.

Most developing, emerging, and transition economies should henceforth have currencies with floating rates. This is the simplest and most obvious lesson of the current crisis. Yet it is strangely absent from most of the rhetoric that has cluttered the world's media this year.

The East Asian victims of currency crises were, like most other nations, on fixed but adjustable pegs to the US dollar or to other major hard currencies or to baskets of these.

Their central banks promised to redeem on demand their own currencies held by anyone, foreign or domestic, in prescribed amounts of hard currencies.

Often the pegs were ranges rather than precise values, and, in many cases, the midpoint of the bracket moved over time at a prescribed speed. The pegged rates were thus not immutable, and central banks could adjust or abandon them at any time, violating their own solemn promises.

Naturally, market participants worldwide speculated on such possibilities. Worse yet, they speculated on what other currency holders thought about the risks of default. Such is the system's inherent source of instability.

Although everyone seems surprised when currency crises occur, they are not at all surprising, and happen at one time or another to almost all fixed-exchange-rate regimes.

In recent decades, such crises have hit European countries (Britain, Italy, Spain, Sweden, Finland), Latin America (notably Mexico in 1994), Russia and other transition economies, and now the Asian tigers.

The gold standard was a fixed-rate system. It suffered terminal collapse in the 1920s and 1930s. The Bretton Woods agreement of 1945 set up a new

---

*   This chapter first appeared as an article in *The Straits Times*, 26 July 1998.

fixed-exchange-rate system, based on the dollar and gold. But this, too, ended in crises affecting the dollar, yen and Deutsche Mark in 1971–3.

Since then, the exchange rates among those three hard currencies have not been pegged, but have floated freely in currency markets. They have fluctuated but there have been no crises.

A recent example is the gradual 50 per cent depreciation of the yen relative to the dollar. Japan's macroeconomic stagnation, of which the fall in the yen is but one symptom, could well be described as a disaster, but it is not a currency crisis like those of its East Asian neighbours.

Floating rates have worked for the Big Three currencies. They would forestall traumatic crises for other currencies too.

Currency values would continue to go up and down, people would continue to speculate, and some of the fluctuations would be unpleasant for the economies affected.

But the trauma of a discrete regime change, a default of solemn official commitments, and the bandwagon momentum of these events, can be avoided.

Foreign leaders who underestimated the risk of short-term loans to Indonesia, Thailand and Korea would have charged higher risk premiums in a floating-rate world.

Those sources of distrust in Asia's economic and financial prospects – some fundamental, some speculative – that triggered the crisis would have pushed down exchange rates in a floating world too, but not by nearly as much as they fell following the collapse of fixed rates.

What explains the prevalence of fixed-rate regimes outside the hard currencies?

For one thing, it is a residuum of Bretton Woods. Through most of the period since 1945, Bretton Woods-fixed rates were protected by capital controls and exchange restrictions.

The International Monetary Fund sought to make currencies convertible in commercial transactions but tolerated regulations of capital account transactions.

Lately, however, economies in all stages of development have been pressured by the world's financial establishments – national and international, official and private – to liberalize their financial markets, allow free foreign access to them, and make their currencies fully convertible.

In many ways, these developments were advantageous to developing and emerging economies, and were welcomed by important local business and political interests. But currencies became more vulnerable as a result, and fixed exchange rates more problematic.

Yet the same authorities which pressed for global financial integration continued to favour fixed exchange rates.

A fixed rate was seen as a 'nominal anchor' against inflation, forcing disciplined monetary and fiscal policies, and touted as an attraction to foreign investors. Today, these arguments have a hollow ring.

Recent short-term bank lending from Tokyo, New York, Frankfurt, and London to East Asian banks and businesses reveal how global financial integration and deregulation made fixed exchange rates more vulnerable.

Short-term capital flows would also have been unacceptable in a floating-rate regime, because they would have threatened to move the exchange rate too far for the health of the economy.

Even with floating rates, the central bank will need hard currency reserves, and will at times need to use them in currency markets. Such interventions are called 'dirty floating', but they are an essential tool of monetary policy.

Every dollar of the short-term debt of, say, a Korean bank was a claim on the Korean central bank's dollar reserves, a claim whose origins were beyond the central bank's control. It is surely unwise to promote or even allow net import of foreign capital in such transient liquid form.

Whatever the exchange rate regime, fixed or floating, governments and central banks should use their powers to steer the import of foreign capital into direct fixed investment, equity, and to a limited extent, long-term hard-currency debt.

LESSON NO. 2

An alternative at the other extreme is to fix the national currency irretrievably to the dollar or some other hard-currency standard.

The trouble with this course is that it surrenders national monetary sovereignty.

Eleven countries of the European Union are in the process of merging their currencies forever into the euro. There are great advantages, political as well as economic, in a broad currency union, as demonstrated by two centuries of the US dollar.

Whether these advantages can be artificially manufactured in a short time among diverse nationalities, governments and economics, remains to be seen.

European nations are surrendering their monetary sovereignty, voluntarily, to be sure. They will no longer have individual monetary policies, or even discretionary fiscal policies, for that matter.

Their economies can no longer adjust to payment imbalances and their macro consequences through exchange rate movements – as the UK, for example, did, very successfully in 1992.

Economists who are optimistic advocates of the euro argue that anything that exchange rate adjustments can do can be done by movements of commodity prices and wages.

This is an application of classical neutrality-of-money propositions, but the evidence is that they work very slowly and imperfectly.

Hong Kong and Argentina are not members of a currency union, but they have fixed their exchange rates permanently to the US dollar. Indonesia toyed with this idea, and Russia seems to be moving in that direction with IMF help.

The idea is to sacrifice every other possible objective of monetary and fiscal policy to the defence of a permanent exchange rate. Indeed, dollars may partly or wholly replace local currency as the unit of account and means of payment. This is the essence of a 'currency board', one well-endowed with reserves of its chosen standard currency to convince its citizens and the world of convertibility. For example, if it takes double- or triple-digit interest rates to attract and hold enough reserves, so be it, regardless of the macroeconomic effects.

Currency boards were originally arrangements to give dependencies of the British empire the illusion of having their own notes and coins while in reality, tying them tight to sterling. The colonies were not meant to have economic objectives of their own.

More generally, the success of the pre-1914 gold standard – equivalently, a sterling standard, under the bank of England's benevolent hegemony – depended on the absence of national economic objectives in the politics of those days, and the willingness of people to accept business cycles as unalterable fate.

Argentina today seems happy to be dollarized, though its unemployment rate is stuck at 12–16 per cent. Likewise, European tolerance of chronic double-digit unemployment rates is the best reason to be confident they will not revolt against the euro.

LESSON NO. 3

Real economic performance – not the strength of the currency, the soundness of banks, or the trading volume on financial markets – is the measure of the success of a nation's economic institutions and policies.

Europe today is obsessed by the question of how strong its currency will be. Will the euro be as strong as the Deutsche Mark it is replacing as the chief European currency? Will it be stronger or weaker than the dollar?

It is within the capacity of the new European Central Bank to raise the value of the euro relative to the dollar as much as it wants.

A strong euro would take high interest rates, but the cost in terms of jobs, exports and growth would be high. Given Europe's high unemployment and lacklustre macroeconomic performance, it would be better off with lower interest rates and a weak currency.

It is foolish to regard the currency markets as though they were Olympic competitions. Currencies are not ends in themselves but means to achieve economic results that really matter.

The same is true of financial institutions and markets in general. Financial globalization – basically the freedom to make any desired financial transaction, regardless of the currencies involved and the locations and nationalities of the transactors – is not an end in itself, but has to be evaluated pragmatically.

A central bank, in order to conduct a monetary policy geared to its own country's economic objectives, must be able to make its interest rates move somewhat independently of world market interest rates.

To prevent arbitrage tending to equate them, a small country needs some obstacles to movements of funds in and out of its currencies.

That is the main purpose of the proposed 'Tobin tax' on foreign exchange transactions and of devices like Chile's extra reserve requirements on foreign-owned deposits.

As I argue above, protection against extreme financial globalization is essential for monetary sovereignty, whether exchange rates are fixed or floating.

LESSON NO. 4

Austerity is not invariably an essential ingredient in solutions of national and international economic crisis and difficulties.

Nor is it always a construction ingredient. Troubled countries need structural reforms, but macroeconomic recovery programmes are the immediate priority.

Whenever a country is in sufficient economic difficulties to attract international front-page attention, the response has a standard format.

People will first say: 'Tough reforms will be needed.' Then they wonder: 'Will the political leaders and the public have the guts to make the painful sacrifices?'

If a currency crisis is involved, the inevitable conditional international 'bailout' is the vehicle for enforcing the required austerity.

In the East Asian currency crisis, the tough macro policies required by the IMF and the US Treasury were intended to restore the confidence of international lenders and investors.

They failed to do so, and indeed the precipitous recessions that ensued had the opposite effects.

These countries had not been guilty of irresponsible and inflationary fiscal and monetary policies, for which austerity is the natural punishment and cure. If their currencies were overvalued, it was more the fault of Japan's stagnation and the depreciation of the yen than of their own policies.

Structural reforms to root out corruption and 'crony capitalism' in these countries are doubtless overdue. But these conditions were not new. They had long coexisted with remarkable economic progress and with stable currencies. How could they suddenly be the cause of currency panics?

Macroeconomic austerity is not a favourable climate in which to begin long-term structural reforms.

In East Asia, the urgent priority is to arrest the plunge in economic activity and start vigorous recovery to restore rates of employment and GDP growth, as happened in Mexico after one year of sharp decline in the wake of its 1994–5 currency crisis.

The same cannot happen in the wounded Asian Tigers unless interest rates are reduced well below the high emergency rates designed to bribe residents and foreigners to hold their local currencies in the face of dismal economic outlooks.

The IMF should support sensible recovery programmes promising assistance to central banks in sustaining interest rate reductions to levels consistent with macroeconomic recovery.

Demand for Asian assets and currencies will be healthier if based on improved overall economic prospects. Also, long-run structural reforms can be undertaken more promisingly in such circumstances.

What about Japan? Its stagnation and intermittent recessions are the results of an incredible, wilful incompetence in macroeconomic policy. What it suffers from is a full-blown case of the Keynesian disease. Misunderstood in the 1930s, this malady led to the Great Depression.

Policy-makers and economists in the 1930s had not yet absorbed Keynes' message. Japanese policy-makers in the 1990s, on the other hand, have no such excuse. Their G-7 counterparts have been urging them to adopt Keynesian policies year after year. (The Europeans should blush when they do so, for their own policies are based on a radically anti-Keynesian view of the world.)

Japan has now made the headlines, often featured as the climax of the contagious Asian virus, but it does not fit that template. It is not running out of reserves; it needs no bailout; austerity and sacrifice are definitely not called for.

What Japan needs is more spending, private and public, on a large and sustained scale, for consumption as well as investment. All the pro-saving shibboleths in Japan must be suspended for a while, until a revived economy restores business expectations and investments.

Much was made of the recent joint US–Japan intervention to lift the yen. This was no help to Japan, which could use the extra net export demand induced by a soft yen.

A stronger yen might reduce America's embarrassing trade deficit, and relieve somewhat the plight of Japan's Asian neighbours and competitors.

Considering Japan's disastrous macroeconomic performance, as well as the apparent inability of the Japanese to enjoy spending money on themselves, perhaps the Japanese government should unilaterally transfer bundles of yen to other Asian countries, as well as poor countries everywhere, for development projects and the relief of poverty, but require that the yen be spent in Japan.

It is interesting to observe the world's official and private financial elite, as well as commentators and pundits, seek refuge from the uncomfortable but essential Keynesian advice they offer Japan, by changing the subject to financial reform, the Big Bang, and the disposition of the half trillion dollars of bad loans on bankers' books. Here is familiar ground for urging courageous reform, sacrifice and pain.

To be sure, reforms are important. The Reconstruction Finance Corporation of 1932 and the Resolution Trust Corporation of the 1980s are two American precedents that Japan can follow. But they delude themselves who think that banking problems caused Japan's macroeconomic disaster, or that its resolution would by itself restore prosperity.

12. Keynesian insights for the Japanese economy*

I have come to these sessions for several years and always enjoyed them. I probably always say the same things; I hope people don't remember. One of the same things I say is that Japanese macroeconomic policy is perversely and inexcusably incompetent, and I surely would say that again. It's true – as Paul Krugman, a fellow participant in this program, has been saying and as I have said here in previous years – that Japan has reinvented the Keynesian liquidity trap It can now reappear in classrooms where it had been long ignored or at best barely mentioned as a curiosum of the Great Depression.

We did have zero interest rates in the United States around 1934–5 – zero short-term interest rates, also much lower long-term interest rates relative to short-term than Japan has now. That leads me to believe that Japan needs to shorten, and in fact monetize, the debt of the government so its yields are not such an obstacle to private credit expansion and economic activity.

As Paul has stressed, the real interest rate in Japan, at least the short-term safe real rate, needs to be negative to spark the economy. Paul therefore calls on the Bank of Japan to create inflationary expectations. I don't think that is within the central bank's capability, given so much excess supply throughout the economy. The markets want to be deflating, and I don't see how government officials can persuade the public to anticipate inflation instead.

There is one way in which monetary policy could still work in Japan. The Bank could engage in open market purchases of dollar instruments with yen. Although the Bank cannot make its domestic rate negative, it can keep it well below the United States federal funds rate. The Keynesian liquidity trap misses this point because it refers to a closed economy. Use of an inter-currency monetary policy expedient wouldn't be popular in America, or in East Asia, where Japanese are the principal competitors of countries still troubled by the crisis to which a previous yen depreciation was a mighty

* Presented at the 9 March 1999, MBA Public Lecture, at the Center for Japan–US Business and Economic Studies, Stern School of Business, New York University; published as 'Reflections on Japanese Political Economy', in Takashi Negishi, Rama V. Ramachandran and Kazuo Mino (eds), *Economic Theory, Dynamics and Markets: Essays in Honor of Ryuzo Sato*, Kluwer Academic Publishers, 2001, pp.468–71.

contributor. The world would not look kindly on a Japanese 'beggar-thy-neighbor' monetary policy.

Expansionary fiscal policy, with cooperative monetary policy helping, is the way out. One idea, which dodges the international objections to a lower yen, is for the Japanese government to give a lot of yen to their East Asian neighbors and trading partners and to tie these gifts to expenditure in Japan. In that way, the grants would help Japan recover from its slump, while benefiting rather than hurting its competitors. The United States Marshall Plan is something of a precedent. There were hints that the Ministry of Finance was working on a program of loans to East Asia; but unfortunately the reaction in Washington was negative. Tied aid is contrary to free trade principles, it is true, but there are good reasons for making exceptions in this case, and anyway the other members of G-7 don't come to this issue with clean hands.

The central message is still that, as Keynes argued, fiscal policy is the answer to liquidity traps, financial or political. The arguments against fiscal policy in Japan, so far as I understand them, are intellectually fallacious; they would receive failing grades in an undergraduate macro exam.

Yes, the saving rate in Japan is high, maybe the marginal as well as the average propensity to save. That's a practical problem all right, but it means that a sizable fiscal stimulus is both necessary and safe. That the public debt is high in Japan – relative to GDP much higher than in the United States and Europe – is not a disaster now or in future. It is a natural consequence of the high saving propensities of the Japanese people. A 100 per cent debt/GDP ratio might not be tenable in America, but thrifty Japanese need some place to put their saving. Otherwise it will go to waste in unemployment and idle capacity – not excess capacity were the economy operating at normal levels, but perfectly useful capacity idled by chronic economy-wide lack of demand and recurrent recession in the 1990s.

The important Keynesian insight is that a high propensity to save will not generate high national saving unless it goes into investment, into accumulation of real capital. The 'paradox of thrift' makes this point in an extreme way. In certain circumstances, when there is no demand for investment around, the economy can be no better off, or even worse off, if a thrifty public cuts consumption. So if you want thrift to be harnessed for the benefit of the people of Japan including the elderly – the demographic change in Japan will be even more pronounced than in America – a high propensity to save does not contribute to this result unless that thrift is translated into real domestic investment or foreign assets. That is not happening now.

How come? I still guess the trouble is a failure of understanding macro-economics and/or a failure of decisive resolution in the Ministry of Finance.

I suspect that many of the world's financial lords are somewhat embarrassed to tell Japan repeatedly at G-7 meetings and elsewhere to adopt a Keynesian solution. Within Europe, central banks and governments think Keynesian theories and policies are absolutely wrong. Despite the remarkable success of pragmatic policies in the United States, true believers in the Invisible Hand reject Keynesian diagnoses and prescriptions. Many observers of Japan have found it intellectually comforting to blame the slump on the plight of the banks, flooded with bad loans dated from the land and equity bubbles and their collapse. They hope that a government-managed and -subsidized rectification of bank balance sheets will trigger overall economic recovery. I think this is a false hope. The bank problem is only a small part of the macroeconomic disaster. It has to be resolved, of course, but resolution is no substitute for the needed fiscal and monetary stimuli.

In restoring the solvency of banks, the procedures followed in the resolution of the debacle of the US savings and loan industry in the 1980s are a good precedent. So are the measures of the Reconstruction Finance Corporation in 1932–3. In return for acquiring banks' bad loans the government should acquire not debt obligations of the banks but preferred stock. That is a better way to enable banks to resume their role in the economy.

Let's move this *tour d'horizon* to the other side of the globe. Western Europe hasn't been doing very well either. One of the more foolish things we read in the financial pages of newspapers or hear in newscasts is that the new euro is a failure because, since its introduction, it has been falling against the dollar. The purpose of an exchange rate is not to go as high as it possibly can relative to other currencies. That can be a recipe for disaster. What happens to the value of the euro is much less important than what happens to the economies of the European Union.

The major problem is chronically high and increasing unemployment, which the Union, the European Central Bank and the member governments all accept fatalistically and for which they all deny responsibility. Franco Modigliani recently organized a manifesto advocating a combination of demand-side and supply-side policies to reduce European unemployment and restore normal economic activity and growth. This was drafted together with other economists, mostly European (I signed on, too). The trouble is that the official policy line in Europe is to outlaw fiscal policy, as in Japan, and to focus monetary policy exclusively on price stability, assuming that governments cannot affect employment, growth and other real magnitudes, and should not try. Thus economic theory, or more likely ideology, is the enemy of successful policy and of economic welfare.

The new social democratic governments in Europe are in this respect a disappointment, accepting passively that macroeconomics is out of their hands. Perhaps frustrated by their impotence within Europe, they have ventured into new architecture for international exchange rates. Unfortunately, their suggestion is misguided. It is to fix the rates among the big three currencies, dollar, yen and euro.

Since 1973, the big three currencies – the dollar, the yen and the Deutsche Mark (*the* European currency prior to the euro) – have been floating in the exchange markets. This regime has done well, in my opinion. There have been no crises. Significant adjustments of the three exchange rates (only two independent ones, as the third can always be derived from the other two) have occurred without headlines and resignations of government officials. For example, the yen of 1997–8 depreciated 40 per cent against the dollar without turmoil. Yet within Europe, the fixed rates of the European Monetary System, led by the Bundesbank, were the source of political and economic crises whenever adjustments of those rates became necessary. The idea of the prime ministers of France and Germany that what is needed now is to fix the world's central currency values is preposterous.

Ironically, it comes just at the time when fixed exchange rates are in bad repute generally because of the currency crises of 1997–9 in East Asia, Russia and Brazil. The US Treasury, the IMF, and world financial opinion are moving towards new world monetary architecture with floating rates for most countries. Exceptions are, of course, within currency unions like Euroland, and 'currency boards' or dollarizations that essentially abandon national monetary policies and substitute major hard currencies for domestic money. These arrangements sacrifice national monetary sovereignty. This is the price of giving absolute priority to exchange rate stability at the expense of macroeconomic stability. In some cases, it may be the best choice, but it needs to be carefully and skeptically thought through.

If national monetary sovereignty is to be preserved at all, world financial markets cannot be completely integrated. Some barriers to cross-currency financial exchanges need to be preserved. The system must allow some deviations of local interest rates and credit conditions from those in New York, Tokyo, Frankfurt and London, some room within which even small-country national central banks can operate in the light of their own countries' circumstances and interests. Integration of finance throughout the world can be of benefit to developing, emerging and transition economies, but not without some limits.

THE ASIAN FINANCIAL CRISIS

The Origins of the Crisis

As general background, remember that a fixed exchange rate, to which a central bank has committed its reserves of hard foreign currency, is always vulnerable. For instance, suppose Korea has promised to pay one dollar for any 1200 won presented to its central bank by anyone, resident or foreign. If people begin to doubt that the Bank of Korea has enough dollars to make good on the promise, they will rush to sell won for dollars. As the Bank's dollar reserves are depleted, it has no choice but to abandon its commitment and the won falls in the market – that is, it takes more, many more than 1200, won to buy a dollar. 'Fixed rate' is a misnomer; the rate cannot be irrevocably fixed unless the won is abandoned in favor of the dollar, just as francs, lire and other European currencies are scheduled to be merged into the new euro.

Short of such unification, 'fixed rates' are better called 'adjustable pegs', and the fact that they can be adjusted, or may have to be, makes them vulnerable to speculation. The situation is like that of an ordinary bank, which has promised to redeem deposits denominated in the local currency in that currency. There are two equilibria: in the good one, depositors are convinced that the bank can and will honor its commitment. Their confidence itself sustains the conditions that fulfill their expectations. In the bad 'equilibrium', banks fail and, after trying desperately to liquidate assets to obtain funds to meet withdrawals, have to abandon their commitments to redeem deposits with currency and have to close their doors.

In the foreign exchange case, the analogous commitment is the central bank's promise to redeem the local currency in the hard foreign currency to which it is pegged. In the good equilibrium, the promise is credible and public confidence sustains conditions that confirm that confidence. In the bad equilibrium, the country defaults on its promise to redeem its currency in hard currency. Panic makes the currency plummet in the free market.

Preceding the East Asian currency crises, banks and businesses in those countries had borrowed heavily short-term in yen and dollars. The local currencies were becoming overvalued, too expensive. Several countries were reporting increasing trade deficits. Japan's chronic business-cycle slump and the depreciation of the yen badly damaged the smaller countries' export markets. Their creditors began worrying that the central banks' reserves would not suffice to repay them. Panic! The currencies fell quickly – much farther than was required to correct the basic overvaluations.

The Bailouts: Diagnosis and Prescription

The highest and most immediate priority of the IMF/US Treasury team was to restore foreign lenders' confidence, to shift their expectations from those of panicky disequilibria to those supporting benign equilibrium with exchange rate stability. The method – honored over the centuries though rarely efficacious – was to impose painful reforms on the government, central bank and economy of each victim country. The trouble with these medicines is that they so damage the economy, at least in the short run, that creditors have every reason to believe the risks are made greater, not smaller. In the recent crisis of Korea and Indonesia, the currencies fell after the 'bailouts' were announced. The customary recipes of austere fiscal and monetary policy were not appropriate in these cases. They punished these economies for crimes they had not committed. They failed to restore market confidence and the credibility of the economies and currency values. Instead, they condemned the countries to deep recessions in economic activity and to severe human suffering, counterproductive both in setting right the financial markets and institutions, and in attracting local political support. The IMF has had to relent somewhat.

The IMF/US Treasury team also detected serious structural diseases, allegedly threatening not just the short-run liquidity of the afflicted countries but their long-run solvency as well. Consequently, the bailout loans were conditioned on long lists of basic reforms. But these alleged maladies were long-standing features of economies whose decades of spectacular growth were until the eve of the crises greatly and openly admired by the same physicians who now prescribed their urgent correction. Though many of the reforms are desirable – in particular those that would make the accounts of businesses and banks much more transparent – recovery from the currency crisis and restoration of normal growth need not wait for their completion.

Among the reforms required by the IMF are further measures of financial liberalization and globalization. As prescription for crises in which spurts of short-term yen and dollar lending to banks and businesses played major roles, these requirements seem ironic, indeed perverse. In order to protect central banks' hard-currency reserves, reform in the opposite direction is indicated: forbid a bank to have, either directly or through its customers, a net short-term debit position in hard currency. Moreover, politically as well as economically, it seems a most inopportune time to encourage sales of local banks and businesses to First-World buyers.

The Future International Monetary System

What exchange rate system will work? One that all too frequently will not work is the adjustable peg system. It is especially difficult to preserve a national currency with a fixed rate or semi-fixed rate system (a moving band) together with fully globalized financial institutions and markets, blind to nationalities of individuals and institutions and to the currencies in which assets and debts are denominated. If a country is to have its own currency and any sovereignty over its own money and interest rates, the government and central bank must have some ways to defend their reserves. Market floating is preferable to pegging, as illustrated by the absence of currency crises among the big three – dollar, yen, Deutsche Mark – while they have been floating relative to one another since the early 1970s. Even so, volatility of market floating exchange rates can be painful. The above proposal to limit private hard-currency short-term debt would be prudent in any exchange regime. Chile's extra reserve requirement on foreign deposits and taxation of currency market transactions are other ways of slowing down movements of short-term funds in and out.

The lords of world finance should overcome knee-jerk notions that currency difficulties always reveal sin and require penance. The Bretton Woods agreement contemplated the IMF as a lender of last resort designed to tide a member country over a liquidity shortfall, whatever its origin. As the recent Asian examples show, countries can suffer liquidity crises through no fault of their own. No-questions-asked drawing rights on the Fund have lagged behind the growth of the world economy and especially the growth of mobile hot money. IMF quotas should be increased. Those who advocate dumping or starving the IMF and leaving everything to the globalized market are spouting ideology, not commonsense economics. The IMF needs more dollars, not fewer. But the IMF should confine itself to its original function, handling liquidity problems, and leave members' long-run structural reforms and developmental capital imports to the other Bretton Woods institution, the World Bank, and to other public and private long-term lenders and equity investors.

13. Currency unions, American v. European*

The United States of America has been a successful currency union for two centuries. Few people – historians, economists or ordinary citizens – doubt that having a single currency, the dollar, contributed mightily to American prosperity and growth. Europeans confident that the euro can do the same for their Union cite the American experience as a precedent.

There are, however, a number of important differences between the two cases. Now that Europe has crossed the Rubicon to currency union, consciousness of these differences provides an agenda for the hard work that lies ahead for the European Monetary Union (EMU) and its members if the new regime is to live up to the hopes of its architects. Although many Union-wide institutions are already in place, other important institutions remain to be designed, negotiated and built.

PHILADELPHIA V. MAASTRICHT

The US Constitution, negotiated in the Philadelphia convention in 1787, came into force in 1789. It vested in the federal Congress the sole power 'To coin Money, regulate the value thereof, and of foreign Coin'. The Constitution also established free trade, travel and migration among the states, and required each state to give 'full faith and credit' to the public acts of other states. There were only 13 states at the time; all the other 37 present members of the dollar currency union joined later as they advanced from territorial status to be admitted as states of the American union. The original states had not had as English colonies their own moneys, and after jointly declaring independence in 1776 their weak Confederation, the Continental Congress, had issued a weak paper currency without gold or silver backing. Both the Confederation and the member states themselves were heavily in debt at the end of the War of Independence. The new federal government established new dollars con-

*   This chapter first appeared as 'Currency Unions, American v. European', in *Policy Options*, Institute for Research on Public Policy, Montreal, May 2001.

vertible into gold and silver, thus indirectly convertible into pounds sterling, and assumed at face value all the debts of the Confederation and the states. This is not what is happening in Europe now. The Treaty of Maastricht is not the US Constitution.

ECONOMIC STABILIZATION TOOLS

Unexpected shocks to economic activity – demographic, technological, political, external – happen all the time. Some will hit all regions within the EU in the same way. Some will hit them in the same direction but with different force. Some will hit them in opposite ways. What tools will the Union and the member states have for moderating or reversing unwelcome business recessions or booms, or adapting to long-run changes in economic performance? How do these compare with the tools of economic policy before Maastricht and with those available in the USA?

CURRENCY VALUATIONS

The 11 members of the EMU are of course surrendering their freedom to change, or to allow markets to change, the values of their currencies with respect to each other and with respect to the dollar, yen and other currencies outside EMU. Members of the European Monetary System, effectively tied to the Deutsche Mark, have mostly become accustomed to forgo this freedom, although several members did resort to devaluation as recently as 1992. At least one, the United Kingdom, seems to have prospered as a result. Anyway, this is not a freedom that American states have, so there will be no difference between continents in this respect.

MONETARY POLICIES

American states can have no monetary policies, and EMU member states will be in the same boat. How about monetary policies at the union levels? Here the powers of the EMU and the US Federal Reserve are comparable. However, the EMU charter directs the European Central Bank (ECB) to aim solely for price stability, presumably on average across its territory. This is not a big change from the de facto European monetary policy under Bundesbank management. The Federal Reserve has more discretion, and indeed is expected under current law to give weight to unemployment and to growth of real gross domestic product. Results since 1982 have been much better both on employment and GDP and on inflation than in Europe. The EMU directive could be particularly damaging to employment, production and income in case of a big inflationary supply shock like the OPEC oil price increases of the 1970s. There is practically very little room for the ECB to differentiate the effects of its monetary policies among member states. This is true of the Federal Reserve, too.

FISCAL POLICIES, CENTRAL

The EU has no fisc, so it cannot have a fiscal policy, either for the Union as a whole or for member states differentially. Central revenues of the Union are not supposed to exceed 1.7 per cent of GDP, and expenditures are similarly limited. The revenues of the US federal government are 21 per cent of GDP, expenditures likewise. Thus the US has considerable scope for fiscal policy, in several ways. Changes in federal government budget deficits or surpluses stimulate or restrict overall spending on goods and services. Expenditure and transfer programs can deliberately help particular states and regions suffering economic reverses. Help to states also comes as a by-product of permanent federal programs. Fully 12 per cent of federal budget outlays are transfers of funds to state and local governments.

A more subtle but very important class of mechanisms are so-called 'built-in stabilizers'. These are programs of federal transfers to state and local governments and to their citizens where the amounts transferred are determined by formulas measuring need: for example, more unemployment compensation when and where there is more unemployment; more federal help to education, the poorer the local communities, more credit to local enterprises, the weaker the local economy.

FISCAL POLICIES, STATES

The EMU rules forbid member states from running deficits larger than 3 per cent of their individual GDPs (thus continuing the Maastricht rule for admission to the Union), under pain of a fine of 0.5 per cent of GDP. This rule applies whether the deficit arose because of economic recession outside the control of the member or because of fiscal profligacy. Moreover, the rule makes no distinction between current and capital expenditures.

US state budgets total 12 per cent of GDP. There are no federal restrictions on state budget policies. Most states are prohibited from running deficits on current account by their own constitutions, although deficits are allowed de facto in business cycle recessions. States are, however, free to finance capital expenditures (for example, schools, highways, housing projects and hospitals) by borrowing.

MARKET MECHANISMS OF ECONOMIC ADJUSTMENT

Optimists about EMU think that they can get along without stabilization policies other than the ECB's commitment to price stability. They would just rely on free markets to make the necessary adjustments to economic disturbances to the Union as a whole or to member states. Prices and wages will, they trust, correct fluctuations in production and employment.

For this to happen, workers and capital must move between industries, occupations, locations and states in response to market signals. They must go where the job and profit opportunities are, and prices and wages must register the right signals to induce them to do so. In the USA, mobility of labor and capital is remarkably fast. Wages and prices are quite flexible, and both workers and business managers respond. Although immense changes in the composition of economic activity are taking place – 'downsizing' is terminating many jobs and plant closings and bankruptcies are always in the news – still new jobs and new businesses keep the overall unemployment rate low and the aggregate profitability of business high.

Most of Europe, however, is suffering chronic double-digit unemployment, and accordingly Europe is producing far below capacity. European economists, bankers and officials blame structural rigidities. Such rigidities are likely to make it difficult for market responses to handle the shocks that are bound to come.

In the best of circumstances, labor and capital will be much less mobile between member states of EMU than between American states. This is not surprising, given in the USA two centuries of free trade and free movement across state lines; a common language and also common or similar laws of contracts, property and bankruptcy; insurance, and professional practices and standards. Institutions of higher education are open to students from all locations and adhere to common academic standards. Social security and elderly health care are federal programs, and other safety nets are joint federal–state policies.

CONCLUSIONS

Europe is much less well equipped to adjust to interregional disturbances to economic activity than the United States both in the strength of forces of market adjustment and in the availability of governmental fiscal responses, automatic and discretionary.

Europe is also less well equipped to deal with worldwide or continental economic shocks than the United States, because of the absence of a federal government with possible fiscal responses, either automatic 'built-in stabilizers' or discretionary policies. As to monetary policy, EMU is tying its own hands behind its back by forswearing any use of central bank powers to affect employment, production and growth.

It may be that the challenge of adapting to an irreversible currency union will bring the farsighted building of institutions needed to make the experiment successful. Let us hope so.

14. Symposium on limiting the moral hazard in international financial rescues*

I do not pretend to have a 'plan' to limit the moral hazard in international financial rescues. While moral hazard is a serious and difficult problem, I am not sure it deserves highest priority among the issues raised by recent currency crises. We do not want to scrap lenders of last resort because moral hazards are intrinsic to them. Limiting the third-party effects of currency crises and of the austere prescriptions for recovery from them is worth putting up with some moral hazard. Maybe the best approach is to limit the probability that international rescues will be necessary.

For most countries fixed exchange rates in their usual form, adjustable pegs (fixed rates that can be changed) are a bad idea. Developing countries would be well advised to follow the example of the major capitalist countries and let their currencies float like the dollar, yen and Deutsche Mark. It is hard to understand why this had not become normal practice long ago. It would have avoided the worst consequences of recent adjustments of exchange rates.

If a country wants to peg its currency, it should be required to make arrangements with the 'peggee' central bank, which would give the satellite central bank a credit line in the reserve currency, to be drawn upon in emergency subject to rules agreed in advance. The idea would be to hold the line while an IMF package can be worked out.

The logic of financial globalization is to increase the substitutability between local assets and debts and those in dollar markets, until the local central bank has no margin within which it is free to determine domestic interest rates. To preserve a local currency with residual monetary sovereignty, some friction in international financial institutions and markets needs to be retained or created. This is true not only in an adjustable peg regime but also in a regime of floating rates, though floating itself is some protection. Protection against speculative inflows can be effected by surtaxes or extra reserve requirements on foreign bank deposits or other

* Symposium held at the Brookings Institution, 4 June 1998.

91

short-term debts to foreigners, as Chile and Colombia have imposed with success to keep out hot money. An international tax on currency transactions would help, but I have no illusions about its prospects. I do hope that Secretary Rubin and his G-8 counterparts would stop asserting that the solution to currency problems is ever more globalization of financial markets and institutions.

The governments, banks and businesses of developing countries should eschew demand debt or short-term debt in hard currencies. Flows of capital to developing countries should usually take the form of fixed direct investment or equity. Banks should not be allowed to have net debtor positions in hard currency. Corporate borrowing in hard currency should be supervised by the central bank.

Clearly, developing countries need to build institutions of financial reform and regulation supportive of modern national financial systems and of independent currencies.

If a crisis occurs, the IMF should shut down trading in the currency under attack and start immediately negotiations with the creditors to prevent panicky withdrawals and non-renewals when trading starts again. This would give other items in the bailout package a chance to work.

PART III

Growth and the Fiscal–Monetary Policy Mix

15.   1960: campaign memo on economic growth and 'Growth Through Taxation'*

MEMO ON ECONOMIC GROWTH

The Need for Faster Economic Growth

Rapid economic growth is the paramount goal of the people of Asia, Africa and Latin America who have yet to participate in the bounty of modern technology. Most of these nations are committed in the struggle between freedom and communism. The political and social forms that these nations assume as their economies develop may determine the fate of

---

*   Chapter 15 is a paper written in 1960. Only a condensed version of it was published at that time, in *The New Republic* under the title 'Growth through Taxation', later republished in 1966 in my collection of essays 'National Economic Policy'. Here it is appended to the full paper, now published for the first time. Let me explain the origins of this paper and the reasons for including it in this book.

The paper was written for John F. Kennedy's presidential campaign. The candidate and his political advisers suspected that the weakness of the national economy, at the time in its second recession of the Eisenhower years, was a promising issue. They were encouraged in this view by their Massachusetts economic advisers, notably J.K. Galbraith and Paul Samuelson. The group felt they needed a background paper on economic growth and policies to encourage it, and on the economists' recommendation Ted Sorenson came to my office at Yale to hire me to do this paper.

The 'growth' at issue was increase in the gross national product (GNP) – 'real', that is corrected for inflation. I thought it necessary to distinguish between short-term year-to-year increases, such as occur during business cycles, and long-term decade-to-decade trends. Policies to affect the GNP in the short run are *monetary*, conducted by the Federal Reserve, our central bank, and *fiscal*, while secular growth depends on advances in technology, productivity, labor supply and capital capacity. The approach was probably too subtle for political campaigning. But it was the paradigm for the policy analytics of the Kennedy administration.

What is more relevant today is that the essay was also a precursor of an important paradigm of the economic policy of the Clinton administration, the concept of the macroeconomic policy *mix*, the relative contributions to aggregate demand of monetary stimulus and fiscal stimulus. In the 1950s, Paul Samuelson and I were beginning to point out that a mix emphasizing monetary stimulus while keeping fiscal policy tight could be favorable for secular growth while maintaining full employment and avoiding recessions. This was argued in my Kennedy paper. This policy mix was successful in the 1990s. (See Alan Blinder and Janet Yellen, *The Fabulous Decade*, Century Foundation, 2001.)

the world. The survival of freedom, in the West as well as in the developing
areas, may depend on the route over which the leaders of these peoples
guide their search for economic growth.

The communists proclaim to the world that they alone have the secret of
rapid economic development. Only communism, they say, can mobilize
economic resources and human energies for this national purpose. Only the
totalitarian discipline can assure sufficient national saving and investment.
Only complete central planning and public ownership can channel capital,
labor and land into the uses of highest social priority. In contrast, democratic government and pluralistic societies are, according to the communists, incapable of the measure of national self-discipline and effective
planning necessary to achieve rapid economic growth.

In confirmation of their claim, the communists point to the success of
the Soviet Union in its economic pursuit of the United States. Recent
unsatisfactory performance of the United States in economic growth lends
credence to the communist position.

By resolving to achieve a higher rate of economic progress, the United
States would show the world that democratic political institutions still can
focus the energies of society on a vital national purpose. By designing and
executing a program to accelerate growth, the United States would show
that political freedom and decentralization of decision do not mean
anarchy and drift but are essential elements of national strength.

The current communist challenge is 180° different from its historical critique of capitalism. We have weathered the earlier challenge and proved the
premise of the critique to be false. Our economy was supposed to be
doomed for inability to solve the problem of chronic insufficiency of
demand and unemployment. In the 1930s this prophecy came dangerously
close to fulfilment. But our institutions were adaptable; our political will
was strong; and we learned how to conquer the threat of unemployment
and stagnation. Now both events and the communist ideology present us
with the opposite challenge – not how to increase consumption spending
but how to increase saving, not how to keep our capacity to produce from
outrunning our capacity to consume but how to make our capacity to
produce growth fast enough to keep pace with the manifold demands upon
it.

Apart from the importance of our example in the worldwide contest of
social systems, we have intrinsic reasons for wishing to increase productivity more rapidly. The requirements on our production are growing, and
they do not wait for our ability to produce. We will need to export not only
example but an increasing amount of capital to the underdeveloped world.
As much as we hope for disarmament, the defense of the Western world
may require both an ever-increasing volume of current production and an

ever-increasing reserve capacity. With the foreseeable growth of our population come expanding needs for education, housing, transportation,
public health, urban redevelopment and medical care. These needs multiply at a time when we still have not overcome backlogs of need due to years
of neglect, myopia and false economy. Along with population growth, we
can look forward to an increase in the proportion of the population outside
the labor force – at school, at home, in retirement – making it the more
urgent to increase the productivity of the labor force.

Even in terms of private consumption, faster economic growth is a
bargain for the American people. The fruits of growth policy would be realized in gains for the consumer within the decade. In addition, larger
amounts would be available for government programs equally important
for the welfare of the citizen. With the gains from growth we can raise to
decent standards throughout the land the opportunities of our citizens for
education, housing, recreation, medical care and social security.

The Cost of Growth

The price of faster growth is a temporary retardation of the growth of consumption. Currently gross national product is about 500 billion dollars,
and of this 65 per cent, or 325 billion dollars, is devoted to private consumption. Since 1953, when the Eisenhower administration took office, the
rate of growth of full employment GNP has been about 3 per cent per year.
(The rate of growth of actual GNP has been smaller than that; we had full
employment in 1953, and we do not have it now.) If the 3 per cent growth
rate were to continue for another decade, full employment GNP would
reach 700 (in 1959 dollars) in 1970. Consumption, maintaining its share at
65 per cent, would reach about 455 billions. If we want faster growth we
must gradually drop the share of consumption, until it becomes, say, 60 per
cent of GNP in 1964. As we do so, we will be able to climb on to faster
growth tracks, 5 per cent from 1964 on. By this process we should attain a
GNP of 821 billion dollars in 1970, of which the 60 per cent devoted to consumption would amount to 493 billions. The two growth paths are compared in Figure 15.1. They start from the same point in 1961, on the
assumption that unemployment is then reduced to 3 per cent. Along the
slow growth path consumption is maintained at 65 per cent and plant and
equipment investment at 9 per cent of GNP. Along the fast growth path,
the proportion of GNP devoted to gross investment in plant and equipment is increased to 12 per cent. The additional outlays that this involves,
above the plant and equipment expenditures assumed for the slow path, are
represented by the shaded deduction from the fast-growth GNP. Even after
these necessary extra investment expenditures are deducted, available

output exceeds slow-growth GNP in 1964 and thereafter. Consumption under the fast-growth program is assumed not to exceed slow-growth consumption until 1966.

The Transition Problem

The principal problem is the transition from a 65 per cent consumption economy to a 60 per cent consumption economy. *After* the transition is accomplished, in 1964 in the example illustrated in Figure 15.1, consumption can rise at the same rate as GNP. Saving and taxes must increase by 40 cents for every dollar increase in GNP, instead of 35 cents as now. This is a significant but clearly practicable increase. But *during* the transition, consumption must be kept from growing as fast as GNP. While GNP rises from 521 in 1960 to 613 in 1964, consumption must rise only from 339 to 368. Thus, during the transition period, saving and taxes need to absorb about 70 per cent of the increase of GNP, including the lion's share of the additional output we will get by reducing unemployment.

The way to accomplish the transition is to introduce in two or three annual steps, beginning in 1961, the additional taxes and saving incentives needed to shift to a 60 per cent consumption economy. The yield of these

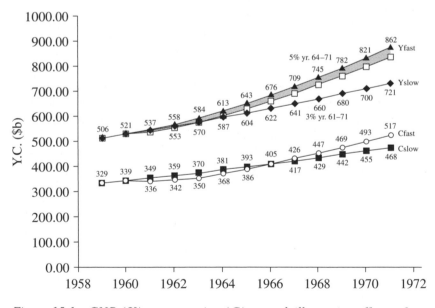

Figure 15.1   GNP (Y), consumption (C), growth illustrating effects of less C, more I

new measures, in saving or in taxes, must in the end amount to 5 per cent of GNP. Perhaps half of this should be introduced in 1961, and a quarter each in 1962 and 1963.

Income Taxation with a Saving Incentive

The amounts needed to finance investment for growth can be saved directly by individuals and offered to investment business firms through the capital markets. Or the saving can be performed indirectly via a government budget surplus; government bonds are retired, and their former holders offer the funds thus released to business firms seeking to finance investment. To the extent that we can induce additional individual saving, we will not have to rely on government saving out of tax revenues.

This is the reason for coupling an increase in individual taxation with an incentive to save. The proposal is to increase the effective individual income tax, either by an increase in rates or by plugging certain loopholes, or both. Simultaneously, taxpayers would be offered the privilege of deducting a certain amount of saving from income subject to tax. The taxpayer would have to support his claim for deduction by reporting changes in assets and liabilities during the year. But he would not have to make such a report unless he desired to claim the deduction. As in the case of other deductions, the burden of proof would be on the taxpayer; he would have to be prepared to support his claim with records, and so on, in case his return was questioned by the Bureau of Internal Revenue. The deduction would not be permitted to exceed a specified percentage of adjusted gross income. Most importantly, only saving in excess of a scheduled normal amount would be eligible for the saving deduction. A standard schedule of normal saving for taxpayers of different income levels and numbers of dependants would be devised. According to this schedule, taxpayers of high incomes would be expected to save a higher proportion of their incomes than taxpayers of low incomes. And taxpayers with large families would not be expected to save as much as single individuals. The purpose of this schedule is to reinforce the incentive to save provided by the deduction privilege. In order to qualify for the deduction privilege, taxpayers below 'normal' will have to bring their saving up above 'normal.' The schedule also is designed to make the scheme equitable as between taxpayers of different economic status. There is no point, either on grounds of equity or as incentive, in rewarding high-income taxpayers for being better able to save. Under the proposal, they will be rewarded only for exceptionally high saving relative to their ability to save. The schedule also avoids the administrative inconvenience of a large number of small claims; taxpayers hopelessly below the scheduled normal will simply pay the increased income tax, without reporting on their saving. Some technical safeguards would be necessary in order to prevent taxpayers from bunching consumption expenditures in one year and concentrating saving in the next year to take advantage of the deduction privilege. For example, it might be sufficient to confine the privilege (after the first year of operation of the plan) to taxpayers who could show that their average saving over two successive taxable years equaled their average scheduled normal.

With what increase in the effective personal income tax should this saving incentive be coupled? Rather than a general increase in rates, I would give priority to reducing some of the erosion of the tax base, to which Pechman has called attention. (See *Tax Revision Compendium*, House Committee on Ways and Means.) In particular:

1. Homeowners should be taxed on an imputed return on their net equity in owner-occupied homes. Deductions for mortgage interest and property taxes should be eliminated. The present provisions discriminate against the occupant of rental housing and permit a large part of personal income to escape income taxation. It may be noted that increase in net equity in the home would count as saving for the purpose of the proposed saving deduction.
2. Capital gains on assets transferred by gift or at death should be subject to capital gains tax. Their present exclusion from tax reduces the yield of the personal income tax, impairs the progressivity of the tax, and introduces undesirable rigidity in capital markets.
3. Deductions for state and local sales and excise taxes should be eliminated. This reform is especially appropriate in a program designed to stimulate saving at the expense of consumption.
4. Interest and dividend income should be subject to withholding tax, and the dividend exclusion and tax credit withdrawn.
5. A taxpayer should be required to pay tax on the total income of all persons for whom he claims exemptions.
6. Stricter enforcement against tax avoidance contrived by disguising personal expenses and income as business expenses is extremely desirable.
7. The whole question of the exclusion from taxation of social benefits and wage supplements needs to be reviewed, in the interests of both equity and revenue. Such a review would encompass the adequacy of present personal exemptions and the equity of the present treatment of single persons and taypayers of various sizes of family. Bringing benefit payments and wage supplements under tax – provided exemptions are fair and adequate – has much to recommend it. For example, it would be possible to dispense with means tests, limitations on earnings of retired persons receiving social security benefits, and other

devices – all difficult to administer and invidious in nature – now required to prevent abuse of social welfare and security programs.

The amount of rate increase necessary depends on how much is done to reverse the erosion of the tax. By one means or the other, we should try to increase the yield of the tax from given GNP by 40 per cent, before allowance for any saving deduction. The actual yield of the tax will not and need not increase by so much, since an increase in saving induced by the scheme is just as useful in financing investment as an increase in tax revenues.

The principal alternatives to the proposed scheme involve direct taxation of consumption, either by a federal sales tax or by a progressive expenditure tax. Both of these would also give an incentive to save in order to avoid or at least postpone the tax.

The easiest device administratively is a federal sales tax. It is objectionable on several grounds. It is regressive and erratic in its burden on individuals and families of different circumstances and abilities to pay. Efforts to mitigate its inequitable impact on low-income consumers and large families by excluding certain 'necessities' from tax are inevitably arbitrary and imperfect. Many items of consumption, in particular services purchased outside regular retail establishments, are immune from sales tax merely for administrative reasons. A final and decisive reason to avoid a federal sales tax is to leave this instrument of taxation to the states. They have urgent needs for more revenue too; it would be unfortunate to discourage them from raising their own levies by a federal sales tax.

While a progressive expenditures tax avoids the defects of the sales tax, it is probably not administratively feasible. Every taxpayer would have to report his income and saving for the year. He would be taxed on his consumption spending, income less saving, or plus dissaving, at progressive rates, with exemptions for dependants, and so on. Every taxpayer would have to provide a complete balance sheet annually – and stand ready to defend it if challenged – in order to establish that he has not consumed from capital in excess of the amount declared. The proposed income tax with saving deduction will accomplish the objectives of the expenditures tax, and it is much simpler to administer.

Contributory Extension of Old Age and Survivors' Insurance

The present program of old age and survivors' insurance (OASI) provides a basic scale of benefits for the entire covered population. As experience has shown, it is a wholly appropriate way to meet the basic needs of retired persons and surviving dependants. Since this is its purpose, the benefits vary in amount with the circumstances of the beneficiary; they are only loosely related to prior contributions of the participant and his employer or to his prior earnings. Indeed the payroll taxes that finance the program apply only to annual earnings below a certain ceiling, now $4800. The spread of private retirement plans to supplement OASI testifies to the strongly felt need of most American families to make systematic provisions for retirement beyond the present governmental program, with benefits which are related in amount to earnings and contributions during working life. The incidence of private pension plans is very uneven; the opportunity to participate in a supplementary program is therefore quite unequally and accidentally distributed among our citizens. Moreover, many private plans are defective; in particular, they do not 'vest' the participant with his and his employer's contributions, but require him to remain in the same employment in order to benefit from the plan. This requirement, however understandable from the employer's viewpoint, is an undesirable interference with the mobility of labor needed in a dynamic economy.

For this reason it would be desirable to introduce an extension of OASI above the present program, which would remain as it is now. The extension would be based on contributions by employer and employee through a tax on earnings above as well as below the present OASI ceiling. The benefits to a participant or survivor would be based on the contributions made. These contributions would be credited with interest and given a purchasing power guarantee. On his retirement a participant would have to his credit a certain sum equivalent in purchasing power to his and his employer's prior contributions plus interest; he would then be paid an actuarially computed annuity, in monthly installments varying in dollar amount in accordance with the Consumer Price Index. Similar arrangements would apply to benefits to survivors of participants who die before retirement. Incidentally the retirement benefits would be the right of the participant on reaching a designated age, even though he continues in gainful employment. Participation in the extended program would be compulsory, except at the choice of employers and employees who substitute for it a private plan of acceptable standards. One requirement for an acceptable substitute private plan would be 'vesting' the employee with all past contributions.

The advantage of introducing this extension of old age and survivors' insurance now is that it would be an important source of the saving we badly need in the 1960s, especially during the transition to a faster growth track. Contributions would begin now. Benefits would not begin until present contributors become eligible. As in the first years of the present OASI program, the amount would run large surpluses. As these are invested in government securities – special ones with purchasing power guarantee – other government securities can be retired, and their former holders will have funds to invest in financing business expansion.

Restraint of Advertising

My third proposal for restraining consumption and stimulating saving is to strike a blow, if only a minor one, at the source of many of the pressures for ever-increasing luxury consumption in our society. Everyone recognizes that advertising in America is excessive. It absorbs a large quantity of talent and productive resources, and to what end? All too often its aim is to generate synthetic and invidious drives for conspicuous consumption and for conformity to an ever more demanding and constantly changing standard of fashion and taste. These efforts distort America's scale of values. What does advertising do for our children's conception of the integrity of the spoken or written word, their image of the good life, their ideal of the successful man or the admirable woman? The proposal is simply to limit the amount of advertising and promotional expenses that can be deducted from corporate income for tax purposes. At present the Treasury pays half of any dollar added to these outlays. The limit would be a reasonable proportion of sales, taking into account the nature of the business and the practice of the firm in a base period. And if the firm feels it must advertise beyond the limit, it may – only without the taxpayer's help. The palatability of this proposal may be greater than at first appears if it is combined with concessions (below) on the corporate income tax to stimulate investment.

Measures to Stimulate Investment

There are two sides to any responsible and consistent policy to accelerate the growth of the productive capital of the economy. One is to increase national saving. The other is to increase investment. They are equally important. Measures to raise the rate of individual and governmental saving will be futile if investment is not stimulated at the same time. If increased saving can find no outlet in investment, it will merely go to waste in unemployment and lost production. Likewise, measures to stimulate investment will simply cause an inflationary scramble, with excessive demands fighting over limited supplies, unless saving to finance the investment is induced.

Easy money and low interest rates

Federal Reserve monetary policy and Treasury debt management should encourage investment by making credit easily available and lowering interest rates. It is important to bring down long-term rates as well as short-term rates. This may involve Federal Reserve purchases of long-term securities, in contravention of its current 'bills only' policy.

The main purpose of such a monetary policy is to stimulate investment in business plant and equipment, and in the inventories associated with growth of national output, and to encourage the capital expenditures programs of state and local governments. The purpose is not to set off a boom in consumers' durables or even in residential housing. It is unlikely that credit will be channeled in those directions if the vigorous measures recommended above to encourage consumer saving are taken. But it is possible – especially if those measures are not fully adopted – that general monetary ease will have to be accompanied by a revival of selective controls of consumer credit and residential mortgage credit.

Improvement of loss-offset provisions in business taxation

A high corporate or personal income tax rate, applicable to profits from business ventures, is not necessarily a deterrent to assumption of the risks of investment. Indeed, to the extent that the taxpayer is able to reduce his tax liability in case of loss, the tax collector is sharing his risks as well as his returns. A corporate or individual investor may well be led to increase the amount of capital he puts at risk by a tax which has the effect of putting part of the risk on the government. For this reason, it is important to broaden the provisions of the tax law that permit the taxpaying firm to reduce its tax liability when it suffers losses. These provisions are of two kinds: those that permit averaging over several taxable years (carry-back and carry-forward of losses) in determining tax liability, and those that permit losses of one kind to be offset against gains and income of another kind in determining the taxable income of any one year. Improvement of loss-offset provisions is a better and fairer device for stimulating investment than reduction of the tax rate. Indeed, with good loss-offset provisions, reduction of the tax rate might not stimulate but reduce business investment.

Tax incentive for high investment

A program for growth requires that corporate business not only invest its own gross saving (depreciation plus retained earnings) but also absorb into investment some of the additional saving offered by individuals as a result of the taxation and saving-incentive policies outlined above. This saving will be available to corporations through financial intermediaries and capital markets, at low interest rates or earning–price ratios. But American corporations, especially in the manufacturing field, are conservative – unduly so – in seeking outside funds for investment. An additional incentive may be desirable to encourage them to invest more than their internal saving, as well as to increase internal saving at the expense of dividends. This investment incentive would be the analogue for the corporation income tax of the saving incentive proposed above for the individual income tax. A corporation would be permitted to deduct from its net income for tax purposes a certain percentage of gross outlays for plant and equipment in excess of a specified amount. The specified amount would be depreciation plus (on the assumption of a 52 per cent tax rate) 48 per cent of net income before tax. As in the case of the individual saving incentive, an averaging requirement would be necessary to assure a genuine increase in investment instead of a mere bunching of investment in a single year to qualify for the tax benefit. This investment allowance would not alter the present provisions of the tax law regarding depreciation; investment against which the incentive allowance is claimed would be eligible for subsequent depreciation in the same manner as other investment. Together with the second proposal, this tax incentive proposal seems to me a more effective and equitable means to increase corporate investment than accelerated depreciation.

An incidental advantage of the proposal is to encourage research and development expenditures complementary to plant and equipment expansion. Research and development expenditures can be charged off as current expense; they make it easier, therefore, to qualify for the investment deduction.

As mentioned above, it would be desirable to reduce the incentive that the corporate income tax gives for advertising outlays and for disguising personal remuneration as business expense.

Expansion of Public Investment and Government Services

The emphasis that has been given to the stimulation and financing of private investment is not intended to minimize the role of expansion of the public sector in a program of economic growth. Expansion of public investment in schools, highways, hospitals, and other construction and hardware is just as essential to economic growth as expansion of private plant and equipment. Improvement of the quantity and quality of education at all levels is, of course, a national need of the highest priority. Research and development is, as the example of the rapid growth of productivity in our most progressive industry, agriculture, demonstrates, a matter of public as well as private initiative.

Nor is economic growth the only reason the public sector needs to obtain a greater share of the nation's productive resources. We have not been spending as much for defense as a prudent concern for national survival dictates. We have not been exporting capital to the underdeveloped world as much as national interest and sheer humanity suggest we should. Within the realm of consumption itself, we have clearly starved public services and facilities at the expense of private spending. For example, we have plenty of cars and time to get there, but too few public recreational areas to drive to.

For these reasons the projected composition of national output (in the *New Republic* article and in Figure 15.1 of this memorandum) allows for substantial increase in the government share. The tax increases recommended are sufficient to pay for increased government activity and to provide a federal budget surplus to help finance expansion of private investment.

Growth, Full Employment and Inflation

The objective of full employment must be distinguished from the objective of growth. There is no automatic correlation between the two. Good things do not necessarily come together. It is possible to achieve one of these objectives, either one, without the other. If we want to attain both, we must deliberately aim for both.

A new administration can and should run the economy at a smaller rate of unemployment than the Republicans have been content to do, 3 per cent instead of 5 per cent. But a vigorous full employment policy, desirable as it is, will not by itself accelerate growth. Let us not delude ourselves on this point. How fast we grow depends on the *composition* of national output, not on its *size*. To raise the rate of growth we must increase the share of output devoted to enlarging future capacity to produce – the share going to public and private investment, research and education. The Eisenhower administration has mismanaged the economy on this count too. Not only have employment and output been too low during the last seven years, but the output we have realized has been misallocated. The administration has improvidently neglected the future. Too little of our national production has gone into uses that promote growth. Too much has been frittered away in frills, fads and gadgets. As a result the economy has been growing too slowly.

How much the restoration of a full employment policy will contribute to growth depends on how it is done. The 20–25 billion dollar increase in output we can get by shifting from a 5 per cent to a 3 per cent unemployment policy is an opportunity to raise the share of output we dedicate to the future. Let the stimulus to the additional output come in the main from new investment spending and new government programs, and full employment policy will also serve the goal of progress. Let the demands that stimulate additional output represent simply further expansion of consumption, and full employment will be achieved without improving the rate of economic growth.

A program for growth – designed to allocate a bigger proportion of national output to growth-generating uses – is not an inflationary program. A responsible policy for growth does not expand investment without also expanding saving, or expand government expenditure without also expanding tax revenues. A coherent policy for growth does not simply stimulate spending for growth purposes, piling these demands on top of demands that already exhaust full employment output. A consistent policy for growth encourages investment spending and enlarges government activity *and* makes sure that the resources necessary to meet these demands are released from less essential uses. Growth policy is necessarily double-edged. Spending must be stimulated in the right directions. But if that spending is to accomplish its aim and not simply lead to inflation, it must be financed by saving and taxes. The financing will not arrange itself; it must be provided by deliberate policy. It is entirely too easy – and perhaps it has too much superficial political appeal – to neglect the financing half of growth policy, emphasizing only the spending half. Republican pronouncements on growth so far give no evidence of economic literacy and responsibility in discussing growth policy. They talk of ways to stimulate corporate investment but not of ways to augment national saving. (Rockefeller talks of 5 per cent to 6 per cent growth rates with no indication of how to finance the spending necessary to achieve it.) Which party is the party of 'fiscal integrity'?

Assuming that we aim in any case at the same level of unemployment – say 3 per cent – the allocation of output achieved by a responsible growth policy is *not* more inflationary than a high-consumption economy. Indeed, a higher rate of growth may mitigate some of the 'cost-push' inflationary pressure associated with a high level of employment. To the extent that the productivity of labor grows faster, a great part of the aspiration of wage-earners for periodic advance in their money wages can be satisfied without price increases.

That kind of inflationary pressure may be somewhat stronger at 3 per cent unemployment than it is at 5 per cent unemployment. The bargaining position of labor relative to employers is naturally greater when unemployment is smaller. This provides another reason for devoting to uses that raise productivity the gain in output due to the higher level of employment

The difficult choice of objective is between high employment and price stability, not between growth and price stability. If the rate of creeping inflation turns out to be too great at 3 per cent unemployment, then we may have to settle for 4 per cent. Whatever compromise of this kind evolves, we are still free to accelerate growth. Whatever the level of employment, we can make output grow faster by putting a bigger share into investment, research and education. Personally, I believe the additional output we can get year after year by maintaining unemployment at 3 per cent instead of 4 per cent or 5 per cent will be well worth the additional inflationary hazard involved, *provided* the additional output is devoted to national needs of high priority, including economic growth.

GROWTH THROUGH TAXATION

The overriding issue of political economy in the 1960s is how to allocate the national output. How much to private consumption? How much for private investment in plant and equipment? For government investment and public services? For national defence? For foreign aid and overseas investment? Though our productive capacity is great and is growing, the demands upon it seem to be growing even faster.

The allocation of resources among competing uses is *the* central and classical theoretical problem of economics. Likewise it is the inescapable central practical problem of a Soviet-type planned economy, or of any economy under the forced draft of total war. Only recently has allocation of the output of the peacetime American economy begun to emerge from economics texts into the political arena, as a challenge and opportunity for democratic decision and governmental action. Public economic policy and debate have long been dominated by other concerns: unemployment, inflation, inequality. The composition of national output has been an unintended by-product rather than a conscious objective of economic policy.

The importance of accelerating economic growth brings the question of allocation to the fore. Can we as a nation, by political decision and governmental action, increase our rate of growth? Or must the rate of growth be regarded fatalistically, the result of uncoordinated decisions and habits of millions of consumers, businessmen, and governments, uncontrollable in our kind of society except by exhortation and prayer? The communists are telling the world that they alone know how to mobilize economic resources for rapid growth. The appeal of free institutions in the underdeveloped world, and perhaps even their survival in the West, may depend on whether the communists are right. We cannot, we need not, leave the outcome to chance.

How can an increase in the rate of growth of national output be achieved? The answer is straightforward and painful. We must devote more of our current capacity to uses that increase our future capacity, and correspondingly less to other uses. The uses of current capacity that build up future productive capacity are of three major types: (1) *Investment*: replacement and expansion of the country's stock of productive capital – factories, machines, roads, trucks, school buildings, hospitals, power dams, pipelines. (2) *Research*, both in basic science and in industrial application, by government, private industry, and nonprofit institutions, leading sooner or later to more efficient processes and new products. (3) *Education* of all kinds augmenting the skill of the future labor force. The competing uses of current capacity are: (1) *Unemployment*: failure to employ current capacity to the full, thus losing potential production. (2) *Consumption*, where most of our resources are engaged, providing us with the goods, services, and leisure that constitute the most luxurious standard of living the world has known.

Since 1953, the economy has been operating at an average unemployment level of 4.9 per cent of the labor force, and the Eisenhower administration seems to regard 5 per cent as a highly satisfactory boom-time performance. A society geared to the objective of growth should keep the average unemployment rate down to 3 per cent. Reduction of unemployment to this level could increase gross national product from the current labor force and capital stock by about $20 billion. But this increase in output will contribute to economic growth only if it is used in substantial part for investment, research, and education; it will make no contribution if it is all consumed. Republican economic policies are highly vulnerable. But critics should eschew the superficial political appeal of the unfounded line that more vigorous pursuit of full employment, with a battery of New Deal antidepression remedies, will by itself assure rapid growth.

To stimulate growth we must somehow engineer two shifts in the composition of actual and potential national output. One is from private consumption to the public sector, federal, state, and local. Domestic economic growth is, of course, not the only reason for such a shift. Increased defence, increased foreign aid, increased public consumption are possibly equally urgent reasons. The second shift of resources that must be engineered is from private consumption to private investment. About three-quarters of gross national product is produced with the help of business plant and equipment. Faster growth of output requires a more rapidly expanding and more up-to-date stock of plant and equipment. Every $1.00 increase of GNP requires in the neighborhood of $1.50 new plant and equipment investment. Thus to raise the rate of growth 2 percentage points, say from 3 per cent to 5 per cent per annum, the share of plant and equipment investment in current GNP must rise by 3 percentage points, for example from 10 to 13 per cent.

Tables 15.1 and 15.2 provide a concrete illustration of the kind of change we need in the relative composition of output if we are serious about increasing our rate of growth. Table 15.1 shows the actual composition of GNP in 1953 and 1959 and a suggested target for 1965. Table 15.2 shows the composition of GNP in the three years with correction for price changes, that is, in 'constant 1959 dollars'. Table 15.4 is based on Tables 15.1 and

Table 15.1 Composition of gross national product in current dollars

	1953	1959 (billions of dollars)	1965 target
Potential gross national product (3% unemployment)	365	500 (104%)	688*
Actual gross national product	365 (100%)	479 (100%)	688 (100%)
Private consumption	233 (64%)	311 (65%)	390 (58%)
Government purchases of goods and services	83 (23%)	98 (20%)	173 (25%)
a. Privately produced	51 (14%)	53 (11%)	88 (13%)
b. Services of government employees	32 (9%)	45 (9%)	85 (12%)
Gross private investment	50 (14%)	70 (15%)	125 (18%)
a. Plant and equipment	36 (10%)	44 (9%)	88 (13%)
b. Increase in inventories	—	4 (1%)	8 (1%)
c. Residential construction	14 (4%)	22 (5%)	27 (4%)
Net private foreign investment	−1 —	−1 —	0 (0%)

Note: *The Council of Economic Advisers now (July 1965) estimates potential GNP for 1965 in current dollars, for 4 per cent unemployment, at $684 billion. However, prices have risen more than I assumed in the tables; consumption prices have risen about 8 per cent since 1959 instead of remaining stationary.

Source: For actual data 1953 and 1959: *Economic Report of the President*, 1960.

Table 15.2   Composition of gross national product in constant 1959 dollars

	1953	1959 (billions of dollars)	1965 target
Potential gross national product (3% unemployment)	417	500 (104%)	650*
Actual gross national product	417 (100%)	479 (100%)	650 (100%)
Private consumption	254 (61%)	311 (65%)	390 (60%)
Government purchases of goods and services	102 (24%)	98 (20%)	145 (22%)
a. Privately produced	59 (14%)	53 (11%)	80 (12%)
b. Services of government employees	43 (10%)	45 (9%)	65 (10%)
Gross private investment	60 (15%)	70 (15%)	115 (18%)
a. Plant and equipment	44 (11%)	44 (9%)	80 (12%)
b. Increase in inventories	1 —	4 (1%)	8 (1%)
c. Residential construction	15 (4%)	22 (5%)	27 (4%)
Net private foreign investment	1 —	–1 —	0 (0%)

Note: *(July 1965): The Council of Economic Advisers' estimate of potential GNP for 1965 at 4 per cent unemployment is $630 billion in 1959 dollars. For 3 per cent unemployment it would be perhaps $640 billion. The difference from my $650 billion target reflects the low investment of the intervening years. But the difference is small and suggests that I underestimated the growth of the economy in the absence of the measures I advocated and, by the same token, probably overestimated their ability to add to the growth rate.

Source: For actual data 1953 and 1959: Economic Report of the President, 1960.

15.2 but brings out the essential point more clearly. It shows how the actual increase in GNP between 1953 and 1959 was allocated among major uses and, in contrast, how we should allocate the growth in output over the next six years if we really want output to grow.

Between 1953 and 1959 potential GNP rose from $365 billion to an estimated $500 billion. The composition of GNP in these years is shown in Table 15.1. The way in which the $135 billion increase was used is shown in the first column of Table 15.4. Some of the potential increase went to waste in unemployment. Of the realized increase, 69 per cent went into consumption, 13 per cent into government activity, and 18 per cent into investment. Unfortunately these calculations *understate* the effective growth of consumption relative to government and investment. The reason is that the prices of goods and services needed for government activity and private investment rose relative to the prices of consumption goods and services. The extent of price increases for the various components of GNP is shown in Table 15.3. For example, the services of government employees (teachers, policemen, clerks and so on) rose in price 34 per cent while consumer prices rose 9 per cent. Although we managed to increase government expenditure for such services by $13 billion, $11 billion of the increase was simply the higher cost of the volume of services we were already getting in 1953 and only $2 billion represented a real expansion of such services. When account is taken of this and other unfavorable relative price changes, some 92 per cent of the growth in output 'in constant dollars' went to consumption; government activity actually diminished; private investment got 16 per cent of the increase in GNP, and none of this increase was for plant and equipment. (See column 3 of Table 15.4.)

Unfortunately, we will probably have to continue to do some running just to stay in the same place. The target suggested for 1965 in Tables 15.1 and 15.2 assumes that prices of goods and services for investment will rise, relative to consumer prices, in the proportions shown in Table 15.3. If consumption prices are kept stable from 1959 to 1965, potential 1965 GNP is estimated at $688 billion. Table 15.1 suggests that we resolve to increase to 25 per cent the government share of that output, and to 18 per cent the investment share. The assumed price increases in those sectors would nullify part of those increases, leaving us a GNP of $650 billion in constant 1959 dollars, with the composition shown in Table 15.2. In order to keep from consuming more than 46 per cent of the projected increase in real output we must restrain consumption to 38 per cent of the growth of dollar output. (See Table 15.4.)

Policy to accelerate growth must be double-edged. On the one hand, it must stimulate the desired government and private expenditures. On the other, it must discourage consumption. Here are some major constituents of a program for growth:

Table 15.3   Price increases of GNP components

	Actual: 1959 prices relative to 1953	Assumed: 1965 prices relative to 1959
Private consumption	1.09	1.00
Government purchases of goods and services		
a. Privately produced	1.15	1.10
b. Services of government employees	1.34	1.30
Gross private investment		
a. Plant and equipment	1.22	1.10
b. Residential construction	1.07	1.05

1. Increased expenditure by federal, state, and local governments for education, basic and applied research, urban redevelopment, resource conservation and development, transportation, and other public facilities.
2. Stimulus to private investment expenditures by:
   a. Federal Reserve and Treasury policy to create and maintain 'easy money' conditions, with credit readily available and interest rates low, especially in long-term capital markets.
   b. Improvement of averaging and loss-offset provisions in taxation of corporate income, in order to increase the degree to which the tax collector shares the risk of investment as well as the reward.
   c. The privilege of deducting from corporate net income for tax purposes a certain percentage of a corporation's outlays for plant and equipment to the extent that these outlays exceed a specified minimum. The specified minimum would be the sum of depreciation and (on the assumption that the tax rate is 52 per cent) 48 per cent of net income before tax. To qualify for the tax concession, a corporation would have to be investing more than its normal gross profits after tax. The concession, and the minimum requirement for eligibility for it, are designed to encourage greater corporate saving, the full investment of internal funds, and, most important, the undertaking of investment financed by outside saving obtained from the capital market. An analogous proposal to encourage noncorporate saving and investment is suggested below.

If these measures were adopted, a reduction in the basic corporate income tax rate, advocated by many as essential to growth, would be neither

Table 15.4 Disposition of increases in GNP

	Current dollars		Constant 1959 dollars	
	1953 to 1959	1959 to 1965	1953 to 1959	1959 to 1965
		(billions of dollars)		
Potential gross national product	135 (118%)	188 (90%)	83 (133%)	150 (88%)
Actual gross national product	114 (100%)	209 (100%)	62 (100%)	171 (100%)
Private consumption	78 (69%)	79 (38%)	57 (92%)	79 (46%)
Government purchases of goods and services	15 (13%)	75 (36%)	−4 (−6%)	47 (27%)
a. Privately produced	2 (2%)	35 (17%)	−6 (−10%)	27 (16%)
b. Services of government employees	13 (11%)	40 (19%)	2 (3%)	20 (11%)
Gross private investment	20 (18%)	55 (26%)	10 (16%)	45 (26%)
a. Plant and equipment	8 (7%)	44 (21%)	0 (0%)	36 (21%)
b. Increase in inventories	4 (5%)	4 (2%)	3 (5%)	4 (2%)
c. Residential construction	8 (7%)	7 (3%)	7 (11%)	5 (3%)
Net private foreign investment	— —	— —	−1 (−2%)	1 —

necessary nor equitable. Indeed the strength of these measures might be greater if the rate were increased.

3. Restriction of consumption, by:
    a. Increase in personal income tax at all levels, accompanied by permission to deduct a certain amount of saving from income subject to tax. Like present deductions for charity or medical care, the saving deduction would be claimed at the taxpayer's option, with the burden of proof on him. A schedule of 'normal' saving for taxpayers of various incomes and family circumstances would be established, and only saving in excess of a taxpayer's 'normal' would be eligible for deduction. A scheme of this kind seems to be the most feasible equitable way to use the tax instrument to favor saving at the expense of consumption.[1]
    b. Improvements in the Social Security system – for example, raising retirement benefits and relating their amount, above a common minimum, to cumulated covered earnings – should be introduced on a quasi-contributory basis. Since the payroll tax contributions then precede the benefits, the funds accumulate and can be an important channel of national saving.
    c. Increases in state and local taxes – property or sales or income as the case may be – to keep pace with the share of these governments in the necessary expansion of the public sector.
    d. Limitation, to a reasonable proportion of sales, of the privilege of deducting advertising and promotional expenses from corporate income subject to tax. No observer of the American scene doubts that advertising is excessive. From the economic point of view, it absorbs too large a share of the nation's resources itself, and at the same time it generates synthetic pressures for ever-higher consumption.

Increased taxation is the price of growth. We must tax ourselves not only to finance the necessary increase in public expenditures but also to finance, indirectly, the expansion of private investment. A federal budget surplus is a method by which we as a nation can expend the volume of savings available for private investment beyond the current saving of individuals and corporations. The surplus must, to be sure, be coupled with measures to stimulate investment, so that the national resolution to save actually leads to capital formation and is not wasted in unemployment and unrequited loss of consumption. It is only superficially paradoxical to combine anti-inflationary fiscal policy with an expansionary monetary policy. The policies outlined above must be combined in the right proportions, so that aggregate demand is high enough to maintain a 3 per cent unemployment rate but not higher. There are several mixtures that can do that job; of them we must choose the one that gives the desired composition of aggregate demand. If the overwhelming problem of democratic capitalism in the 1930s and even the 1950s was to bring the business cycle under social control, the challenge of the 1960s is to bring under public decision the broad allocation of national output. Fortunately the means are at hand. They are techniques well within the peacetime scope of government. We can do the job without the direct controls of wartime – priorities, rationing, price and wage controls.

The means are at hand; to use them we will need to muster more wisdom, maturity, leadership, and sense of national purpose than we displayed in the 1950s. A program like the suggested 1965 target, which allows an increase of per capita consumption at about 1 per cent a year, is scarcely a program of austerity. Indeed it would not feel austere even if the growth of gross output per head were held to 1½ per cent per annum. We are used to institutions that let us realize in increased consumption about two thirds of increases in output. But let people earn the incomes associated with a 2½ per cent rise in output per capita, and the measures necessary to keep their consumption from rising faster than 1 per cent may seem burdensome sacrifices. Our communist competitors have an advantage. Since they do not pay out such increases in output as personal incomes in the first place, they do not have the problem of recapturing them in taxes or saving. That problem we cannot escape in a free society. Unless we master it, we shall not fare well in the competition for economic growth and national survival.

NOTE

1. For a further discussion of this proposal, see James Tobin, 'Taxes, Saving, and Inflation', *American Economic Review*, 39 (December 1949), 1223–32.

16. The monetary and fiscal policy mix*

AGGREGATE DEMAND AND SUPPLY

In this lecture, I shall discuss the strategy of what economists call *demand management* – the policies of the government, including the Federal Reserve, that affect the aggregate spending of the population on goods and services and so act upon the economy. I refer to the economy as a whole, not to particular products or markets.

I distinguish *demand* from *supply* in the following sense: During business cycles the economy is not always constrained by its capacity to produce, its supply potential. Cyclical fluctuations reflect variations, for one reason or another, in the overall demand for goods and services, and thus for workers to produce them. In the long run, however, the output of goods and services in the country is clearly limited by the capacity of the economy to produce.

'Supply-side' economics concerns the growth of productive capacity. 'Demand-side' economics, my main focus in this lecture, has to do with the management of the economy, not for accelerating its long-run capacity growth, but for stabilizing the business cycle and avoiding excesses of unemployment on the one hand and inflation on the other. The two 'sides' are, however, related in a way that I will be discussing and trying to describe. Some strategies of short-run demand management are better for long-run growth than others.

In recent years, I think it is fair to say, the capacity of the economy to produce goods and services – potential output – has not been the binding constraint on the real output of the United States economy. Rather, the constraint has been the adequacy of aggregate demand to purchase the output of the economy. This has been true since 1980, when we fell into the first of two recessions that occurred in rapid succession. We began recovering from the second one at the end of 1982, but we haven't yet fully recovered. For more than two years the rate of utilization of the economy's

*   This chapter first appeared as an article in the *Economic Review*, August/September 1986, pp.4–16.

potential has been flat; only 80 per cent of industrial capacity has been uti-
lized, recently even less. Normal capacity utilization in our economy in
prosperity has been at 85, 86 or 87 per cent. The unemployment rate of
workers has been stuck for more than two years at 7 per cent of the labor
force, plus or minus a couple of tenths, more often plus than minus. There
is no evidence that 7 per cent is as low an unemployment rate as we can have
today without setting off inflation. It's hard to find any bottlenecks or scar-
cities or shortages in this economy, or any tendency for wages to accelerate.
The inflation rate has been extremely well-behaved, even after the end of
the deep recession of 1981–2. This means that ever since 1979, demand
management, or short-run stabilization policy, which is the main business
of the Federal Reserve, has been the decisive determinant of unemployment, capacity utilization and the growth of real GNP.

DEMAND MANAGEMENT, FISCAL AND MONETARY

Two major instruments of demand management are available to the central
government in the United States and other advanced economies: on the one
hand, monetary policy and, on the other, fiscal policy. Reference was made
in the introductions to my service in Washington on the President's Council
of Economic Advisers. At that time we on the Council were doing a teaching job. We had an important student, the President of the United States,
John F. Kennedy, who seemed not to have absorbed a lot of economics in
his undergraduate training. He was a good student and able to learn fast,
and we were good teachers, I must say. We knew we were getting somewhere
one day when he said, 'I think I now know the difference between monetary policy and fiscal policy. Monetary policy begins with an "M," and the
chairman of the Federal Reserve is [William McChesney] Martin, so that's
monetary policy. What we do in the budget must be fiscal policy.' These two
instruments of demand management policy are the ingredients I refer to
when I speak of 'the mix.'

How does the use of these two instruments work on aggregate demand?
Fiscal policy involves spending money. When the government spends more
money directly on goods and services – mainly armaments these days – or
transfers money to the beneficiaries of Social Security and other programs,
aggregate demand for goods and services increases. You may or may not
like particular programs, but how the money is spent does not matter for
our immediate purpose. What matters is the additional overall spending on
goods and services. If you don't believe that defense spending is stimulating, I invite you to come to Connecticut or Massachusetts to see that econ-

omies supplying defense-related products do prosper. Tax reductions work the same way. People generally spend a large fraction of their tax savings. For example, in 1981 we had a mammoth reduction in income taxes under the Economic Recovery Tax Act of 1981. To be sure, it was advertised by the administration and in the press as a supply-side tax cut. Its philosophy was to increase incentives for working more, saving more, producing more, and taking more risk. Thus it was meant to be a policy to increase the capacity of the economy, its productivity, its potential output. In the immediate circumstances of the day, however, when the potential output of the economy was far above its actual performance, it worked to increase spending. The recipients of the tax cut didn't know that they weren't supposed to spend the proceeds, and so they spent them. Thus it worked as a demand-side stimulus.

Monetary policy generally works in ways that lower or raise interest rates and raise or lower market values of bonds, stocks, and other assets. Through these effects, monetary policy stimulates or restrains spending for investment goods – for house building, business plant and equipment, and inventories.

EXCHANGE RATES AND AGGREGATE DEMAND

There is one other mechanism by which monetary policy works to expand or restrict demand, a mechanism fairly new in American experience – and in world experience. Recent events have given a striking demonstration of its power. It works through the balance of exports and imports in foreign trade. Because of the floating exchange rate regime in which the United States and other countries have been operating since 1973, along with the amazing international mobility of funds, immense amounts of money can move rapidly across the exchange rates from, say, dollar assets into yen assets or vice versa, or into and out of pound-sterling, Deutsche Mark assets, or others. Recently we have had a textbook example of this mechanism, which, I must say to the credit of us economists, was well understood in theory before it actually occurred with such remarkable fidelity.

In the 1980s, thanks to our monetary and fiscal policies, interest rates in the United States were high, even higher than interest rates in other advanced economies. They attracted funds across the currency exchanges into dollar assets, often US Treasury bills and bonds but into the whole range of dollar-denominated assets as well. Likewise, they deterred Americans from lending funds overseas. The result was a big demand for dollars relative to other currencies, which bid up the price of a dollar in yen and other major currencies. The dollar became costly to foreigners; other currencies became inexpensive to Americans. The further result was that people didn't buy many American goods, while we bought a lot of foreign goods at bargain dollar prices. We developed the massive surplus of imports over exports that is still reported every month.

Here, then, was a powerful mechanism by which a monetary policy that actively raised interest rates affected demand for US goods and services. By reducing exports and raising imports, it diverted American demand to foreign goods instead of goods produced by American labor and capital. That supplemented the normal, old-fashioned way tight monetary policies and high interest rates work, by restricting residential construction and business investment.

THE FISCAL/MONETARY POLICY MIX

In discussing the policy *mix*, I want to give the word a precise meaning. I am not talking about a mix-up between the two policies, although that may often occur. I am not referring to the two policies in a general way. I make a precise distinction between the total stimulus administered by the two policies and the relative contributions of each of the two policies to that total. It's as if you have two types of medicine: first you ask what is the total dose of the two medicines together; and second, how is the dose split between the two medicines Right now I want to address the second question, how the dose is split between the two medicines – the mix.

Figure 16.1 relates the after-tax interest rate in the economy and the real (inflation-corrected) output of the economy. The horizontal axis represents output, real GNP, labeled 'Y'. The vertical axis is the interest rate after tax: $(1-t)\,r$, one minus the tax rate, that quantity times the interest rate. The *IS* curves for investment and saving, tell how the interest rate has to move for given monetary and fiscal policies in order to induce the amount of spending that would buy exactly the output measured on the horizontal axis. Each IS curve is sloping down, because lower interest rates are needed to get people to spend more money. When interest rates are low, people spend more money on investment and borrow more for consumption as well. The down-sloping effect also comes through exports and imports, as I already explained. Lower interest rates mean the dollar is cheaper, and that helps our exports relative to our imports. All these effects together make an *IS* curve slope down, as shown.

This figure shows a whole family of *IS* curves Some are higher than the others and further to the right. The position of a curve depends on government policies. (Other things too can affect the position, but for our purposes the point is that the position depends on policies). Specifically, the

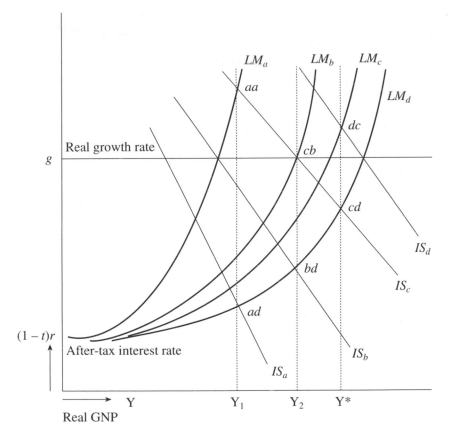

Note: The diagram shows how the same GNP values, Y_1 or Y_2 or Y^* (full employment output), can be achieved by different mixes of monetary and fiscal policies. Fiscal policy determines which *IS* locus the economy is on: curves higher and to the right result from easier fiscal policies. Monetary policy determines which *LM* curve the economy is on; curves lower and to the right represent easier monetary policies. The horizontal line at *g* depicts the real growth rate of GNP. As discussed in the text, an after-tax interest rate above *g* means that federal debt grows explosively indefinitely.

Figure 16.1   Policy mixes, interest rates and GNP

position of an *IS* curve depends on fiscal policy. Each of the *IS* curves could be regarded as being drawn for a particular budget program, encompassing the federal tax system, the expenditure budget, the legislation determining transfer entitlements like Social Security. Curve IS_a is a relatively tight budget policy, whereas IS_b is somewhat looser, with more spending or lower taxes or both. IS_c and IS_d are even looser, even more stimulating. Think of the effects of the Reagan Administration's budgets from 1981 on as moving up to the right shifting to higher *IS* curves by decreasing taxes and increasing defense expenditures.

Now consider the *LM* curves, which are determined by our friends of the Fed. Any one such curve answers the following question: given a certain amount of money that the Fed is willing to provide to the economy, what will happen to interest rates if output should increase? The curve says the interest rate will go up. Why? Because banks have only so many reserves, and households and businesses have only so much money in the banks and in their pockets and tills. Higher outputs mean higher levels of business activity and more competition by borrowers for the limited amount of funds that the Fed is willing to supply. That competition will raise interest rates. Economists typically label this sort of relationship, depicted by the LM curves, '*LM*' for liquidity, money.

Just as there is a family of *IS* curves, so there is a family of *LM* curves. In this abstract representation, fiscal policy chooses a member of the *IS* family, as I already explained. Monetary policy chooses a member of the *LM* family. If the Federal Open Market Committee, which meets every five or six weeks in Washington, decides to be more generous to the economy in the amount of money it provides, it will move to a *LM* curve further to the right and down; any given output of income will be associated with a lower interest rate. Easier monetary policy moves the economy's *LM* curve to the right and tighter monetary policy moves it to the left. As all economics students know, economists like intersections of curves, such as those that show the price of peanuts and the quantity bought and sold where a peanut demand curve crosses a peanut supply curve. Here we are interested in the intersection of a *IS* and a *LM* showing the interest rate and output generated by the corresponding fiscal policy and monetary policy. In Figure 16.1 there are lots of such intersections, indicating that there are several ways of achieving the same output, the same value of *Y*. All of these policy combinations deliver the same total dose, but the mixes differ. Different mixes of fiscal and monetary policy can generate the same aggregate demand, the same output, the same employment and unemployment, and the same capacity utilization rate. For example, the output represented by Y_2 can be created by the combination of monetary and fiscal policy designated by *bd* as well as by the combination marked *cb*. The higher intersection has a tighter monetary policy, and thus a higher interest rate and a relatively easier fiscal policy than *bd*. The intersection *bd*, on the other hand, has an easier monetary policy and a tighter fiscal policy, defined by a *IS* curve to the left.

Keeping Figure 16.1 in mind, let's think about what has happened in the United States during the last few years. Through a combination of policy decisions starting in 1979, we arrived at high intersections. That is, monetary policy was tight and fiscal policy was easy compared with mixes that could have produced the same output. The same Y could have been achieved with a different mix of policies.

Figure 16.2 makes the same point in another way. The horizontal axis represents fiscal policy. Moving to the right means easier budgets with

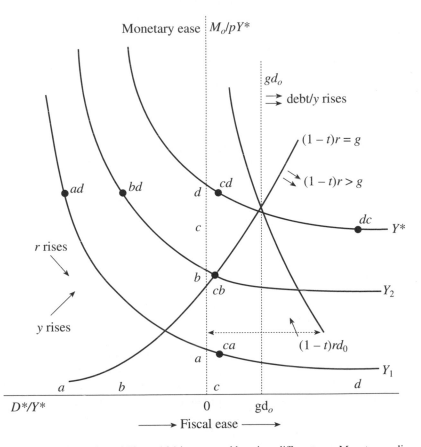

Note: The information of Figure 16.1 is presented here in a different way. Monetary policy is measured by the ratio of the monetary base, in real terms, to potential output pY^*. Isoquants – combinations of the two policies that yield the same real GNP – are pictured for Y_1, Y_2 and Y^*. Points of intersection in Figure 16.1 are placed here also and labeled the same $(ad, bd, \text{etc.})$. The vertical line gd_o tells how big a deficit will keep the debt–GNP ratio at d_o, given GNP growth at rate g. The downward-sloping curve $(1-t)rd_o$ is the interest cost of the existing debt d_o. The upward-sloping curve $(1-t)r = g$ is the boundary between stable (above) and unstable (below) debt–GNP ratios, as explained in the text.

Figure 16.2   Fiscal and monetary policies and GNP outcomes

lower taxes, more spending. and bigger deficits. Monetary policy is on the vertical axis. Going up means easier monetary policy, with the Fed providing more money relative to total output. The downward sloping curves in this diagram are called isoquants (same quantity). All the points on one of the downward curves are different ways of getting a given output Y_1. All the points on the next downward curve Y_2 represent combinations that produce the common result Y_2. The two Y_2 mixes we singled out in Figure 16.1 are both shown here, too, as *cb* and *bd*. One of them has easy fiscal policy and tight money and the other has tight fiscal policy and easy money. Then there is Y^*, which represents full capacity output – not the forced economic mobilization that occurred during World War II but the highest output a peacetime market economy can expect without having a resurgence of accelerating prices, rising inflation. (I don't know how large that is nor do I know what the corresponding lowest inflation-safe unemployment rate is. I was arguing with the local Fed people this morning about whether that figure is closer to 7 or to 6 per cent or even lower than that now. As I said earlier, I am sure it's not as high as 7 per cent).

PRICES VS QUANTITIES: THE COMMON FUNNEL THEORY

If our objective is just to determine output, our two policies evidently give us more degrees of freedom than we really need. We have at least two instruments – maybe more, considering that there are different kinds of taxes and expenditures, and several monetary tools. Since we have more tools than we need, why cannot we achieve some other goal at the same time? We know that the the main constraint on demand, output, and employment is the danger of inflation. Why not use one instrument to control inflation and the other one to get a desirable level of output and employment? For example, why not keep inflation down by tight money while we push output up by easy budgets? Why not manipulate the mix of the policies to combat inflation and unemployment simultaneously? That would be ideal. Unfortunately, the world is not made that way – at least according to the strong belief of most macroeconomists.

This belief I call the 'common funnel theory,' illustrated in Figure 16.3. Fiscal and monetary policy together determine aggregate dollar spending for GNP. They do not, however, determine how dollar spending is divided between prices and quantities. The common funnel theory goes as follows: Consider an injection of spending in dollars into the economy. Its size matters for prices and quantities. But whether it comes from the Fed or the budget doesn't matter; it produces inflation and unemployment in the same combination either way. In Figure 16.3 we see that money is being provided by the Fed (M), while fiscal stimulus is being poured in (V). They go into a mixing pot, turning pink. Then they come out in the form of prices and quantities. It does not matter from what source they came in, whether from fiscal stimulus or the Fed; they come out in the same proportions in changes in prices and changes in quantities.

Those proportions do depend on the state of the economy. If the economy is tight in terms of capacity utilization, then most of the demand goes into prices and little into quantity. If it is slack in terms of capacity utilization and labor employment, then the injections will show up mostly in quantities and only slightly in prices. The price/quantity outcome depends on the state of the economy, not on the sources of the demand or the policies that generated the demand.

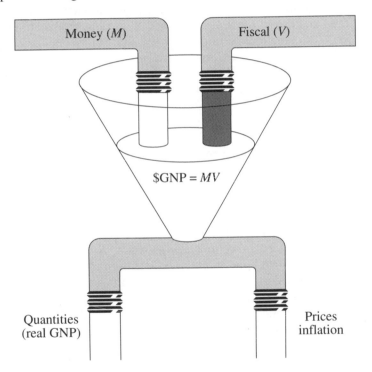

Note: This schematic diagram illustrates the point that the mix of price/quantity outcomes is independent of the sources of aggregate dollar demand. Monetary policy affects the supply of money and fiscal policy its circuit velocity. It is the product MV (money supply times circuit velocity), which is equal to dollar GNP, that represents demand for goods, services and labor and induces output and price responses from businesses and workers.

Figure 16.3   The common funnel theory

Thus it is not true, according to the common funnel proposition, that the Fed has a particular handle on prices and the budget a particular handle on quantities. Some people in Washington thought that in 1981 or at least said that, but it flies in the face of most evidence and theory about how the economy works. We cannot solve the unemployment/inflation dilemma by mixing monetary and fiscal policy in different proportions.

EXCHANGE RATES AND INFLATION

One necessary amendment to this discouraging proposition arises in international trade through the implications of floating exchange rates for macroeconomic policies, mentioned above. To understand this amendment let's go back to my previous story, in which tight money produces high interest rates and causes the dollar to shoot up in value relative to foreign currencies. This made foreign imports – Toyotas, Sonys, European vacations – cheap in dollars to Americans and helped our process of disinflation. The cheapness of foreign goods, which enter our price indexes in some proportion, gave us some relief from inflation in the early 1980s. That mechanism is now working in the opposite direction as the recent depreciation of the dollar becomes reflected in dollar prices of imports and exports.

This consequence of floating exchange rates is a point in favor of a tight money/easy fiscal mix. Relative to other mixes, it will have higher interest rates with the same outcome in employment and output, the same Y in Figures 16.1 and 16.2. This mix will be somewhat less inflationary, or more disinflationary, than a mix in which low interest rates are the result of easy money combined with a tight fiscal budget

But there is a catch, as we are now learning. A high exchange rate obtained through higher interest rates is only temporary. We can't live with massive import surpluses forever. At some point – a point we recently reached in the United States – the exchange rate has to go down again, the dollar has to depreciate. As that happens, we have to give back the price reductions we earned earlier by artificial appreciation of the currency. After all, the same movements of exchange rates that made things cheap for us made things dear for other countries. This game is not one that all countries can play at the same time. One reason that Japan and Germany objected to the high value of the dollar is that it made not only American imports but also oil, which is also invoiced in dollars, much more expensive in yen and Deutsche Marks.

For these reasons, I do not regard this qualification to the common funnel theory as a really important consideration in deciding on the monetary–fiscal mix. The gains in inflation control from choosing one mix rather than another to achieve the same output and employment are likely to be small and temporary for the United States

POLICY MIXES, CROWDING OUT, AND LONG-RUN GROWTH

How do we decide the mix of policies? Assume that someone has decided on the total dose, that is, the path of GNP and unemployment. What is a socially rational choice of the mix of policies to support that decision? The mix does make a difference, much more for the long run than for the short run. At the beginning of the lecture, I pointed out that demand management strategy does affect the long-run capacity of the economy to produce. The policy mix makes that connection. The reason is that the *composition* of national output will be different with a different mix, even though *aggregate* GNP is the same with one mix as with another. The tight money and easy fiscal mix emphasizes consumption relative to investment – consumption by government and by private sector relative to future-oriented uses of national output. High interest rates deter investment, while an easy fiscal stance encourages consumption through tax cuts, high transfer payments, or high government current expenditure. True, government purchases are not always for consumption; if the government were running deficits to accumulate public capital that would enhance the productivity and capacity of the economy over the long run, this characterization would not be valid.

Recently, the federal government has been financing current expenditures by deficit spending, and the Federal Reserve has countered the expansionary effects of this fiscal policy by high interest rates. The result is a larger consumption component of output than with a different policy mix. High interest rates have 'crowded out' some domestic investment and a spectacular amount of foreign investment. By running big trade deficits, we are spending the overseas capital we previously acquired and going into debt to the rest of the world. This is just as damaging to the future prospects of Americans as failing to replace worn-out or obsolete capital equipment at home. Although our record of domestic capital formation in the last several years is not bad, we have financed it essentially by mortgaging productive assets to the rest of the world. That cannot be regarded as future-oriented activity. Whether domestic or foreign investment is crowded out, future generations pay the price.

Suppose we had achieved the same recovery since 1982 with a tighter budget and an appropriately easier, lower-interest rate, monetary policy. Then we would not have suffered such big deficits in our balance of trade.

We would have had as much, perhaps even more, domestic investment, and it would not be mortgaged to the rest of the world. That is one reason why I and many other economists have strongly preferred a mix easier in money and tighter in budget.

STABLE AND UNSTABLE POLICIES

There is another reason for that preference. Freedom of choice among policy mixes is not unlimited. The mix chosen in the United States, at least until recently, is one that cannot be sustained. Let me explain: A substantial part of the federal budget is payment of interest on the national debt Suppose that the interest rate the government has to pay on the debt is higher than the rate of economic growth. Suppose, realistically, that the Treasury's average interest rate is 7 per cent, while the economy is growing in current dollar GNP at 6 per cent per year, with 3 per cent inflation and 3 per cent real growth. Even if the budget is otherwise balanced, this disparity alone will make the debt grow by 7 per cent while GNP will be growing by only 6 per cent As the debt grows faster than GNP, the interest burden will grow further, so that the deficit and debt become still larger relative to GNP. This accelerating process will continue year after year. This would be true even if the first of the government budget were exactly balanced, but of course that has not been the same. A deficit in the 'primary' budget – that is, exclusive of debt service – makes the process more explosive. The ratio of debt to GNP rises indefinitely, faster and faster, as does the deficit a share of GNP. An even larger share of the population's saving is diverted from productive investment at home or abroad, into financing the federal government. As 'crowding out' becomes more and more severe, the interest rate itself rises. The policy mix becomes a still tighter money, easier budget combination. The circle is really vicious.

Note the horizontal line or curve on Figures 16.1 and 16.2. These depict the boundary I have just been discussing: crossing it leads to the vicious circle just described. The boundary traces the limit at which the interest rate becomes the same as the growth rate. If you go to mixes tighter in monetary policy and looser in fiscal policy, you enter the unstable territory of exploding debt.

THE POLICY MIX IN THE UNITED STATES TODAY

Table 16.1 presents some data on the United States' federal debt and deficits since 1952. It shows the ratios of federal debt (to the public) to GNP at the beginning of each of several periods. In 1952, for example, the public debt was 65 per cent of one year's gross national product. As the table shows, the ratio declined until 1980, to about 22 per cent. The debt–GNP ratio actually started declining right after World War II, which had raised the ratio to 120 per cent. While many people think the federal government has been following profligate fiscal policies continuously, as long as anyone can remember, at least since the Great Depression, the table shows that this charge is far from true. The debt grew more slowly than GNP from 1946 to 1980.

Things changed radically in the 1980s. In the last five years the debt to GNP ratio has risen to 38 per cent That is a big increase, though 38 per cent is still not a disastrously high number. We have had higher numbers before without disaster; nonetheless, in the 1950s and 1960s the ratio was declining, while in the 1980s it has been rising.

Table 16.1 also shows the primary deficit in percent of GNP. This is the deficit we would have had if there had been no outstanding debt at the beginning of the period. For example, in the first period, 1952 to 1957, the primary budget showed an average surplus of 0.6 of 1 per cent of GNP. It continued in surplus or close to balance in all periods through 1974. In 1986 prior to Gramm–Rudman, however, the primary deficit would have been 2.7 per cent of GNP, the largest ever in peace time. The next column shows the total deficit including interest payments on the debt, again in percent of GNP. The total deficit, which was very close to zero in the 1950s and 1960s, has risen to about 5 per cent of GNP. Most of the increase occurred after 1980. Much of it, as the table shows, is due to the tight money/easy fiscal mix, which brought high interest rates and in turn a tremendous surge of interest payments compared to the years before 1980.

Column 4 of Table 16.1 shows the 'Real Deficit'. Applying inflation accounting principles to the government budget and its debt means counting only real interest – the difference between the interest rate and the inflation rate – as a cost to the government The implicit assumption is that the public's latent demand for government debt will cause people to save enough to maintain their holdings of the debt in real terms. In other words, people are assumed to understand that part of the high nominal interest they receive just pays for the loss in the real principal value of government securities due to inflation. Inflation accounting gives lower deficit figures, but the pattern shows a very sharp increase since 1980.

Columns 5 and 6 of Table 16.1 compare the real growth rate of the economy with the interest rate the government has to pay on its debt. I pointed out earlier the danger that confronts us if the interest that the Treasury has to pay (allowing for taxes) exceeds the growth rate of the economy. We were never close to that point until now; we crossed the line

Table 16.1 Federal fiscal history and projections

| | (As per cent of GNP) | | | (Per cent Per Year) | | (Per cent) |
	(1) Debt beginning of period	(2) Primary deficit	(3) Total deficit	(4) Real deficit	(5) Net real interest rate assumed	(6) Growth of real GNP	(7) Equilibrium debt/GNP ratio
1952–57	65	−0.6	0.3	−1.0	−0.7	2.8	−17
1958–66	48	−0.5	0.1	−0.8	−0.7	3.4	−12
1967–74	36	0.3	1.1	−0.5	−2.8	3.8	5
1975–79	23	1.4	2.5	−0.8	−2.8	3.5	22
1980–85	22	2.6	4.5	2.7	0.3	1.9	45
1986	38	2.7	5.2	4.0	3.4	3.0	unstable
1991 A	35	−1.9	0.0	−1.4	1.5	3.0	−126
1991 B	35	−0.7	1.4	0.0	2.0	3.0	−70
1991 C	35	0.2	2.5	1.1	2.5	3.0	35

Notes:
1991 A Balanced budget, G–R–H.
1991 B Balanced budget, correcting interest for inflation (4%).
1991 C Stabilizing debt relative to GNP.

Source: Author's calculations. Before 1980, originally presented in *Towards a Reconstruction of Federal Budgeting*, The Conference Board, 1983, pp.51–9.

some time between 1980 and 1985. Before 1980 real GNP growth always exceeded interest cost by a wide margin – you get the same answer by comparing nominal interest rates and dollar GNP growth. But since then the comparison turned the other way, and these circumstances produced the unstable vicious spiral I described. This mix of monetary and fiscal policy simply cannot be allowed to continue indefinitely.

The last column is a bit more esoteric. It addresses the question: Is there a value at which the debt–GNP ratio would settle down permanently, as long as the parameters of the budget and the economy remained constant? If so, what is it? The answers depend on the values of three parameters: the primary deficit in ratio to GNP, x; the net (after-tax) interest rate $(1-t)r$; and the rate of growth of GNP, g. The answer to the first question is 'yes', if $(1-t)r$ is less than g, as was true in every period except 1986. The answer is 'no, unstable,' if $(1-t)r$ exceeds g. as in 1986. When a numerical answer to the question exists, it can be calculated for each period from the parameters of the period. Those numbers are shown in column 7. The negative numbers are especially hypothetical. Their significance is that the debt–GNP ratio would rapidly decline and, in principle, would settle down only if and when the government became a creditor rather than a debtor.

Three possibilities are shown for 1991 in Table 16.1. All of them assume that through fiscal year 1990 deficits will be reduced according to the Gramm–Rudman–Hollings schedule, enough to lower the debt–GNP ratio to 35 per cent. The first scenario, A, assumes the Gramm–Rudman–Hollings target of a balanced total budget by conventional accounting will be met in 1991 and ever thereafter. As the applicable row of Table 16.1 shows, this is a very austere regimen, requiring a primary surplus of 1.9 per cent of GNP, about $120 billion in 1991. A less austere policy would be to balance the budget calculated according to inflation accounting. The result is given in row B. The third possibility is to let bygones be bygones and be satisfied to maintain a 35 per cent debt–GNP ratio. As row C shows, this could be approximated just by balancing the primary budget. The total deficit would then be 7 per cent of the debt, 2.5 per cent of GNP; the real deficit would be only 1.1 per cent of GNP.

Table 16.2, borrowed from an article by Barry Bosworth in *Brookings Bulletin* of Winter/Spring 1986, offers additional relevant insights into our topic. Bosworth's numbers show for several periods national saving relative to net national product (NNP). (NNP is smaller than GNP by allowing for capital consumption.) National saving is composed of two parts, 'private' (inclusive of state and local governments) and federal. In the 1950s private saving amounted to about 8.4 per cent of NNP, but the government had a small deficit, and so national saving was 7.7 per cent of NNP. Similarly in the 1960s and even the 1970s the national saving ratio was still close to 8

Table 16.2   National saving and investment as percentage shares of net national product, 1951–85

	National Saving			Net Investment	
	Private	Government	Total	Foreign	Domestic
1951–60	8.4	−0.7	7.7	0.3	7.4
1961–70	9.2	−1.0	8.1	0.6	7.6
1971–80	9.7	−2.0	7.7	0.3	7.4
1981–85	8.6	−4.7	3.9	−1.3	5.2
1985	8.8	−5.4	3.4	−3.1	6.5

Source: Barry Bosworth, 'Fiscal Fitness: Deficit Reduction and the Economy', *Brookings Bulletin*, Winter/Spring 1986, Table 1, p.5.

per cent Throughout these decades net national saving went both into domestic investment and, via trade surpluses, into increasing the nation's net claims against the rest of the world. Once again, the drastic change occurred in the 1980s. Federal dissaving offset more than half of private saving. Foreign investment, in consequence, turned strongly negative, and, even so, domestic investment fell relative to NNP.

These dismal outcomes are the result of the policy mix. The mix of fiscal and monetary policy we have drifted into in recent years is bizarre, extreme, and unprecedented. It has had very unfortunate consequences. This policy was meant, according to the rhetoric of 1981, to increase investment. It was supposed to be oriented toward using resources in ways that would increase productivity and long-term growth. The results are just the opposite. Fully 97 per cent of the additional output the country has been able to produce since 1978 or 1979 has been consumed, either publicly or privately.

How did we manage to adopt such a bad policy mix? Tight monetary policies were used to bring down inflation after 1979, and real interest rates have never been the same. Then came the reckless budget policies of the 1980s – big tax cuts and rapid growth of defense spending.

Changing this policy mix is a high priority. We seem to be embarked upon a course that will tighten the budget under the gun of Gramm–Rudman. I do not myself believe Gramm–Rudman is a good way to correct our fiscal policy, and I think the target of balancing the conventional budget is over-kill. I believe the federal government needs more tax revenue, but this is not the forum for arguing these points.

In any case, let me emphasize, fiscal correction is only half the needed remedy. The other half is up to the Federal Reserve, to whom I never fail to give advice, generally unheeded, when given the chance. As budget policy is tightened, monetary policy must be eased and interest rates substantially lowered. Otherwise, we will not achieve the same results in output and employment as under the present mix. Indeed, there is ample evidence now that the overall dose of stimulus from the two policies together is inadequate. It's not enough to keep the economy from outright recession. It needs to be rescued from stagnation. It is not enough to keep the unemployment rate near 7 per cent and capacity utilization at 78 per cent. The economy can do better than that without courting renewed inflation. In the present circumstances fiscal policy obviously can make no contribution to the resumption and completion of the recovery; it will instead be moving us the other way. Prosperity is the responsibility of the institution playing host to us today, the Federal Reserve System.

EDITOR'S NOTE

This article, based on a lecture delivered by Professor James Tobin in May 1986, inaugurated the Atlanta Federal Reserve Bank's distinguished lecturer series. Those attending included both professional economists and the general public. The lecturer sought to present macroeconomic analysis familiar to many economists for a lay audience. The views expressed are Professor Tobin's, not those of the Federal Reserve Bank of Atlanta.

Professor Tobin analyzes the macroeconomic impacts of monetary and fiscal policies. Within limits the same short-run paths of gross national product (GNP) and employment can be achieved by different 'mixes' of the two policies. But a mix of high real interest rates and large budget deficits, though it temporarily dampens inflation, has adverse long-run consequences. Carried to the extremes of recent US policies, such a mix, if continued, would lead to unending rises in the ratio of public debt to GNP, in interest rates, and in 'crowding out'.

APPENDIX

The formulas used for the calculations reported in column 7 of Table 16.1 are as follows: Let d be the speed at which the ratio d is rising. The other symbols were defined in the text, p.131. Then,

$$d = x + [(1-t)r - g]d.$$

This tells us immediately that d will be rising if neither x nor $[(1-t)r-g]$ is negative and if one or both of them is positive. We can also see, by putting d equal to zero, that the equilibrium or stationary ratio d^* is $x/(g-r)$. Therefore,

$$d = [(1-t)r - g](d - d^*).$$

Equation (16.2) tells us that if $[(1-t)r-g]$ is negative d moves toward its equilibrium value d^*. If $[(1-t)r-g]$ is positive, however, it moves away from d^*, which is then an uninteresting unstable stationary point.

17. Can we grow faster?*

The capacity of the American economy to produce and to grow is commanding unusual attention. Current rates of growth of real (that is, inflation-corrected) gross domestic product (GDP) are in the range of 2 per cent to 2.3 per cent. They compare unfavorably with the 3.9 per cent spurt from 1982 to 1989 and the 3.5 per cent to 4.0 per cent average rates sustained from 1946 to 1972. 'A rising tide lifts all boats' was a favorite aphorism of John Kennedy and Lyndon Johnson. Were the economy to grow 3.5 per cent per year from 1996 to 2050 instead of 2.3 per cent, GDP in 2050 would be $68 trillion instead of $36 trillion. This 86 per cent gain would solve a host of problems, notably Social Security and Medicare, that now look intractable. Such is the magic of compound interest.

That greater national output and faster GDP growth are desirable does not mean they are feasible. It is too much to expect that any government action can raise the GDP growth rate forever, or until 2050, or indeed for more than a few years. Maybe good policy can raise the *level* of GDP for years ahead, but generally not its *growth rate*.

To keep raising GDP year after year, it would be necessary to keep repeating the dose of good policy.

Consider, for example, a commonly asserted cause-to-effect chain resulting from a cut in marginal income-tax rates. People choose to work more; employment and GDP rise. The change in behavior takes a bit of time, maybe a year or two. During this period, growth rates are higher. But once workers' adjustments are complete, the rates of grow of employment and GDP revert to what they were before. Employment and GDP remain at higher levels; but to boost them again, tax rates would have to be cut again.

The same is true of other 'pro-growth' medicines, like those involving Federal Reserve interest-rate reductions or cuts in budget deficits. Proposals billed as growth-increasing are more accurately GDP-increasing; the increases in growth rates are transient.

Pro-growth prescriptions stress incentives to produce more. At the same time, they typically augment purchasing power in the hands of households and business firms, thus expanding aggregate demand for goods and ser-

*   This chapter first appeared in Jerry Jasinowski (ed.), *The Rising Tide: The Leading Minds of Business and Economics Chart a Course Toward Higher Growth and Prosperity*, John Wiley and Sons, 1998, pp.27–46.

vices. Frequently actual GDP rises in response. To assess accurately the results of these policies, it is crucially important not to interpret demand-side effects as supply-side successes. Unfortunately confusion of supply and demand, the most fundamental distinction in economics, is all too common in public and political discussion.

DEMAND AND SUPPLY: BUSINESS CYCLES AND SUSTAINABLE GROWTH

In this article, I try to set forth a coherent framework in which levels and growth rates fall into place and supply side and demand side are kept straight.

The economy is subject to two supply constraints. One is the level of its capacity to produce goods and services. The other is the rate at which this capacity is growing. The output of the economy in a given year is limited by its available productive resources – labor, capital goods, land and other natural resources – and by their productivity. This constraint determines potential gross domestic product (PGDP). PGDP grows as population and labor force grow, workers improve in skill, capital is accumulated, and scientists, inventors and innovative entrepreneurs create new products and technologies. These factors change quite gradually. In Figure 17.1, the smooth track is the estimated PGDP (log scale), full employment output from 1952 to 1995. The slope of this track is the PGDP growth rate, shown as 2.3 per cent recently.

The PGDP growth rate can be decomposed into growth of labor input in hours per year and growth of productivity per hour. In the glorious quarter-century after World War II, both components were 1.75 per cent to 2.0 per cent per year; now they are 1.0 per cent to 1.25 per cent. The slow-down in labor-force growth is demographic: birth rates are low; and a large number of women are joining the workforce. It is not a matter of political concern, although income tax cuts are touted as a work incentive. No pro-posals to subsidize childbearing or open the gates to immigrants are on the table. Instead, the hand-wringing is about the decline in productivity growth since about 1973. It happened in other advanced capitalist democ-racies, and its causes are mysterious.

Most of the time the economy is not operating at full potential, but with excess unemployment and idle industrial capacity. Actual GDP falls short of PGDP – as shown by the wiggly track in Figure 17.1. The shortfall (indi-cated by the shaded area), of actual from potential, the GAP, is the busi-ness cycle. Occasionally the GAP is negative – the economy has overshot its normal capacity, as in the escalation of the 1966–9 Vietnam war. Figure 17.2 shows how fluctuations in the GDP GAP and in unemployment are

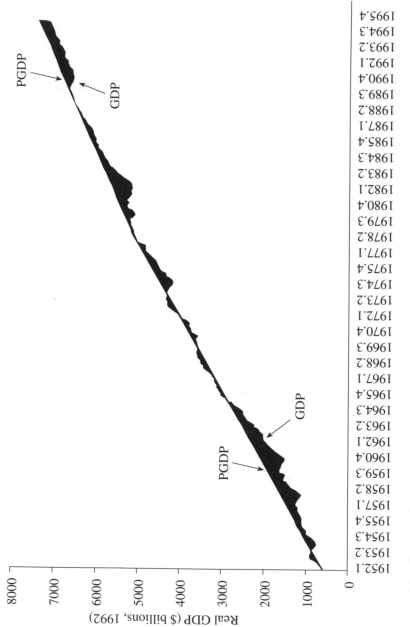

Figure 17.1 $\ln(GDP)$ and $\ln(PGDP)$, 1952–95

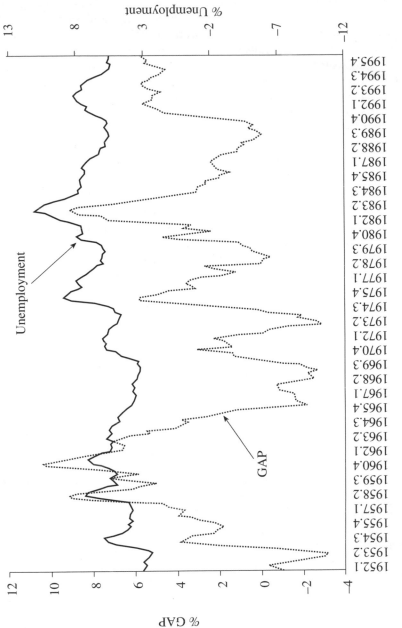

Figure 17.2 GDP GAP and unemployment rate, 1952–95

137

synchronized, with the GAP's amplitude from two to three times that of the unemployment rate a regularly known to economists as Okun's law.

Business cycles, created by ups and downs in GAPS and unemployment rates, reflect fluctuations in *demand*, that is, in spending on goods and services. When actual GDP falls short of potential, the *supply* constraint is not binding. Aggregate demand is now calling the tune. New demands can be met as employment of labor and utilization of capital are increased. A business-cycle recovery, from 1982 to 1989 or from 1992 to 1996 is a *demand-side* phenomenon, an expansion of *demands* for goods and services and for the workers to produce them. Frequently government policies provide stimuli – in the 1980s tax cuts, defense expenditures and eased monetary policies. During recoveries, GDP growth rates are high, unsustainably high.

The PGDP growth rate, the 2.0 per cent or 2.25 per cent or 2.5 per cent, is often called *sustainable* growth. It is the growth of GDP at which the unemployment rate and the GAP remain constant. Along the PGDP path, the GAP is not just constant; it is zero. Along a lower parallel path with the same growth rate, the GAP would also be constant, but it would not be zero; it would be, say, 3 per cent or 5 per cent. The economy is not limited to sustainable growth unless it is operating at full capacity. By the same token, it cannot grow at an unsustainable rate once it reaches the PGDP path.

THE NAIRU AS CAPACITY CONSTRAINT

What determines the capacity constraint? For a large and diverse market economy, it cannot be a simple, measurable physical limit. A peacetime free-market economy cannot mobilize the nation into the kind of three-shift, everybody-works command economy that won World War II. The symptoms of a normal economy overheated by excess demand are escalations of price and wage inflation. The unemployment rate is an important barometer of inflation pressure. When unemployment and GAP are low, employers have both means and incentive to bid up wages, and workers have more bargaining power. Product prices rise along with labor costs.

What numerical unemployment rate defines full employment and corresponds to PGDP? What is the lowest inflation-safe unemployment rate, the notorious NAIRU, the nonaccelerating inflation rate of unemployment? The theory is that, at unemployment rates lower than the NAIRU, rates of wage and price inflation rise. Before 1995, the consensus estimate of the NAIRU was 6 per cent. Now that unemployment has been below 6 per cent since August 1994 without evidence of 'accelerating' inflation, NAIRU estimates are being revised downward, and PGDP correspondingly revised upward.

Much of the concern and anger evoked by low growth rates is misdirected. In reality the critics are complaining about the NAIRU: the number is too high or the very concept is flawed. If the NAIRU constraint on GDP were relaxed, GDP could grow faster, but only temporarily. For Chairman Alan Greenspan and his colleagues at the Federal Reserve Board, it is the NAIRU – not the 2.0 per cent to 2.5 per cent ceiling on sustainable (PGDP) growth – that stands in the way of monetary stimulus of demand. Were they convinced that the economy had room for noninflationary expansion, they would presumably accommodate or actively stimulate extra demand, which is what they have done the past two years.

The important truth in the NAIRU concept is that GDP cannot be expanded indefinitely by demand stimulus. The practical issue is the location of this constraint. Are we now at or above potential output? Or is there still room for expansion?

The NAIRU is not a precise number so that a further tenth of a point reduction of unemployment suddenly and irretrievably unleashes a torrent of inflation. Rather, it is the midpoint of a zone, within which the lower the unemployment rate, the more widespread and likely are inflationary pressures. And the numerical value of the NAIRU is not an eternal constant. It moves with economic, social, technological, and demographic change. Evidently, it was about 4 per cent in the 1950s and early 1960s, rose to 5 per cent and then to 6 per cent or higher in the 1970s, before drifting down recently.

Neither econometricians nor central bankers know for sure where the NAIRU is at any particular time. Alan Greenspan and his fellow policy makers on the Federal Open Market Committee must balance two risks. On the one hand, they might be keeping unemployment unnecessarily high, depriving the economy of extra output there for the taking. On the other hand, the economy may already be at or below the NAIRU, so that expansionary monetary policy would accelerate prices and necessitate a corrective spell of tighter money and higher interest rates. The policy choice depends both on the Fed's estimates of this tradeoff of risks and on its relative value weighting of the two evils, unemployment and inflation.

Consider, for a moment, enough monetary demand stimulus to cut unemployment by half a point over one year, which would raise GDP by 1 per cent ($75 billion). During the year, the growth rate would be a point above the sustainable rate. The addition to the level of GDP would persist year after year, although the GDP growth rate would revert to its sustainable rate.

This policy would be inflation-safe if the NAIRU had fallen to a bit below 5 per cent, a possibility suggested by the striking absence of inflationary

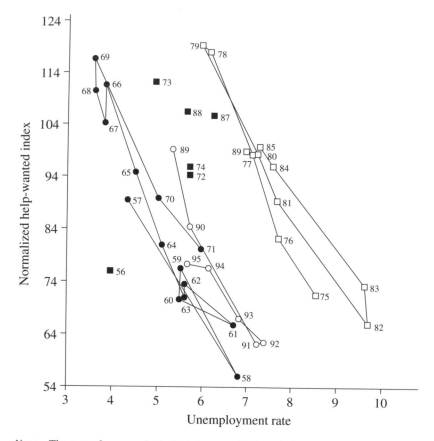

Note: The proxy for vacancies is the help-wanted index relative to the labor force. The curve for the 1950s and 1960s was favorable for combining low vacancies with low unemployment and low inflation. The situation deteriorated in the 1970s and the curve for the 1980s was unfavorable. However, in the 1990s the curve appears to have shifted back to the benign curve of the 1960s.

Figure 17.3   Help-wanted index and unemployment rate, 1956–94

pressures at unemployment rates as low as 5.3 per cent. Other statistics suggest that labor markets are not as tight as unemployment rates alone might indicate: the increased prevalence among the unemployed of job losers relative to job leavers, and the abnormal scarcity of vacancies indicated by help-wanted advertisements. See Figures 17.3, 17.4a, and 17.4b.

Yet no one can guarantee that the NAIRU is not still close to 6 per cent. If so, the one-year stimulus policy would bring higher inflation and tighter monetary policy.

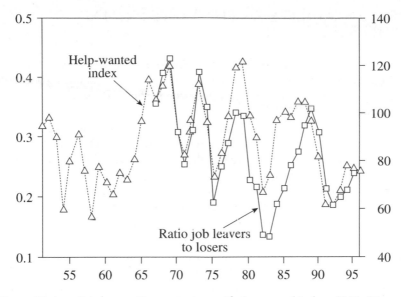

Figure 17.4a   Job leavers/losers ratio and help-wanted index, 1951–95

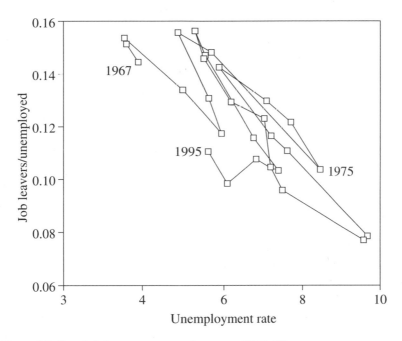

Figure 17.4b   Job leavers v unemployment, 1967–95

PRICE STABILITY AS THE FED'S PRIMARY OBJECTIVE

Since 1983, the Fed has pragmatically fine-tuned the macroeconomy, balancing the two objectives of high employment and low inflation. As a result US, macroeconomic performance has been by far the best among the G-7 countries.

Nevertheless an increasingly strong movement among financial leaders, central bankers, and conservative economists throughout the world is dedicating monetary policy to 'price stability' ahead of all other goals. Inflation hawks want stable zero inflation. The objectives of the Employment Act of 1946, 'maximum employment, production and purchasing power,' would be scrapped – a very serious mistake. The cost in jobs and GDP of lowering the inflation trend from its present 3 per cent to 0 per cent would be considerable. Some of the cost would be permanent, not just transitional. The reason is that the relative wage adjustments inevitable in a dynamic economy are easier to make if they do not entail absolute cuts in money wages in declining sectors. Therefore, they can be made with less unemployment when average inflation is moderately positive than when it is zero or negative (Akerlof *et al.*, 1996).

In any case, zero inflation is an amorphous concept. Alan Greenspan is prominent among the many students of price inflation who believe that official price indexes overstate inflation by anywhere from 0.6 to 2 percentage points a year. Yet there is danger that inflation hawks inside and outside the Fed will weaken its resolve to keep the economy moving even as fast as current estimates of its sustainable rate of growth, and indeed possibly will dilute its determination to avert outright recession. Under a new doctrine labeled 'opportunistic disinflation' leaked from the Fed, patches of softness in the economy would be seen as opportunities to whittle away at the inflation trend, rather than as occasions for expansionary policy.

FISCAL AUSTERITY AS GROWTH POLICY

Monetary policy cannot be expected to lift the long-term sustainable growth rate. The Fed's role is to make sure that any productivity gains occurring spontaneously or as a result of supply-side policies are realized in jobs and output and do not go to waste in recessions and unemployment.

What policies can raise the level of capacity output or its rate of growth or both? Several proposals are prominent in current policy debates: (1) reducing federal budget deficits and balancing the federal budget; (2)

cutting taxes, in particular marginal tax rates; and (3) downsizing government, in particular federal nondefense expenditure programs.

Advocates of fiscal austerity see it as positive supply-side policy, on the grounds that it increases the proportion of national output invested in productive future-oriented activities instead of present-oriented consumption. These activities include business acquisitions of plant and equipment, residential construction, and purchases of consumer durables. Some of these government outlays are capital investments. In addition, no less important is the human capital embodied in the education, skill, and health of the population, especially the young. And one component of national wealth is the country's accumulation of claims on foreigners net of their claims on us.

Government deficit spending, it is argued, crowds out private investment by diverting private saving to purchases of government securities. As a result aggregate national saving and investment are diminished and budget balance then augments the supply of saving available to finance productive private investments. Also, interest rates in the capital markets fall to attract the additional private demands that can now be accommodated. As these investments come on line, capacity output (PGDP) is increased by their (marginal) productivity. In the end, workers' productivity and wages increase, because they are equipped with more and better tools.

This is a good story if properly used, but it has a few pitfalls. First, the payoffs from durable long-term investments will be spread over many future years. Gains to PGDP will scarcely be perceptible within normal political horizons. A balanced budget by 2002 would, by my back-of-an-envelope calculation, raise PGDP in that year by 1 per cent or 2 per cent. This is the estimated result of reducing the federal debt outstanding in that year by 12 per cent of PGDP and nearly 85 per cent of that amount of private wealth into productive domestic capital and the rest into repayment of foreign debt. Public-debt interest rates would have to fall by 50 to 150 basis points to induce these reallocations. If it is assumed that if a three-point increase in the percentage share of national saving and investment in PGDP, relative to what would take place otherwise, continues, PGDP will eventually be another 6 per cent or 7 per cent higher. Increases in per capita consumption would be much smaller, only 1 per cent or 2 per cent, because the gains in PGDP cannot be maintained unless most of them are reinvested.

Second, as an example of a general point I made at the beginning of the article, higher national saving and investment is a recipe for a higher level of PGDP, not for a permanent increase in its growth rate. It is true, that while this new higher level is being approached, the rate of growth will be a bit higher, more so for PGDP than for consumption. But the rate of growth will taper off. This process follows conventional neoclassical growth theory, which takes the view that the sustainable growth rate depends on demographic and technological factors independent of saving rates. Younger economists, using endogenous growth theory, seek ways in which growth rates are permanently changed by changes in national saving rates, but these attempts are still too speculative to guide policy.

Third, if the budget is balanced at the expense of public investment programs, the eventual economy-wide benefits are diminished by the losses of the social returns on these programs. The fervent apostles of budget balance stress that government debt will place burdens on our children and their children, who will be taxed to meet interest charges. Many of these children, however, would lose much more if deficits were attacked by cutbacks in public outlays for education, nutrition, and health. Since the federal government does not distinguish capital and current account budgets, as state governments do, all line items are fodder for the deficit cutters.

Fourth, the potential gains from fiscal austerity will not be realized unless the economy continues to operate at capacity. The immediate impact of cuts in deficit spending is demand-side-contractionary. They reduce spending on goods and services and destroy jobs. If taxes are raised, taxpayers curtail spending. If transfers to the aged, the poor, and the sick are diminished, the beneficiaries cut their spending too. If military procurement and highway- or school-building are slashed, the impacts are direct and obvious. The social gains of austerity require that the resources released by these contractions, or their equivalent, be employed elsewhere, producing the desired new investments. This is the task of monetary policy. It's up to the Fed to engineer the declines in interest rates needed to offset the fiscal contractions. This transition was accomplished smoothly in 1993–4, and little active help from the Fed was needed. This may not always be so, however.

TAX CUTTING AS GROWTH POLICY

Fiscal austerity is the priority of one school of conservative economics. Another school, loyal to the supply-side doctrines of Reaganomics, urges tax cutting as the centerpiece of macroeconomic policy. What are the mechanisms by which cuts in tax rates are supposed to generate additional national output, higher growth of output, and, as by-products, extra tax revenues? The proponents appeal to incentive effects – simple and obvious, the stuff of Econ 101, as University of Chicago economist and Nobel laureate Gary Becker is endlessly reported to have said.

Faced with a lower marginal tax rate, individuals will work more hours per week, more weeks per year, more years per lifetime. They will save more because the government will take less of their interest, dividends, and capital gains. They will invest more in businesses, real estate projects, and education and gaining because they will be allowed to keep more of the profits, rents, and extra wages. Supply-side effects of this kind are basic economics. No one doubts their existence, but there are other effects too. The question is how important the incentive effects are, and what they add up to in relation to PGDP. The empirical evidence does not justify counting on these changes in human behavior to achieve any noticeable increase in PGDP or its rate of growth.

Consider, for example, a 15 per cent income-tax cut for a married couple with two dependent children with pretax income, all wages, of $35000. In 1995, the family paid $2767 in income taxes (zero on the first $16550 and 15 per cent on the other $18450), and $2677 in payroll taxes (excluding the half paid by employers), totaling $5444, 15.6 per cent of pretax income. The couple's marginal tax rate was 22.65 per cent, the sum of a 15 per cent income tax and a 7.65 per cent payroll tax. A reduction of 15 per cent, 2.25 points on the income-tax rate, would lower the family's marginal tax rate to 20.4 per cent, enabling it to keep 79.6 cents of an extra dollar earned, up 2.25 cents (2.91 per cent) from the former after-tax gain of 77.35 cents. These marginal improvements are supposed to be an incentive for family members to seek more work (which proponents assume they will find). Even if they work no more hours, however, and even if their pretax income remains $35000, the family benefits. A reduction of 2.25 points (15 per cent of 15 points) on the income-tax rate gives the family $415 a year (2.25 per cent of $18450), a take-home gain of 1.4 per cent.

The example illustrates the point that tax-cut proposals are not purely incentives to change behavior. They give taxpayers more after-tax income even if they do not change behavior. These benefits have 'income effects' that counter the incentive effects and may even overcome them. Households might choose to work less, not more. This is the more likely event if, in addition to tax-rate cuts, the legislation offers new tax credits or deductions. This too is taught in Econ 101.

What is the empirical evidence for this view? A Congressional Budget Office study (1996) reviewed empirical analyses of the effects of tax-rate changes on aggregate labor supply in hours. Its conclusion was that a 1 per cent increase in after-tax wage rates would lift labor supply by 0 per cent to 0.3 per cent. The incentive effect – *substitution elasticity* in economists' jargon – lies between 0.2 per cent and 0.4 per cent; the *income elasticity* lies between −0.2 per cent and −0.1 per cent. In the example, the 2.91 per cent increase in take-home wages could be an incentive for an increase in hours of work between 0.58 per cent and 1.16 per cent, while the income effect could take away from 0.14 per cent to 0.28 per cent. Adding $1000 in tax credits would magnify these income effects by 3.33 times, burying the incentive effects. No supply-side miracles here. And even if positive supply-side effects dominate, they are one-shot increases in labor supply and GDP, not permanent increases in growth rates.

Some tax cuts are designed as investment incentives. As demand stimuli, they have the virtue of expanding PGDP at the same time. This was the purpose of the investment tax credit introduced by the Kennedy administration and turned off and on and off several times since. There is evidence that a good share of the intended response to the ITC was lost in subsidizing ongoing gross investments rather than in incremental ones and in higher prices of capital goods.

On the macroeconomic scene, the supply-side payoffs of capital investments occur gradually over future years, while the demand impacts are felt immediately. If there is no room in the economy, the Fed will raise interest rates and no net increase in aggregate investment will occur. As the Fed knows, investment booms can be just as inflationary as consumption booms. A true progrowth policy, in times of full employment, would offset tax-cut investment incentives by cuts in government consumption spending or by tax deterrents to private consumption.

Incentives for investment are fruitless without saving to match. When labor and other resources are idle, investment spending can put them to work and saving from the new wages and profits will do the job. Consumption will increase along with saving and investment, as long as there is room in the economy for both. At full employment along the PGDP track, however, lower national consumption is a requisite of higher national saving and investment. At full employment, there is no way new investment spending itself can generate the needed saving.

Tax-cut incentives for household saving are popular in Congress. IRAs for a variety of ostensible purposes are multiplying. As growth policy via higher national saving and investment, IRAs are likely to be useless or perverse, for two reasons. One is that taxpayers can usually qualify for tax benefits while consuming no less, or often more; they qualify for IRAs, for example, by using funds they already have, obtain by borrowing, or would save anyway. The other is that the lost tax revenue raises government dissaving, unless Congress offsets it by raising other taxes or cutting expenditures.

A similar problem afflicts proposals for large-scale cuts in capital-gains tax rates. The rationalization is that it provides incentive for investments, especially innovative entrepreneurial ventures. Risk-taking investors themselves might be somewhat ambivalent about the rate cut, because it means that government will absorb a smaller fraction of losses as well as of gains. Nevertheless, this rationalization does not apply to the trillions of unrealized capital gains on assets acquired in the past. Cutting the tax due on their realizations just gives windfalls to their holders, windfalls likely to raise consumption spending. (It's true that tax collections will increase in the short run, as owners who have locked in appreciated assets seize the opportunity to sell them.)

The best way to provide a tax incentive to save rather than consume is to allow a deduction of *net* saving – purchases of capital assets net of borrowing and asset sales – in reckoning taxable income. To minimize windfalls to taxpayers who would be saving anyway, the deduction should be given only for the excess of net saving over a threshold that would rise with income.

The difficulty of targeting tax incentives to particular purposes afflicts many actual and proposed rate cuts, credits and deductions, and many outright subsidies too. For example, though meant for students unable to afford college or other post-high school education, or to attend private elementary or secondary schools, subventions to everyone who enrolls are mostly windfalls to persons who would attend these schools anyway. There are sharper, more discriminating tools available.

'DOWNSIZING' GOVERNMENT AS GROWTH POLICY

Budget balancers and tax cutters agree on the ultimate goal of downsizing civilian government. They frequently try to reach the goal by squeezing government between the pincers of tax cuts and budget balance. Their idea is that an economy with small government is more productive than an economy with large government, even if the budget is balanced in both. Both groups rationalize their view by citing the inefficiencies and distortions of higher taxes, a view that is often reinforced by the allegation that government expenditures are inherently wasteful. There are many anecdotes but little evidence to support so sweeping a generalization. European countries with larger civilian governments have had higher growth rates than the United States and have been more successful in other dimensions. A discriminating approach to costs and benefits would give governments credit for supplying public goods, coping with 'externalities,' and maintaining social safety nets. In the United States today, further cuts in federal discretionary nondefense programs are bound to come mostly from public investments – in education, R & D, public health and safety, medical research, environmental protection, and infrastructure. It is hard to see how such downsizing can increase potential GDP or speed up economic growth.

KEEP DEMAND-SIDE AND SUPPLY-SIDE EFFECTS STRAIGHT

Whatever their supply-side effects, tax cuts are demand-side stimuli unless they are matched by concurrent cuts in government spending. Deficit-increasing tax cuts may be welcome when the economy is operating short of potential; they can help arrest recessions and fuel recoveries. But in times of full employment, with the economy constrained by the NAIRU, the Federal Reserve will oppose additional aggregate demand by raising interest rates. The tax cuts will mainly raise consumption, while the hikes in interest rates will curtail investment. The net result is unfavorable to growth.

Supply-siders invariably count demand-side effects in support of their supply-side proposals. They often cite the increases in GDP and tax revenues that accompanied the Kennedy–Johnson tax cut of 1964. This legislation, proposed as early as 1962, was primarily designed as a demand-side stimulus to keep a cyclical recovery going, reduce unemployment to the 4 per cent then regarded as the NAIRU (though not so named), and close the GDP GAP. Matching cuts in spending were not proposed. Supporters of the tax cut claimed that some productivity by-products would result from incentive effects, which broadened congressional support. The measure had its intended demand-side effects, but there is no evidence that it increased potential GDP. When Vietnam war spending was added to the budget in 1966, the economy was overheated and inflation rose for the rest of the decade.

Worse still, supply-siders are grossly mistaken to claim the 1983–9 recovery as a vindication of Reaganomics and to assert that the same recipe can now lift growth rates again. The 1981 tax cuts and the buildup of defense spending were fiscal demand stimuli unprecedented in peace time. With unemployment and excess capacity at their highest rates since the Great Depression, the economy could easily meet the new demands upon it. Inflation, which had touched double digits in 1979–80 and fallen to 5 per cent in the subsequent recession, actually continued to abate during the 1983–9 recovery. Interest rates declined too; the Federal Reserve was accommodative. As the 10 per cent GDP GAP of 1982 was closed, actual GDP grew 4.4 per cent per year, about 2 points above the sustainable PGDP rate. It is ridiculous and dangerous to advocate repeating in 1996 the Reaganomics policies of the 1980s. The slack that was in the economy in 1982, when unemployment exceeded 10 per cent, is not there now, when unemployment is only 5.3 per cent.

Nothing at all happened on the supply-side in the 1980s; neither PGDP nor its rate of growth were raised. Reagan's fiscal policy powered the demand-side recovery of the 1980s, but it was not essential. The US economy recovered from its seven previous postwar recessions without anything resembling such drastic policies. The Federal Reserve could have managed a 1980s recovery by itself; absent the bizarre fiscal policies, there was plenty of room for lowering interest rates further. Claims from Laffer curve adherents that expansion of the tax base would overcome the deficits resulting from the tax cuts were emphatically falsified. The economy of the 1980s was tilted toward private consumption and defence, at the expense of investment – the economy was not pro-growth, but anti-growth. The reckless experiment left the federal government with a large debt and a heavy burden of interest payments.

CONCLUSIONS

Although politicians freely promise faster growth, government has no handy set of tools for effecting it. The Federal Reserve can possibly raise GDP somewhat by further exploiting the apparent downward drift in the NAIRU; but the Fed cannot raise the economy's rate of growth for very long. Fiscal austerity, balancing the federal budget, can increase national saving and investment, with modest eventual payoffs in higher GDP and consumption. But public investments of high social productivity should not be sacrificed in the name of budget balance. Supply-side tax cuts are not likely to achieve the gains in output and growth their advocates claim. In practice, these measures often result in less work, less saving, less investment rather than more. Past tax cuts might appear to some to have had positive macroeconomic results, but these were due to demand-side stimuli in periods of economic slack.

The search for a holy grail that will lift permanently the growth rate of productivity seems hopeless. This melancholy conclusion deprives the pro-growth apostles of the miracles of compound interest in calculating the payoffs of their policies in 2050. True supply-side policies are hard work, painstaking and slow, as distinct from free-lunch, supply-side fantasies.

A list of sensible policies, one might say conservative policies, includes basic science, R & D, education and training, public infrastructure, and carefully designed incentives for both private and public sectors to consume less, and save and invest more. If everyone is patient with gains measured in tenths of a percentage point over the coming decades, these policies can pay off. With luck, new technologies may bring dramatic *improvements* in the growth rate. The computer and communications revolutions may well bear fruit in the next century.

Meanwhile, the United States is probably doing better economically than its people think. Our macroeconomic performance is the envy of Europe and Japan. The complaint that Americans are worse off than in the 1950s does not bear close scrutiny. Just compare the inventories of consumer durables '*the typical family*' had then and has now. Statistics of GNP, family incomes, and real wages would look better if the admitted bias toward upward changes in price indexes were corrected. With a stroke of a pen we could have 3.5 per cent growth.

We have yet to figure out how to cope with the developments in demographics and medical science that raise the proportion of the aged in the population and make it possible but costly to keep them alive and healthy. This issue, a compound of good and bad news, raises problems in all advanced capitalist democracies, problems that are not just the fault of spendthrift politicians.

The United States stands out from other democracies in ways that should not be sources of pride: our acute poverty, inequality and insecurity. Nothing in economic science and economic history says that these are inevitable by-products of overall prosperity and growth, or that good economic performance is incompatible with progressive taxation, a decent safety net and a public sector large enough to deal with the host of environmental and social problems that markets by themselves cannot solve.

REFERENCES

George Akerlof, William Dickens and George Perry (1996), *The macroeconomics of low inflation*, Washington, DC: Brookings Institution. Congressional Budget Office (1996), 'Labor supply and taxes', January.

18. Supply constraints on employment and output: NAIRU versus natural rate*

'POTENTIAL OUTPUT' AND THE TWO-REGIME MODEL

Every macroeconomic theory needs a concept of the economy's productive capacity, the overall constraint on the effectiveness of increasing aggregate demand in increasing actual output and employment. This is not a technocratic physical limit, such as could be relevant to a wartime emergency. In the United States in World War II the entire population was working overtime, unemployment was 1 per cent, plants were operating on shifts around the clock, and quantitative controls dictated by central government priorities displaced market prices and wages in allocating resources. This regime performed miracles. In 1944, nearly half the GNP was commandeered for war, and the remainder was greater than the entire prewar GNP. Clearly, this kind of economy is infeasible in peacetime.

What we mean by potential GDP in peacetime is what a market economy, without rationing and other quantitative controls, with households and businesses making most of the decisions affecting prices and resource allocations, can produce. Accordingly, capacity *Net* Domestic Product is sustainable GDP minus allowance for the depreciation and depletion of productive resources. These are not unambiguous concepts, because there is generally no sharp dividing line beyond which additions to demand cease to induce response in increased production.

That is why it is natural to define the capacity constraint in terms of the effects of additional demand on prices (including nominal wage rates). In Keynes's *General Theory* (1936), potential output corresponds to *full employment* of labor, and the tell-tale symptom of excess demand is inflation. In the *General Theory*, any stable level of aggregate demand and

* This chapter was originally presented at the international conference in memory of Fausto Vicarelli, Rome, 21–3 November 1998, and published in G. Gandolfo and F. Marzano (eds), *Economic Theory and Social Justice*, Macmillan, 1998.

output short of full employment will be accompanied by stable prices. However, moving closer to full employment would raise prices. That is, the stable price level will be higher at a higher stable aggregate demand level. The picture is asymmetrical. Deflationary gaps in demand show up in shortfalls of actual output from full employment output but not in prices, whereas inflationary gaps of demand affect prices but not output. The notion that the economy can be in either of these two regimes, demand-constrained or supply-constrained is, an important and useful doctrine, central to Keynes's thought and to the meaning of the word 'general' in his title. Of course, he believed that mature capitalist economies are usually demand-constrained.

COST-PUSH, DEMAND-PULL AND PHILLIPS

In the middle 1950s, American experience posed problems for this Keynesian model. Inflation arose and persisted at levels of GDP and employment that, on the basis of earlier observation, were thought to be well short of full employment. This inflation was dubbed 'cost-push' in distinction to the inflation we economists thought we understood, 'demand-pull.' Naming a phenomenon does not explain it, and there was no theory of cost-push inflation.[1]

Then came A.W. Phillips (1958) and his curve.[2] Stretched far beyond the author's intentions, this seemed to blur the distinction in a sensible way. The strength of cost-push depends on the pull of demand, as measured by the gap, positive or negative, between capacity output and actual output. That gap, in turn, is closely related to the unemployment rate, a relationship quantified by Arthur Okun for the Council of Economic Advisers in 1961 (*Economic Report of the President*, 1962, pp.49–56; Okun, 1962). The Phillips curve provided a continuous relationship of wage inflation to unemployment. Assuming that prices of value added are normal labor costs per unit output marked up to cover fixed costs and capital costs, price inflation mirrors wage inflation less the trend of productivity growth.

One trouble with this development was that it left full employment undefined. Should it correspond to the unemployment rate at which wage inflation would just equal productivity growth, so that price inflation would be zero? This definition just revived the original problem: GDP at that unemployment rate did not look and feel like full employment. But if full employment was further up the Phillips curve, how far? And would not the Keynesian hypothesis that prices are stable when demand falls below full employment GNP have to be abandoned? Or alternatively the notion of a sharp dividing line between the two regimes, demand-determined and supply-determined, could be discarded in favor of the idea of a zone of more and less full employment.

THE PRICE–WAGE FEEDBACK

Phillips himself, Lipsey (1960), Samuelson and Solow (1960), and many other economists who adopted the Phillips curve recognized that wage inflation, a determinant of price inflation, would itself be affected by price inflation. There are two reasons for this reverse effect: workers seek compensation for increases in consumer prices, and employers are more willing to pay higher nominal wages when product prices are higher. In the early 1960s, statistical Phillips curve fits on American postwar data were very good. When lagged price inflation was added as a regressor, its coefficient was significant but also significantly less than one. The notion of a long-run Phillips curve, the locus along which the dependent variable wage-change was the same as the independent variable price-change minus the productivity trend, was introduced. The long-run curve was steeper than the short-run Phillips curve, which assumed the inflation feedback term to be constant. As years passed and added observations in more inflationary environments, estimates of the feedback coefficient gravitated to one, making the long-run Phillips curve vertical and undermining the notion of a policy tradeoff between unemployment and inflation popularized by Samuelson and Solow (1960).

THE NATURAL RATE

Came then the natural rate of unemployment. Phelps (1967) and Friedman (1968) maintained that rational behavior precluded any long-run tradeoff, a conclusion strengthened by regarding the inflation term on the right hand side of the Phillips wage equation as expectation rather than sluggish adjustment, and as rational rather than adaptive expectation. Thus was the sharp dividing line earlier provided by Keynes's concept of full employment restored, but in new guise with important differences. At Friedman's natural rate of unemployment, Friedman's full employment, it is not the price level but the inflation rate that is stable. The rate is determined by the growth in money supply and in nominal aggregate demand, possibly but not necessarily zero. Friedman's price dynamics are, unlike Keynes's, symmetric: when monetary policy produces unemployment less than the natural rate, inflation increases without limit, and when monetary policy produces unemployment that is unnaturally high, inflation decreases indefinitely.

Friedman describes the natural rate of unemployment as 'the level that would be ground out by the Walrasian system of general equilibrium equations, provided that there is embedded in them the actual structural characteristics of the labor and commodity markets, including market imperfections, stochastic variability in demands and supplies, the costs of getting information about job vacancies and labor availabilities, the costs of mobility, and so on'. By characterizing the natural rate as Walrasian equilibrium, Friedman endows it with the usual optimal properties. The proviso is understandable, if not excusable. Without the non-Walrasian elements listed, the natural rate would be zero; if markets cleared, there would be no unemployment and no unfilled vacancies. But the proviso is a tall order. Generations of economists have not found an equilibrium system that embeds all those bothersome phenomena.

Keynes too recognized that there would be non-zero unemployment – frictional unemployment – at what he called full employment. He too finessed explanation of the size of frictional unemployment. He regarded full employment as optimal: 'I see no reason to suppose that the existing system seriously misemploys the factors of production which are in use . . . It is in determining the volume, not the direction, of actual employment that the existing system has broken down' (Keynes, 1936. p.379). Keynes identified full employment with the 'classical' equilibrium of the aggregate labor market, defined as that volume of employment at which the marginal product of labor equals the real wage equals the marginal disutility of work. Unlike Friedman, of course, Keynes regarded involuntary unemployment, the demand-constrained regime, as the usual state of affairs.

Friedman was a short step away from the New Classical doctrine that markets are continuously clearing and grinding out optimal moving equilibria solving the Walrasian equations. That leads to the conclusion that actual unemployment, whatever it is, is natural or 'full'. I recall seeing in 1982 a message on the blackboard in the economics graduate students' lounge at Stanford saying, 'The Bureau of Labor Statistics announced this morning that the natural rate of unemployment is now 9.4 per cent.'

THE NAIRU

Franco Modigliani, I believe, originated the NAIRU concept – non-accelerating inflation rate of unemployment (Modigliani and Papademos, 1976). At first he called it simply NIRU, non-inflationary rate of unemployment'. Somehow it got changed in common usage, presumably to reflect better the 'accelerationist' theory. I believe that the whole purpose of the concept was to escape the normative equilibrium connotations of the natural rate. The NAIRU is, like full employment, a barrier to expansion of demand and in some sense a boundary between regimes. But it need not be the best of all possible worlds, and departures from it need not have Friedman's dynamic consequences. It is a mistake, I think, to regard NIRU or NAIRU just as neutral synonyms of natural rate.

My own interpretation of the difference between NAIRU and natural rate is as follows. The NAIRU does not assume a Walrasian equilibrium, in which markets, in particular labor markets, are being cleared by existing prices and wages. Instead it assumes an economy in which at any time most markets are characterized by excess demand or excess supply at prevailing prices. Applied to labor markets, excess demand means a preponderance of job vacancies over unemployment, and excess supply means the opposite. The distribution of markets, weighted by the number of workers or jobs in them, depends systematically on the strength of aggregate demand relative to potential GDP. That is, the weighted number of excess demand markets, relative to excess supply markets, will be greater the higher is aggregate demand.

The NAIRU is the unemployment rate at which the inflation-increasing effects of the excess-demand markets just balance the inflation-decreasing impacts of the excess-supply markets. Unlike the natural rate, this is a balance among disequilibrium markets, a stand-off between those in excess demand and those in excess supply. The existence of markets in diverse circumstances is essential for the NAIRU. Unlike the natural rate, the NAIRU could not be modeled as a single economy-wide market or representative agent.

The distribution of these markets as function of aggregate real demand I take to be a characteristic of an economy that remains fairly constant within the time span of a business cycle and indeed changes only slowly from cycle to cycle. However, this does not mean that the identities of the markets within the distribution is constant or slow-changing. Markets are always interchanging places, as a result of never-ceasing intersectoral flux of microeconomic demands and supplies. This flux is quite consistent with the maintenance of a fairly stable macroeconomic environment.

THE BEVERIDGE CURVE

A Beveridge curve plots, for the economy as a whole, vacancies against unemployment, both as percentages of labor force. Observed Beveridge curves can be thought to be generated by the multi-market disequilibrium model just described, in the following way. It is convenient to think of each market at a given time as characterized by either vacancies or unemployment (or by neither) but not by both at the same time. Indeed, that might be the

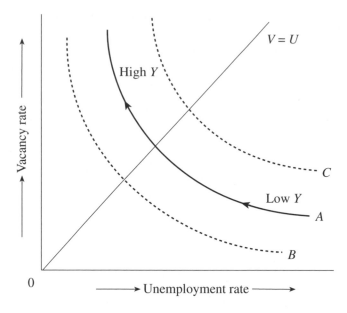

Note: Points above the *V=U* line are full employment by Beveridge's criterion. (In practice, however, empirical measures of *U* and *V* are not commensurate. Indicated movement along curve *A* from low *Y* to high *Y* represents increase in aggregate real demand. Shift to curve *C* represents deterioration of labor market, leading to greater frictional or structural unemployment, likely also to an adverse shift in Phillips curve and NAIRU. Shift to curve *A* is benign.

Figure 18.1   Beveridge curves in theory

definition of an atomic market. Then, for the economy as a whole, vacancies are the sum of excess demands over all excess-demand markets, and unemployment is the sum of excess supplies over all excess-supply markets. As aggregate demand is hypothetically raised from low to high, relative to potential output, excess supplies fall, excess demands rise and markets move from excess-supply to excess-demand status. Consequently total vacancies increase and total unemployment decreases. The resulting Beveridge curve is downward-sloping, and in practice concave (Figure 18.1).

The coexistence of unemployment and vacancies is a sign of frictional unemployment, which could be measured in principle as the amount of unemployment at the point on the curve where *V=U*. Beveridge (1945) did not invent the curve that bears his name, but he did define full employment as a situation in which unemployment is less than vacancies.

A movement along a Beveridge curve up and left arises from expansion of aggregate demand. An outward and upward shift of the curve increases frictional unemployment and raises the rate of vacancies associated with any given rate of unemployment. This might come about from an increase in the dispersion of excess demands and supplies across the markets, because of less efficient matching by labor markets or because of slower response of workers in moving from weak to strong markets. 'Structural unemployment', the label frequently given to unemployment not remediable by aggregate demand, might be an extreme case of frictional unemployment.

THE NAIRU AND THE PHILLIPS CURVE

A Phillips curve plots, for the economy as a whole, percentage increase in average wage rates against the economy-wide unemployment rate. Observed Phillips curves can be regarded as having been generated by the same model that generates the Beveridge curve. For each market there is a function that translates excess demand or supply into a market-specific wage change, to which is added the common ongoing average wage change. (Figure 18.2 shows wage change in a single market as a function of excess demand or supply in that market. For each level of aggregate demand there is a point on the Beveridge curve and also a corresponding average wage change, which can be plotted either against the aggregate unemployment rate, as does the Phillips curve, or against aggregate vacancies. Since vacancies and unemployment are symmetric indicators of disequilibrium, it is logical to associate wage pressures with both of them. Just as unemployment might be expected to induce workers, individually or collectively, to moderate the terms on which they are willing to work, so vacancies might be expected to induce employers to bid higher for labor. See Baily and Tobin (1977) for statistical wage-change regressions on both vacancies and unemployment. An upward shift in the Beveridge curve, signifying an increase in frictional unemployment, should mean an increase in the wage inflation associated with a given rate of unemployment.

The old-fashioned neoclassical view of the mechanics of adjustment to excess supply or demand in individual markets was simply that prices would rise or fall as a positive function of excess demand (regarding excess supply as negative excess demand). Traditionally, this was just assumed to be a plausible characteristic of competitive markets, but it is also a likely implication of models of optimal price and quantity adjustments by individual market participants. In any case, the average wage increase would be greater the more the distribution of labor markets was weighted in favor of excess-demand markets. Phillips (1958) and Lipsey (1960) took this approach as the obvious logic of the Phillips curve.

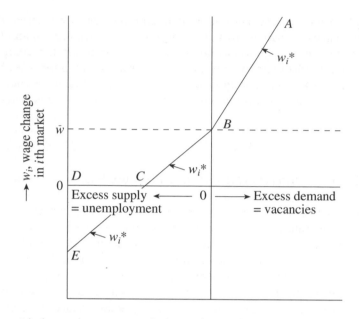

Note: $\bar{w}$ is the ongoing average nominal wage change of the economy. To this is added or subtracted w_i^*, a function of excess demand or supply in market i. As average wage-change rises or falls, point B moves with it. The function depicted is a broken line with steeper slope for excess demand than for excess supply. This is realistic but inessential. Temporary resistance to negative w_i is indicated by substitution of $ABCD$ for $ABCE$ as the wage-change function.

Figure 18.2   Wage change as function of excess demand or supply

In addition, there would usually be in each market a non-zero wage increase or decrease related to the growth of productivity in that market and to the ongoing economy-wide pattern and expectation of wage and price inflation or deflation. This would occur in the absence of excess demand or supply.

The NAIRU is the rate of unemployment that generates no change in the average wage change. At the NAIRU the excess-demand and excess-supply markets' components of wage change average to zero. Does this model imply that the 'long-run' Phillips curve is vertical at the NAIRU, just as it is vertical at the natural rate in the Friedman–Phelps model? The answer is 'not always'. The multi-market stochastic macro-equilibrium model allows for a different possibility, about to be explained.

NOMINAL WAGE STICKINESS AND THE COSTS OF ZERO INFLATION

An important difference of Keynesian from neoclassical economics is that Keynes was explicitly describing a monetary economy, in which markets set *nominal* prices. Neoclassical economics is a theory of real or relative prices, essentially multilateral barter. Dudley Dillard (1988) convicted it of 'barter illusion'. Keynes considered it likely that adjustments of money wages to excess demand or supply would be sluggish, especially downward wage adjustments to excess supply of labor. This should not be considered as money illusion or as a characteristic of market-clearing equilibrium in any individual market or of Walrasian equilibrium in the whole economy.

Empirical evidence for downward wage stickiness is overwhelming. Availability of replacement workers outside the factory gate is almost never an occasion for employers to cut wages. At the same time, there is evidence that nominal wages will give way to save insiders' jobs when the employing company can convincingly claim financial distress and can threaten imminent shutdown. Perhaps the Phillips curve is a reclining 'S', with a long fairly flat middle, between sharp rises in inflation at low unemployment and falls at very high unemployment.

In Tobin (1972) I set forth a model of temporary downward nominal wage rigidity, namely that a market's wage change would be the maximum of 0 and w^*, where w^* is calculated from the formula above, shown in Figure 18.2, the sum of the change related to excess supply or demand and the common economy-wide pattern, but could be zero continuously for only a finite time. Thus, if a market remained in a situation of large excess supply and w^* negative, eventually the money wage would fall and this source of unemployment-inflation tradeoff would cease. However, if microeconomic flux always puts another market into a similar excess-supply situation, some element of downward rigidity is always there, enabling an increment of aggregate demand to reduce unemployment permanently while increasing inflation permanently, or making a permanent increase of unemployment a cost of lowering the ongoing inflation trend.

This curvature in the long-run Phillips curve exists only at low inflation rates. If the economy's average wage inflation is high enough, there will never be any real wage adjustments in any markets that cannot be made without negative wage change, simply by falling behind the general pattern.

A recent paper at the Brookings Institution (Akerlof *et al.*, 1996) presents a similar model, and estimates and tests it empirically, finding that the model even explains the combination of rising unemployment and galloping deflation in the Great Depression in the United States. The authors estimate that, at present, pushing the price inflation trend in the United States to zero from 3 per cent would cost an additional full point of unemployment every year. By Okun's law, this is a permanent 2 or 2.5 per cent loss of GDP. This Brookings paper seems to be tempering the enthusiasm for literal price stability in the United States.

UNCERTAINTY ABOUT NAIRU AND POLICY TRADEOFFS

Where the NAIRU is at any given time is quite uncertain. Evidently, it rose in the United States after the 1960s, when 4 per cent seemed a good guess. NAIRU was widely estimated as 6 per cent at the beginning of the 1990s. This was the Federal Reserve's belief. But the Fed has allowed unemployment to decline almost to 5 per cent during the present recovery without hitting the monetary brakes. No significant inflationary consequences have followed. It seems that NAIRU has declined. Other indicators of labor market tightness – a low help-wanted index, a proxy for vacancies, and a low ratio of job leavers to job losers – suggest that the current environment is like the 1960s, when the NAIRU was 5 per cent or less. (See Figures 18.3 and 18.4.)

Natural rate theory implied that there is no durable policy tradeoff between unemployment and inflation. New Classical Macroeconomics and Real Business Cycle Theory went one step further, asserting there is no temporary tradeoff either. Nominal stickiness is, as argued above, a reason for curvature of the long-run Phillips curve at low rates of inflation. In any case, the uncertainty of the location of the NAIRU, whether it is a constant or a function of the unemployment rate, is an independent source of policy tradeoff.

This tradeoff is between two risks. Associated with any actual unemployment rate, and thus indirectly with the monetary policy that supports it, are a range of possible discrepancies of actual unemployment from the unknown NAIRU. If the NAIRU is higher than the actual rate, the cost is higher inflation. If the NAIRU is lower than the actual rate, the costs are the jobs and output unnecessarily forgone. The lower the actual unemployment rate chosen, the more likely the first kind of error and the less likely the second kind. The central bank has to balance the probability-weighted disutilities of the two kinds of errors.

Events will provide information for a new policy decision. If, for example, more inflation occurs than the central bank bargained for, the policy makers will presumably decide to aim for a higher unemployment rate. Some commentators appear to regard NAIRU as a threshold to a

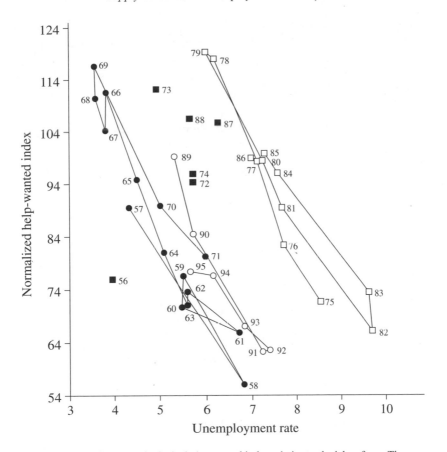

Note: The proxy for vacancies is the help-wanted index relative to the labor force. The curve for the 1950s and 1960s was favorable for combining low vacancies with low unemployment and low inflation. The situation deteriorated in the 1970s and the curve for the 1980s was unfavorable. However, in the 1990s the curve appears to have shifted back to the benign curve of the 1960s.

Figure 18.3   Empirical Beveridge curve points: USA, 1956–95

burst of wage–price spiral exceedingly difficult and costly to reverse. Worse yet, it may be like the virus of a dread disease, which does not break out for a long time. Accordingly, they counsel a very conservative policy. But there is no convincing evidence of that kind of asymmetric discontinuity as between the two types of error.

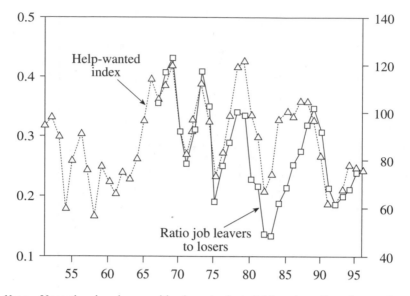

Note: Unemployed workers are either leavers, who quit jobs voluntarily, or losers, who were laid off. When labor markets are tight, the leavers/losers ratio could be expected to be high because workers can quit with reasonable expectation of finding another job. The figure shows that this ratio confirms the message of Figure 18.3. The ratio has recently been rising but in 1995 it is still quite low considering how low unemployment is.

Figure 18.4   Job leavers/losers ratio and help-wanted index, USA, 1967–95

THE NEED FOR ACTIVE MACRO POLICY

Do we need policy to stay at the NAIRU, that is to return to it promptly whenever an aggregate demand shock pushes the economy away from it? Or, if you prefer, is the natural rate equilibrium stable without the help of active monetary or fiscal policy? This is the big issue of macroeconomics, the debate between Keynes and Pigou, carried on by their followers. Does flexibility of nominal prices and wages guarantee that enough aggregate real demand is automatically restored to return the economy to full employment?

Much of the profession nowadays believes that, years ago, the Pigou effect or real balance effect settled that issue once and for all. However, I think Irving Fisher (1933) was right. I would recast his argument in Keynesian terms. The propensity to spend from wealth is systematically greater for debtors than for creditors, enough so to overcome the small amount by which nominal creditor positions exceed nominal private debts, the monetary base plus part of other government debt. Moreover, Fisher was right too that the process of deflation is like an increase in the real rate of interest and is devastating for demand for goods and services. The dynamics of the relation of aggregate demand to disinflation and inflation may well be destabilizing. As Keynes argued, there are good reasons for stickiness of nominal wages; it is not money illusion. At the same time, he argued, more flexibility of nominal wages may be ineffectual or even counterproductive.

No wonder that exponents of New Classical Macroeconomics and Real Business Cycle Theory evade the problem by assuming perfect flexibility in the sense of continuous instantaneous market clearing, so that excess demands and supplies never occur for even a second of real time. Actual is always Potential. Real demand shocks never occur; that is, incipient shocks are instantaneously absorbed by market-clearing price settings.

Since 1982, the Federal Reserve has fine-tuned its monetary policy, expressed in the Federal Funds rate on base money. As a result, the US economy recovered from the deep 1981–2 recession and a shallow 1990–91 setback, and achieved virtually full employment with low inflation, a macroeconomic performance much superior to that of Europe or Japan, where monetary policies are much less activist and much more subservient to monetarism and New Classical theories, and much more dedicated to price stability to the exclusion of high employment and output. Actually the United States passes all the Maastricht tests, which no EU member save Luxembourg can meet.

NOTES

1. Charles Schultze (1959) examined the supposed two kinds of inflation and concluded that the problem was the sensitivity of key industrial sectors to increases in demand when the economy as a whole was not at full employment, plus the asymmetrical insensitivity of prices and wages to decreases in demand.
2. Irving Fisher (1925, 1926) anticipated Phillips, showing with American data that the price changes and either the volume of trade or the volume of employment were negatively correlated. These articles were scarcely noticed, while Phillips's article came at a time when the subject was at the forefront of professional and political attention.

REFERENCES

Akerlof, G., W. T. Dickens and George Perry (1996), 'The Macroeconomics of Low Inflation', *Brookings Papers on Economic Activity*, 2.
Baily, M.N. and J. Tobin, (1977), 'Macroeconomic Effects of Selective Public Employment and Wage Subsidies', *Brookings Papers on Economic Activity*, 2, 511–41.

Beveridge, W.H. (1945), *Full Employment in a Free Society*, New York: W.W. Norton.
Dillard, D. (1988), 'The Barter Illusion in Classical and Neoclassical Economics', *Eastern Economic Journal*, October–December, 299–318.
Economic Report of the President (1962), Washington: US Government Printing Office.
Fisher, Irving (1925), 'Our Unstable Dollar and the So-called Business Cycle', *Journal of the American Statistical Association*, June, 179–202.
Fisher, Irving (1926), 'A Statistical Relationship between Unemployment and Price Changes', *International Labour Review*, June, 785–92.
Fisher, Irving (1933), 'The Debt–Deflation Theory of Great Depressions,' *Econometrica*, October, 337–57.
Friedman, Milton (1968), 'The Role of Monetary Policy', *American Economic Review*, March, 1–17.
Keynes, J.M. (1936), *The General Theory of Employment, Interest and Money*, New York: Harcourt Brace.
Lipsey, R.G. (1960), 'The Relation between Unemployment and the Rate of Change of Money Wages in the United Kingdom, 1861–1957: A Further Analysis', *Economica*, February, 1–61.
Modigliani, Franco and Lucas Papademos (1976), 'Monetary Policy for the Coming Quarters: The Conflicting Views', *The New England Economic Review*, March–April, 2–35; reprinted in *The Collected Papers of Franco Modigliani*, vol. 3, Cambridge, Mass: MIT Press, 1980, pp.186–219.
Okun, Arthur M. (1962), 'Potential GNP: Its Measurement and Significance', *Proceedings of the Business and Economics Section, American Statistical Association 1962*, 145–58; reprinted in J.A. Pechman (ed.), *Economics for Policymaking: Selected Essays of Arthur M. Okun*, Cambridge, Mass: MIT Press, 1983.
Phelps, E.S. (1967), 'Inflation and Optimal Unemployment Over Time', *Economica*, August, 254–81.
Phillips, A.W. (1958), 'The Relation between Unemployment and the Rate of Change of Money Wages in the United Kingdom, 1861–1957', *Economica*, November, 283–299.
Samuelson, P.A. and R.M. Solow (1960), 'Analytical Aspects of Anti-Inflation Policy', *American Economic Review*, May, 177–94.
Schultze, Charles L. (1959), 'Recent Inflation in the United States', Study Paper No. 1 for Joint Economic Committee, Congress of the United States, US Government Printing Office, Washington.
Tobin, J. (1972), 'Inflation and Unemployment', *American Economic Review*, March, 1–18.

19. Monetary policy: recent theory and practice*

1 THE DEMISE OF MONETARISM

Milton Friedman's monetarism provoked hot debates on the conduct of monetary policy from the 1950s through the 1970s. The monetarists wanted the central bank to stop setting interest rates and instead to target growth in a monetary quantity, a stock of money by one or another definition, from the monetary base to intermediate aggregates as inclusive as M2 and M3. For hitting at least some of these monetary targets setting a money-market interest rate might be the operating mechanism. (The alternative could be quantitative control of the bank reserves portion of the monetary base, as practiced by the Federal Reserve 1979–82.)

Monetarist proposals differed in the horizon over which a money stock growth rate would be fixed. Friedman himself sometimes advocated setting it permanently, once for all at the estimated growth rate of the real economy. In practice, numerical money stock growth targets were reconsidered every year or even every quarter. The Full Employment and Balanced Growth Act of 1978, the 'Humphrey–Hawkins' Act, required the Fed to report them to Congressional committees every six months. Thus they could themselves be intermediate instruments designed to achieve the broader economic goals of the legislation. The use of money stock targets spread throughout the central banks of the world. The main purpose was to overcome the inflationary bias alleged to result from operating by discretionary movements of interest rates.

In the last two decades the sway of mechanical monetarism of this kind faded away. A principal reason was institutional change, which made the velocities of the various Ms even more variable and uncertain than they already were. Money substitutes multiplied, and definitions of Ms could not keep up. Regulatory reforms and market developments allowed market-determined interest to be paid on deposits that had formerly been interest-free or subject to legal ceilings.

*   This chapter originally appeared as a prologue to H. Wagner (ed.), *Current Issues in Monetary Economics*, Physica-Verlag, 1998, and was Cowles Foundation Paper no. 975, Cowles Foundation for Research in Economics at Yale University, 1999, pp.1–21.

One proposal to avoid the problems created by volatility of money velocity V was to target nominal gross domestic product, that is M times V, instead. The implicit terms of trade between rates of growth of price level P and real GDP Y, in responding to a shock to MV would then be 1 per cent to -1 per cent, and this might result in excessive short-run volatility of Y and P. This whole approach to monetary policy seems to have lost support, as it came to be understood that central banks did not need the discipline of intermediate M-growth targets to achieve more fundamental goals, including the control of inflation.

2   CURRENT ORTHODOXY IN MONETARY AND FISCAL POLICY

The dominant trend in the theory and practice of monetary policy over these last two decades has been its dedication to price stability. Central banks from New Zealand to the Finland have undertaken this commitment, either by mandates of their governments or by exercises of independent discretion granted them by their governments. Now the new European central bank will be bound by its charter to maintain the purchasing power of the euro, the coming single currency of the European Union (EU).

It is significant that these targets are stability of the price *level*, not of the rate of inflation. Inflation is not to be stabilized at a positive rate, by holding unemployment at the 'natural rate' or the NAIRU (the 'non-accelerating inflation rate of unemployment'), or at a negative rate either. No, it is to be stabilized at zero. This implies that any inflation that occurs as a result of supply or demand shocks, domestic or foreign, must be sooner or later expunged. A less draconian monetary strategy would accept price level increases resulting from big shocks as permanent and seek to avoid subsequent inflations. Even if inflation stability were accepted as a target, it is likely to be asymmetrical. That is, monetary policy would oppose a shock increasing the rate of inflation but would welcome a disinflationary shock.

The corollary to dedicating monetary policy to price stability is official indifference to real macroeconomic outcomes – employment and unemployment, real domestic product and its growth rate. These are likely to be ignored or drastically subordinated in the priorities of most central banks today. At best, they will suffer from lexicographic ordering. That is, real outcomes become a policy concern only after the central bank, and the government too, are confident that the price stability target is met.

Fiscal policy, reflecting the same values and priorities, and the same macro theory, is also unavailable to stabilize real national output against cyclical fluctuations. The same orthodoxy that minimizes the role of real economic performance in monetary policy insists on fiscal discipline regardless of the state of the economy. Indeed, not only is active fiscal stimulus to reverse cyclical recession and promote recovery outlawed, but also active fiscal contraction is required to overcome deficits that arise endogenously from recessions and feeble growth. Formal rules to enforce fiscal as well as monetary austerity in the coming euro regime of the EU are provided in the Treaty of Maastricht.

Under the Treaty the member states will have no autonomous macro policy instruments, not monetary policy, not exchange rate depreciation or appreciation, not budgetary policy. Their governments' debt interest rates will be those of the EU central bank plus allowances for maturities and risks reflecting judgments of rating agencies and financial markets. Absent the governmental, political, and fiscal institutions possessed by the authorities of federations like the United States, Canada and Germany, the EU's macro policy will be limited to its central bank's tough stance. They are bound to be both Europe-wide and interregional shocks, both demand and supply. The architects of the new regime are placing extraordinary faith in the flexibility, mobility, and resourcefulness of the peoples of the continent.

The Bank of Japan has long followed monetarist policies, pursuing price stability via intermediate targets for non-inflationary growth of monetary aggregates. At the same time, the Japanese Ministry of Finance is extremely allergic to budget deficits, even those produced by economy-wide slowdowns. The Ministry especially disdains Keynesian countercyclical fiscal policies. Thus Japan, like Europe, eschews macro policy, in faith that the economy will achieve optimal results on its own.

3   ORTHODOX MACROECONOMIC DOCTRINE

The macroeconomic theories underlying these policy rules are those of the anti-Keynesian counterrevolutions, Monetarism and the New Classical Macroeconomics. The fundamental proposition of these new orthodoxies is that real outcomes are invariant to price levels and inflation rates. Actually this was a pre-Keynesian old classical proposition, though more modestly interpreted to refer to long-run tendencies rather than to be literally true every day of the year. The old 'classical dichotomy' is now read to mean not only that real outcomes cannot be improved by monetary policies that increase prices and inflation – you cannot ride up Phillips's famous curve – but also to imply that counterinflationary austerity will be costless in real income, consumption and social welfare.

Acceptance of New Classical doctrine in official financial policy-making circles was mightily promoted by the unhappy macroeconomic history of the 1970s. Prices accelerated first as a consequence of demand shocks from the Vietnam war, then as a result of supply shocks, the two oil price boosts of 1973–4 and 1978–9. Counterinflationary monetary policies led to four recessions, in 1969–70, 1973–5, 1979–80, and 1981–2, and to postwar record highs in United States unemployment rates in 1975 and 1982. 'Stagflation', the simultaneous occurrence of high unemployment and high inflation, seemed to be a 180-degree refutation of Keynesian Phillips-curve predictions. In the New Classical version of these events, easy monetary policy – notably Federal Reserve expansionary measures in the election year of 1972 – received the blame. The supply shocks, unprecedented in peacetime, are completely omitted from the ideological histories of the period. Yet the deep and lengthy recessions that accompanied the central banks' concerted attacks on inflation, beginning in 1979, were scarcely confirmations of the New Classical claim that disinflation is costless.

4   THE UNITED STATES, AN EXCEPTION IN MONETARY POLICY AND IN RESULTS

The United States is a striking exception to the fashion of designating price stability as *the* target of monetary policy.

Faced with inflation rates above 10 per cent in 1979, it is true, the Federal Reserve shifted its tactical operating instrument from money-market interest rates (the Treasury bill rate, and the market rate on overnight interbank loans of 'federal funds' – bank reserve accounts in Federal Reserve Banks), to bank reserve aggregates. For three years, 1979–82 the ultimate policy target of the 'Fed' was to bring down inflation. By mid-1982, inflation had fallen to 5 per cent and unemployment had risen from 6 per cent to 10.5 per cent. At this point the Fed under Chairman Paul Volcker reversed course, returned to its previous interest-rate operating procedure, and initiated and managed a six-year recovery, which reduced unemployment below 6 per cent while inflation continued to decline.

Under Volcker's successor Alan Greenspan, United States monetary policy has continued to be balanced and pragmatic. It has been directed to reduction of unemployment rates and of the 'gap' between potential and actual GDP, as well as to stabilization of inflation. Indeed, Congress has mandated such an approach. The Employment Act of 1946 commits the Federal government, including the Federal Reserve System, to pursuit of 'maximum employment, production and purchasing power.' The 'Humphrey–Hawkins Act' specifically directs the Fed to aim at both unemployment and inflation goals. This Act's numerical targets, 4 per cent for each, were long ignored as impractical, but now they do not seem so outlandish. Radical Right Republicans have in recent years introduced legislation to repeal these Acts and to replace them with a pure price stability mandate. The proposal has supporters within the Federal Reserve System and in private financial circles. However, it seems unlikely to be adopted, anyway so long as the economy's macro performance in the present regime continues to be so spectacularly successful.

In contrast to the United States, European and Japanese central banks and governments did not try to return to the high growth rates, with low unemployment and inflation, which characterized their spectacular quarter-century of postwar reconstruction and prosperity, 1947–72. They did not even try to recover the real economic ground they lost in the 1970s and early 1980s. Instead they concentrated on eliminating the slightest chance of any resurgence of inflation. European unemployment has risen to 12 per cent in 1997, compared to 4.7 per cent in the United States. Inflation in Europe is no lower than in America.

Japanese unemployment numbers are chronically low, because redundant workers are kept on payrolls; but the increase in underutilization of workers is comparable to Europe. Indeed Japan has managed to have a full-blown depression for the past four years, with periods of negative growth and negative inflation. As a result of lack of demand, not because of deliberate expansionary monetary policy, short interest rates have fallen virtually to zero. Thus monetary policy has become impotent, even if the central bank should want to use it to rescue the economy. Thus has Keynes's *liquidity trap*, thought even by Keynes himself to be an anomalous and rare curiosity confined to severe depressions, come to life once more. The Finance Ministry, unwilling to fill the breach in aggregate demand and distressed by the fiscal cosmetics of a stagnant economy, acts perversely to raise taxes and cut spending. Japanese savers move the funds no one wants to borrow at home into dollars, causing the yen to depreciate (losing 40 per cent of its dollar value since 1995), generating an ever larger trade surplus, welcome within Japan as needed demand but unwelcome to the USA and other trading partners. It would be hard to find a case of worse macroeconomic policy. As terribly costly as it has been to Japan itself, it has been much more disastrous to other economies of East Asia, as events in late 1997 have shown.

5 APPLYING RULES WITH DISCRETION

'Rules versus discretion' in monetary policy has long been a topic of debate and research. In Tobin (1983), I argued that a mechanical rule blind to actual economic events and outcomes could not work, and for that reason alone would not be tolerated by central bankers, governments and electorates. Any rule would have to be responsive to observed economic information. However, it would be impossible to anticipate all events that might require policy adjustments and to specify in advance the correct direction and size of the response to each. Actual responses would have to depend on the best estimates and judgments of the policy makers at the time – in that sense, discretion. For this reason, I stressed, as I have here, the prime importance of choices of targets and operating procedures for monetary policy, rather than 'rules', counting on the central bank to find, in varying circumstances, the ways of pursuing the goals.

According to Taylor (1993), 'If there is anything about which modern macroeconomics is clear . . . – and on which there is substantial consensus – it is that policy rules have major advantages over discretion in improving economic performance.' At the same time Taylor interprets 'rules' in a way that allows, indeed requires, large doses of discretion in their application. Starting from the side of the debate opposite to mine, he seems to arrive at the same place. Follow the spirit, the intent, of a rule, he says, and do not be bound by a particular quantitative formula. Use such a formula perhaps, but as just one element in the set of indicators considered in periodic decisions on settings of the operating variables of monetary policy, whether quantitative aggregates or interest rates.

A major reason for the modern consensus for rules over discretion, as Taylor remarks, is to sustain the 'credibility' of the policy makers, specifically avoiding 'dynamic inconsistency'. I have never believed that monetary policy makers are organically vulnerable to such irrationality or addicted to playing a deceitful game to override public preferences. I am sure that they do not consciously seek to mislead the public into expecting future price stability in order to fool workers into working more than they really wish to. On the contrary, central bankers are obsessively concerned with the future consequences of their actions and the possibility that something they do now will set a bad precedent. Anyway, Taylor agrees that formal rules are not essential to credibility.

Taylor suggests a simple monetary policy formula for the United States:

$$r = p + 0.5y + 0.5(p - 2) + 2,$$

where
r is the federal funds rate in per cent per year,
p is the rate of inflation (of the GDP deflator) over the past four quarters,
y is the per cent deviation of real GDP from target.

Target GDP would be its value at full employment, that is, NAIRU. Potential GDP in this sense has been growing at 2.2 to 2.5 per cent per year.

This 'rule' embodies the balanced pragmatic two-goal policy I above attributed to the Fed since 1982. Taylor shows that his 'rule' fits actual data quite well. As he recognizes and illustrates, nevertheless, its message has to be modified in case of observed or expected exogenous shocks, and the formula itself has to be corrected as new data accumulate. In fact, if the Fed had implemented his equation from 1993 through 1997, the economy would have suffered unnecessarily high unemployment and lost about 2 per cent of GDP per year. The reason is that in 1993 and indeed until 1996 the NAIRU defining Potential Output was thought to be at least 6 per cent, whereas in the event it turned out to be at most 5 per cent and probably lower. Greenspan was right to use discretion, as new observations suggested that more output could be produced without inflationary danger.

6 THE MYSTERY: WHY AND HOW DOES MONETARY POLICY RULE THE ECONOMY?

The interest rate on overnight loans of federal funds is, as explained above, the Fed's instrument of policy. It is a market rate, which the Fed controls by buying or selling Treasury bills (in usual practice with agreements to repurchase them) at its intervention rate, nowadays publicly announced. At scheduled meetings eight times a year – and occasionally at other times – the Federal Reserve System's 'Federal Open Market Committee' (FOMC) reconsiders and sometimes changes the intervention rate, generally by 25 or 50 basis points, rarely by more.

The tail wags the dog. By gently touching a tiny tail, Alan Greenspan wags the mammoth dog, the great American economy. Isn't that remarkable? The federal funds rate is the shortest of all interest rates, remote from the rates on assets and debts by which businesses and households finance real investment and consumption expenditures counted in GDP. Why does monetary policy work? How? It's a mystery, fully understood by neither central bankers nor economists.

There are two lines of explanation: substitution chains and policy expectations. Expectations are very powerful, but they cannot work unless chains of asset substitution really do occur. That is, FOMC actions today, in conjunction with other economic observations, convey information about future monetary policies and future federal funds rates and thus affect the entire current spectrum of interest rates and asset prices. The process involves reshufflings of portfolios in response to changes in market interest rates and asset prices, actual and expected: banks' reserves and loans; bank deposits, bonds and equities; debt instruments, equities and real properties.

It would do portfolio managers, entrepreneurs, and consumers no good to understand Alan Greenspan if his actions really do not matter – unless they matter *just because* everyone thinks they do. We think we know that monetary policy is not just a bubble. We think we know from experience, as in 1931–3, 1973–4, 1979–83, that the Fed can if it wants take really big actions with immense consequences, and these demonstrations support the belief that even its modest everyday measures are important. That belief makes the central bank's job much easier. But it does not permit us, or the central bank, to expect precision from formula rules like Taylor's, as good as his is.

Why do the Federal Reserve and other central banks intervene only in financial markets for the shortest and most liquid nominal assets, those closest to the monetary base, far from the frontiers between financial markets and economic agents' expenditures on GDP goods and services? It was not always thus. In the past, central banks have discounted illiquid commercial loans, and even brokers' customer loans, and have conducted open market operations in long-term government bonds. In the present free-market mood of capitalist democracies, central banks want to be as unobtrusive and neutral as possible.

However, there are times when interventions closer to the real economy would be desirable. The present impasse in Japan is an example. Central bank operations in short safe liquid assets are mired in the 'liquidity trap'. Because of the unfavorable and risky business outlook and the unsound balance sheets of the banks, loans to businesses and households are expensive or unavailable. The Bank of Japan has operated in the stock market in the past, and maybe the time has come again for bold moves.

More generally, operations in long-term bonds could help get cyclical recoveries going when lenders are slow to reflect easing of short-term rates. Inflation-indexed government bonds are desirable instruments for open market operations, because they are closer to real goods and services than are nominal bonds. With fiscal policies no longer eligible for countercyclical stabilization, and with the globalization of financial markets threatening national financial sovereignty, innovative thinking about the tactics and structure of monetary operations is urgently needed. This is especially imperative in Europe, given the novel challenges facing the new EU central bank.

REFERENCES

Taylor, J.B. (1993), 'Discretion versus Policy Rules in Practice', *Carnegie–Rochester Series on Public Policy*, 23, 194–214.

Tobin, J. (1983), Monetary Policy: Rules, Targets and Shocks', *Journal of Money, Credit, and Banking*, 15, 506–18.

20. Whatever happened to fiscal policy?*

Bobby Heilbroner and I were undergraduate economics students at Harvard in the late 1930s, I in the class of 1939 and he one year behind, and we both went on to Harvard graduate school. I don't remember that we were in the same classes, but we certainly grew up in the same exciting intellectual climate of those days on that campus. We and most of our fellow students were attracted to economics by deep concern about the state of the world and by hope that economics could explain what had gone so terribly wrong and point the way to remedies. Capitalism was on trial, and whether it could survive and deserved to survive was far from clear. Democracy and liberty, weakened by economic failures, were under mortal attack. Economics as a social science was in crisis, as its practitioners and apprentices debated how to make it relevant to the fateful times. Harvard was the principal American scene of the Keynesian revolution.

The challenges of our student days have shaped our careers, Bob's and mine, although in quite different ways. Bob has thought and written deeply about capitalism and about the relation of our profession to the economic order. He is unique, and we are all greatly in his debt. He and I do have in common the Keynesian lessons we learned or figured out for ourselves. Among them was the use of fiscal policy as a tool of economic stabilization, of minimizing involuntary unemployment. Bob Heilbroner has been an eloquent apostle of 'fiscalism', as in the short and clear book he and Peter Bernstein wrote for general readers, puncturing prevalent fallacies and myths.

Time was that the federal government budget was a recognized instrument in the macroeconomic policy arsenal in the United States, espoused and used – though not always enthusiastically and consistently – by all presidents from Roosevelt to Carter (with the possible exception of Ford). Recessions were an occasion for tax cuts or expenditure increases, even in the Eisenhower and Nixon administrations. Deficits that arose from revenue losses and transfer outlays resulting from the weakness of the

*   This chapter was first presented at the Heilbroner Celebration, New York, 12 November 1998.

economy were generally tolerated, for fear that measures to correct them would weaken the economy further. Since 1980, however, presidents and Congresses of both political parties have eschewed countercyclical finance in single-minded pursuit of budget balance. Even the built-in stabilizers provided by the endogenous responses of the budget to business recessions came to be regarded as problematic rather than helpful. In our days we considered the tax increases and expenditure cuts of Presidents Hoover and Roosevelt at the depths of the Great Depression wrong-headed errors; their perversity would have been laughable had it not been so disastrous. Now such policies are orthodox virtues.

The Reagan administration was a watershed. Its overriding fiscal objective was to cut back government, both taxes and expenditures, at least civilian expenditures. Its audacious new strategy in fiscal politics was to cut taxes first, and use the deficits resulting from its own tax cuts and its defense-spending spree to force spending cuts. That strategy was eventually quite successful. As deficits zoomed to unprecedented heights relative to GDP, and the administration and Congress fought about spending priorities and economies, macroeconomic use of fiscal policy was officially rejected in favor of fiscal discipline. Of course, the 'tax cut first' strategy was patently a violation of fiscal discipline. That was explained away on supply-side grounds. These tax cuts were not Keynesian facilitators of demand-side spending; they were supply-side incentives to productivity, work, thrift, entrepreneurship and risk taking. Through these effects, they might even, according to Arthur Laffer and other gurus, generate more tax revenue than they initially lost. Since the beneficiaries of the tax cuts did not know they were not to respond in demand-side ways, they actually were Keynesian stimuli as long as the matching cuts in government expenditures were not achieved.

At the same time, the Reagan and Bush administrations and the Congressional Republicans tried repeatedly to pass a Balanced Budget Amendment. Just the threat was a blow to rational fiscal policy. While a big reason to oppose the amendment was to preserve the possibility of compensatory macro fiscal policy, opponents of the amendment also needed to argue and if possible to demonstrate that Congress was capable of fiscal discipline without constitutional compulsion.

In western Europe from the 1970s on, Keynes was way out of fashion, and supply-side enthusiasm did not encompass Reagan–Laffer-like excuses for transitional deficits. The Maastricht conditions for membership in the monetary union prescribed limits on deficit-to-GDP and debt-to-GDP ratios, with no concessions to business cycles and macroeconomic stabilization. These restrictions continue in the new Euroland. They rule out fiscal policies, other than austerity and discipline, in the 11 member states. The

European Union itself has no federal government. Without a fisc you cannot have a fiscal policy. Monetary policy is also tightly constrained, virtually untouchable by political governments, individual states or the EU. Obviously, the individual states, having no currencies, have no monetary powers; their central banks have become branches of the new European Central Bank, analogous to the 12 district Federal Reserve banks. The European Central Bank is independent of the member governments and is directed by its charter to gear its policies solely to price stability. The theory to be tested is that in an environment of steady sound policies, macroeconomic prosperity will take care of itself. Not even Keynes's 'classical' opponents were so supremely confident in market capitalism. To a considerable degree, the new classical theory has already been applied and tested in the European Monetary System run by the Bundesbank over the last two decades, with chronic double-digit unemployment as the result. Will Euroland do any better?

Japan in the 1990s has been a textbook Keynesian case of urgent need for expansionary fiscal policy. The economic trend has been dreadful: chronic stagnation punctuated by recessions and incomplete recoveries. Incredible mismanagement in macroeconomic policy succeeded in bringing about a 'liquidity trap', a Keynesian *curiosum* seen nowhere else since the 1930s. Aggregate demand was so weak that short interest rates fell to zero and are stuck there. Real rates, however, are positive, reflecting deflationary expectations and heightened business risks. Banks became acutely risk-averse, making loan rates too big a hurdle for businesses. For some Japanese savers, overseas interest rates rather than domestic near-zero rates are the operational opportunity cost. Anyway monetary policy is quite impotent, unless the Bank of Japan would sell yen for dollars. Depreciation of the yen, inducing a still larger trade surplus, would help Japan but would not be popular in the United States and East Asia. The situation is made to order for expansionary fiscal policy. That is what Japan's G-7 partners urge, though they would never prescribe such a thing for themselves. That is what, despite repeated promises and announcements by Japanese prime ministers, never seems to survive the all-powerful bureaucrats of the Finance Ministry. They argue that, given the frightening aging of the population, the country needs more saving, not less. That may be true, but fiscal austerity may well achieve less national saving rather than more. Sometimes Keynes's 'paradox of thrift' is right.

In contrast to Europe and Japan, the United States has enjoyed spectacularly successful macroeconomic management since 1994. But it was monetary rather than fiscal policy that did the trick. The Federal Reserve slowed the economy down in 1988, and the Bush administration suffered a sluggish economy and an actual recession. In 1992 and 1993, some economists, myself included, advocated temporary modest fiscal stimulus, say 1 per cent of GDP, advising President-elect Clinton to begin the public investment programs he favored while deferring the taxes to pay for them. However, the new Treasury team, Robert Rubin and Lawrence Summers, persuaded the new president that the 'markets' would react more kindly to fiscal austerity. They argued that the resulting lower interest rates would be sufficient macroeconomic stimulus. Both the public investment program and fiscal stimulus were scrapped. From a Keynesian viewpoint. the Rubin–Summers proposition was fallacious, unless the Federal Reserve stepped in with substantial monetary stimulus to offset the demand contraction brought by the fiscal austerity. But the economy did well. Federal Reserve Chairman Greenspan delivered stimulus, but not until 1995. The fruits were low unemployment, low inflation and steady growth.

This performance was accomplished along with an eventual budget surplus, as the stubborn Reaganomics deficits were vanquished by the fiscal by-products of continuing prosperity. Clearly, deficit spending was not essential for prosperity. Thus were vindicated the views that Paul Samuelson and I espoused 30 or more years ago, namely that a given macro outcome, as measured by GDP and unemployment and prices, can generally – not always, but usually – be achieved by a variety of mixes of monetary and fiscal policy. The choice among the viable policy mixes can then be made in the light of other criteria or constraints. For example, a tight money/easy fiscal combination might be favorable for balance of payments, while an easy money/tight fiscal policy mix would foster investments leading to long-run productivity gains and growth. Maybe this 'neoclassical synthesis' – Paul's term – is not Keynesian for Heilbroner and Bernstein or for Robert Eisner or for New School economists, but I think it would not have been foreign to Keynes, a very worldly philosopher who really did believe in monetary as well as fiscal policy in normal circumstances. I have always been allergic to the popular journalistic dichotomy, Fiscalism (Keynes) versus Monetarism (Friedman). Milton Friedman and his followers were monetarists all right, and denied the macro significance of fiscal policy. But neither Keynes nor Keynesians like me were fiscalists; we defended the macro relevance of fiscal policy but did not deny the macro importance of monetary policy.

I plead guilty to having written, together with Bob Solow, the policy-mix doctrine into the 1962 *Economic Report of the President*. In 1960, I had published an article titled 'Growth through Taxation' in *The New Republic*. In the 1960s, the prescription could not be carried out, because the Federal Reserve and the Treasury thought a lower interest rate would cause gold to move overseas, a catastrophe that frightened President Kennedy. Today, fortunately, we have floating exchange rates, which augment the macro potency of monetary policy. Surely the Clinton–Greenspan policy mix, with relatively low interest rates and high ratios of market valuations of corporate capital to replacement costs (the Brainard–Tobin 'q') are much better than the Reagan–Volcker mix of the 1980s, when real interest rates were much higher than in other cyclical recoveries. (Not Volcker's fault, he had little choice.)

As Jan Tinbergen taught, surely it is generally better to have two instruments than one. It may enable policy makers to hit two targets, not just one. Not always, however, as he also taught. For an important example, it is not possible to overcome the cruel inflation/unemployment tradeoff by tinkering with the mix of monetary and fiscal policies. Inflation and unemployment outcomes are both functions of the level aggregate demand, regardless of what policy mix is supporting that level. What we at Yale know as the Common Funnel Theorem says that demand is demand: whatever its source it is channeled through the same funnel into the markets where its impacts on quantities relative to prices are determined. (A bit of an exception occurs insofar as a mix weighted toward monetary policy will raise import and export prices.)

Of course, as the current plight of Japan dramatically illustrates, there can be liquidity trap times when monetary policy is powerless to lower interest rates. And there can be bouts of business pessimism when lowering rates is 'pushing on a string'. Small countries on fixed exchange rates with free international flows of funds are pretty much deprived of monetary sovereignty, but they are unlikely to have much discretion in fiscal policy either.

A long-recognized practical and political difficulty of fiscal policy is the delay in implementing a budgetary change. It usually takes legislation, followed by administration, and by the time it is applied the conditions that motivated it may have vanished or reversed. In contrast, monetary policy can turn on a dime. Presidents Kennedy and Johnson requested Congress to delegate power to institute temporarily a pre-defined cut in income taxes, without success. It was not even possible to obtain 'fast tracks' for presidential requests for such cuts. Anyway economic theory, with some empirical support, has cast doubt on the potency of clearly temporary income tax cuts: better to reduce temporarily taxes on purchases of consumption goods or investment goods, exploiting substitution effects instead of income effects. President Johnson's temporary income tax cuts, President Carter's small one-shot demogrants, and President Bush's temporary suspension of withholding were none of them resounding successes.

The budgetary struggles in the United States since 1980 made flexibility in fiscal policy especially difficult. The energies of President and Congress were concentrated on controlling expenditures and revenues, whatever the macroeconomic climate. After efforts to legislate deficit outcomes, as in

Gramm–Rudman–Hollings, failed, Congress imposed on itself strict multi-year ceilings on various components of the budget. These obstacles to expenditure increases and tax cuts brought the budget into surplus territory; they still apply.

Shortly after the Heilbroner celebration, the death of Robert Eisner deprived the profession and the nation of one of its finest economists and, in particular, of a faithful and indefatigable voice for rationality in fiscal policy. He never failed to point out that the shibboleth of budget balance was an irrational constraint on fiscal policy, and on the size and composition of government expenditures and revenues. He stressed the importance of recognizing, in public finance as in private finance, the difference between capital and current outlays, and the potential contributions of public investments to national well-being and growth. Whatever the macroeconomic state of the economy, those contributions may justify either the taxes or the interest-bearing bond issues to pay for them. Whether a formal capital budget is the way to implement these principles is a difficult issue of practical politics.

Whatever happened to fiscal policy? To begin with, some Keynesian advocates of fiscal policy as *the* instrument of macroeconomic stabilization overplayed their hand. While there are situations in which fiscal policy is the only feasible instrument, they are unusual, as Keynes himself recognized. Extreme 'fiscalists' seriously underestimated the potency, for good and bad, of monetary policy, just as monetarists underrated fiscal measures. On the one hand, the deficit spending of the Reagan era, a peacetime record fiscal stimulus to aggregate demand (though billed as supply-side), was successfully moderated by cautious Federal Reserve policy during the cyclical recovery of the 1980s, resulting in unusually high real interest rates. On the other hand, Federal Reserve policy in the 1990s kept recovery and expansion going despite the budget-balancing fiscal policies of the Clinton administration. Keynesians who argued that policy makers could and should choose among various mixes of fiscal and monetary policies were vindicated.

The reckless fiscal initiatives of Reaganomics distracted political attention from demand management and concentrated debate on the size and composition of federal budgets and their implications for resource allocation and social justice. Once budget balance became the prime goal, there was no room for considerations of stabilization. The long-recognized practical difficulties of discretionary fiscal policy were magnified, especially if the limited effectiveness of temporary stimuli were considered. Of course, the size and scope of government expenditures and revenues are themselves terribly important subjects, much in need of rational economic analysis to counter slogans and shibboleths.

21. Clinton's second term and the American economy*

Bill Clinton could not have asked for a better election year economy: unemployment averaging 5.2 per cent, the lowest since 1973; 10.7 million new jobs since 1992, a gain of 9 per cent; inflation steady around 3 per cent per year; stock market booming and interest rates low; consumer and business confidence high; the budget deficit cut four years in a row, falling 63 per cent to $107 billion, 1.4 per cent of GDP. 'Are you better off than four years ago?', Clinton asked the voters, and they answered 'Yes!'

Presidents get credit and blame for whatever happens, whether they deserve them or not. Alan Greenspan's Federal Reserve deserves credit for managing the 1992–6 recovery from 'Bush's recession'. Many inflation hawks, some inside the Fed, thought unemployment rates below 6 per cent were dangerous, but Greenspan and company have let unemployment fall towards pre-1970 rates as long as wages and prices remain well-behaved.

For deficit reduction, Clinton can claim credit. Early on, Treasury Secretary Rubin persuaded the president to concentrate on deficit reduction. Clinton gave up fiscal stimulus to pep up the sluggish economy, scrapped his promised 'middle class tax cut', and abandoned his public investment initiatives. His fiscal package passed Congress without a single Republican vote. The gamble worked, both economically and politically. The economy recovered, the bond market cheered, and middle class voters did not revolt.

In macroeconomic performance the United States is the most successful advanced economy in the world. America meets all the Maastricht tests for monetary union, which no actual EU member except Luxembourg has yet passed. What now? The prospects are for continued strong macroeconomic performance. Recovery is virtually complete, evolving into sustainable growth, with low inflation and low unemployment. No inflationary shock that might provoke the Fed to slam on the brakes is on the horizon.

Yet, as Clinton starts 'building a bridge to the 21st century', he and the nation face some difficult economic problems. First, the sustainable growth

*   This chapter was first published in *Bulgarski Business*, Bulgaria; *Belorusskaya Gazeta*, Belarus; *Economist*, Bosnia; *Delo*, Slovenia; *Der Standard*, Austria; *Il Sore – 24 Ore*, Italy; *Nepszabadsag*, Hungary; *Romania Livera*, Romania.

rate of the economy is pitifully low, not more than 2.5 per cent per year, compared to 4 per cent plus in the golden age – 1946–72. Demographic slowdowns of labor force growth account for some of the difference. What is disturbing is the post-1972 slowdown in productivity, from 2.5 per cent to 1 per cent. This translates into anemic growth in real wages, for many workers stagnant or declining wages.

Dissatisfaction with slow growth is widespread. Republicans tried unsuccessfully to exploit it, reviving discredited 'supply-side' claims that drastic tax cuts would raise growth substantially and permanently. This time the public did not bite. But speeding up growth remains high on the national agenda. It takes more saving and investment, better education and training, and innovative research and development. Government policy tools are limited, and results come unspectacularly.

Second, inequality of income and wealth in the United States, already much more pronounced than in other advanced democratic capitalist nations, has been dramatically increasing. The percentage of families, and especially children, living in poverty remains disturbingly high. Many unskilled jobs pay ever-lower wages. Income differentials associated with higher education have risen drastically. No one knows what to do; many conservatives see no problem.

American workers compete with low-wage labor abroad and with immigrants at home. In the 1996 political campaigns, resentments and exaggerations of import competition surfaced in economic nationalism, espoused by Pat Buchanan and Ross Perot on the right and by trade union leaders on the left. President Clinton, on the other hand, remains committed to the internationalist trade policies of his first term (NAFTA, GATT), combined with bilateral negotiations to 'open foreign markets'. He can probably count on the leaderships of both parties in Congress. Immigration is another story. The president agreed to some restrictive legislation he would like to reverse; this will be a contentious issue with Republicans.

Third, the president and both parties in Congress are committed to balancing the budget in 2002. The economic purpose is to rechannel private saving from deficits to productivity-enhancing investments. Standard economics says that this switch will, at least temporarily and modestly, augment growth – provided that the Fed makes sure that fiscal cutbacks are not wasted in recession and unemployment, and that the expenditures cut are not public investments of high social productivity. Clinton would like to squeeze expenditures on education, environment, science, technology and infrastructure into his budgets.

Budget room will be scarce for many other worthwhile programs, among them aid to poor countries, where the USA is scandalously stingy; paying dues in arrears to the United Nations; creating jobs for mothers who will, under the cruel welfare 'reform' Clinton signed in 1996, be denied public assistance for themselves and their children.

Budget balance in 2002 is well within reach. But entitlements for the elderly, Social Security and Medicare, threaten severe fiscal imbalances later in the 21st century. The issues are hypersensitive, but President Clinton and both parties in Congress are under great pressure to agree on long-run solutions.

Fourth, health care reform may return to the national agenda. Clinton's revolutionary proposal failed in Congress in 1994 and contributed to the Republican sweep in the 1994 congressional elections. The problems still exist. The number of Americans with no medical insurance is 20 per cent and still rising. Many families feel insecure about the availability and cost of unregulated private insurance.

For President Clinton, the objective of the first term was re-election, and the objective of the second term must be a high place in history. How? He has not said. Foreign policy? After a slow start, Clinton had his successes. But the intractable regional crises in the world today are land mines for the leader of the one superpower, especially when his own public is turning inward. Domestic policy? In the campaign, he spoke eloquently of America's future but confined himself to a few modest and inexpensive proposals, mainly tax concessions and subsidies for children, students and schools. Lacking any major innovation that could carry his name, like Franklin Roosevelt's Social Security and Lyndon Johnson's Medicare, Bill Clinton may have to settle for competent management of the status quo. Unfortunately, the next four years may well be dominated by the allegations of wrongdoing by the president, Mrs Clinton and their associates in Arkansas and Washington.

22. Fiscal policy: its macroeconomics in perspective*

In making a major cut in federal income taxes the centerpiece of his program, George W. Bush has followed two influential precedents, one of Democratic Presidents Kennedy and Johnson in 1962–4 and the other, of course, that of Republican President Reagan in 1981. Candidate Bob Dole obeyed Republican tradition by proposing in his 1996 campaign a 15 per cent across-the-board cut in income tax rates. Instead, the re election of Bill Clinton continued the regime of fiscal discipline and monetary wisdom begun by Treasury Secretary Rubin and Federal Reserve Chairman Greenspan in 1993. The economy and the federal budget were doing so well in election year 2000 that it seemed unlikely that young Mr Bush could be elected, much less succeed in reviving Reaganomic fiscal policies. Yet now, in 2001, it seems quite probable that a substantial permanent cut in income taxes will be enacted, along with an emergency package to encourage spending soon this year.

The story of macroeconomic and fiscal developments over the last 40 years is an amalgam of economic theory, politics, and ideology. I admit to being both a Keynesian and a neoclassical economist and both a liberal and a conservative in public policy. I was an adviser to President Kennedy, and an informal consultant to other Democratic candidates. Win or lose, my advice was very often not taken.

JFK'S TAX CUTS AND THEIR UNHAPPY SEQUEL

In 1962–4, when JFK first considered and then recommended cutting taxes, the economy was hesitantly recovering from the 1959–60 recession. Kennedy's first measures were incentives for business plant and equipment investments, accelerated depreciation allowances and tax credits. The major tax legislation, in 1964, was intended to keep the recovery from petering out prematurely. Unemployment had fallen from 7 per cent at JFK's

---

*   This chapter first appeared as 'Fiscal Policy: Its Macroeconomics in Perspective, 2001', *The Politic: Yale's Journal of Politics*, 1(1), Spring 2001, 14–17.

inauguration in 1961 to the 5–6 per cent range, but the administration's target was 4 per cent. It was reached in 1965. The stimulus of the tax cut was unexpectedly augmented by spending for Vietnam. The combined spending was excessive, reducing unemployment to a point below the 4 per cent target and unleashing unwelcome inflation in 1966–8. President Johnson belatedly and reluctantly was persuaded to prevail on the Congress to raise taxes temporarily in 1968. It was too late, and the Nixon administration inherited a difficult economy. Moral: unforeseen events may make you regret a permanent loss of federal revenue, and it is awfully difficult ever to raise taxes. This is even truer now that any tax increase is a deadly sin in the litany of the GOP.

REAGAN'S 1981 CUT: SUPPLY-SIDE REFORM WAS DEMAND STIMULUS INSTEAD

Ronald Reagan's tax cut took effect in the depths of the worst recession since World War II. Unemployment had hit double digits. This was the cost of the crusade of the Federal Reserve under Chairman Paul Volcker against an inflation that itself had in 1979–80 hit double digits. The tax cut was a big stimulus to consumer and business spending, reinforced by Reagan's buildup of the US military.

The period 1981–8 was one of recovery from the recession, bringing unemployment back down to 6 per cent. The high year-to-year rates of increase of economic activity and real gross domestic product (GDP) during such business-cycle upswings reflect the reemployment of idle resources, both workers and industrial capacity. This additional output growth is the essence of prosperity. But this pace cannot be sustained. Once the economy returns to full employment, the economy can grow only at its long-run sustainable rates of increase in the supplies of economic resources and, especially, in their productivity.

The architects of Reaganomics styled themselves supply-siders. They scorned the demand-side theories and policies they attributed to John Maynard Keynes and to his 'liberal' followers, whom they held responsible for the stagflation of the 1970s. In their view, the Federal Reserve could and should control inflation by stabilizing the supply of money, as preached in the monetarism of Milton Friedman. Keynesians were, they argued, dangerously wrong to think that demand-side stimuli to spending could lift employment, GDP and economic welfare. Instead, what the country needs are policies to enhance supply, in particular by lower taxes, providing incentives to work, save, innovate and take risks. That was the spirit and the purpose of the Reagan fiscal policy.

In practice, Reaganomics turned out to be the biggest and most success-ful demand-side fiscal gambit in peacetime US history. What it was not was what it was intended to be, a supply-side transformation of the economy. There was zero evidence that the American economy's capacity to produce goods and services *at full employment* was any greater at the end of the 1980s than would have been prophesied a decade earlier without Reagan fiscal policy. The trend of productivity growth was the same as before.

These supply-side failures may seem surprising, since income tax cuts were meant to embody incentives for more productive and innovative behavior. Unfortunately, these cuts in tax rates also bring windfalls for past behavior that has already taken place. For example, offering concessions for capital gains on future acquisitions of assets might be socially useful, while reduc-ing taxes on gains realized on holdings bought years ago clearly is not. The test is whether the taxpayer must, in order to benefit, change his behavior in the desired supply-side direction. If yes, the touted incentives work. If no, the individual taxpayers' gains have to be defended otherwise, as deserved and just. Undergraduate microeconomics students know the difference between the 'income effects' and 'substitution effects' of variations in prices or taxes. The substitution effects are responses to incentives, but they are often out-weighed by income effects in the perverse direction. Income effects may sometimes be what the doctor ordered: more consumer spending. But those effects can overwhelm supply-side objectives. A cut in marginal income tax rates may elicit more work from some taxpayers, but workers whose taxes are reduced anyway may take some of their gains in leisure. The same objections apply to tax credits intended to induce desirable behavior, for example saving or paying school and college tuitions. These devices have long been favorites of politicians in both parties. The trouble is that they are often windfalls for persons who would behave in the desired way without any subsidies, who are already saving or paying tuitions. The government loses revenue, or other taxpayers pay more, or other programs are curtailed. Yet the intended objec-tives are not achieved. Individual Retirement Accounts (IRAs) are a flagrant example. The investing taxpayer acquires tax-free accounts, not by saving more, the raison d'être of the program, but just by cashing in other assets or borrowing. Despite repeated giveaway subsidies of this kind, the United States remains a very low-saving country.

THE MACRO POLICY MIX: DID GREENSPAN MAKE FISCAL POLICY OBSOLETE?

Prosperity per worker was greater in 1989 than in 1981 not because of a supply-side revolution but because of demand-side stimulus. That is, consumers and businesses and governments were spending more and putting to work previously idle workers and plants. The Reagan fiscal policy certainly helped bring about those happy results. Was it necessary?

Not according to modern mainstream macroeconomics, which would say that Federal Reserve monetary policy could have done the job on its own. Indeed, Fed Chairman Paul Volcker, who after all was the author of the 1978–82 recessions, decided in 1982 that he had won the war against inflation and pressed the lower-interest button for recovery. Both fiscal and monetary policies are demand-side instruments (not to say that they might not also have supply-side effects). The two instruments are in various possible degrees alternatives to one another in federal government policy to control aggregate demand. Choosing the mix of the two instruments is a most important policy decision for president, Congress and Federal Reserve. Different mixes can have equivalent effects on spending and demand and thus on business-cycle developments, and yet differ significantly in other important respects.

In the 1980s, President Reagan and Congress ran an easy fiscal policy and forced Volcker's Fed to keep the recovery from overheating by following a tighter, higher-interest monetary policy than usual in previous business-cycle recoveries. Contrast the Clinton–Greenspan policy mix of 1993–2000, tight budget and easy money. The Reagan–Volcker policy mix tilts the composition of national output to consumption by citizens favored by tax concessions and to national defense and other increased government programs away from business and public investments deterred by high interest rates and scarce loan finance. The 1990s economy with the Clinton–Greenspan policy mix was, in most reckonings, much the happier time.

Sometimes a low-interest monetary policy is infeasible. The burden of demand-side measures to achieve or maintain full employment then falls on fiscal measures, and among those often on tax relief. In the early 1960s, the Federal Reserve and the Treasury felt that defense of the gold standard value of the dollar forced them to keep US interest rates competitive with those in Europe and Japan, compelling greater reliance on tax cuts in the mix of policies for domestic prosperity than would otherwise have been desired. In the USA in the Great Depression of the 1930s and in Japan in the 1990s, monetary policy became virtually impossible because interest rates were as low as they could go, zero on safe short-term paper. This predicament was known to economists as Keynes's 'liquidity trap', from which fiscal stimulus was the only way out.

Governments and legislators often feel that their central banks are keeping interest rates too high, monetary policy too tight. In 1991–2, President George H.W. Bush thought that Alan Greenspan's Fed was unduly cautious in stimulating recovery from recession. The Bush camp blamed the sluggish economy for its defeat in the 1992 election. At the same time, fiscal initiative was limited because the Democrats, controlling the Congress, were tired of Reaganomic budget deficits and indeed forced President Bush *père* to sign a budget containing a small tax increase. This episode is probably one reason that President Bush *fils* is stressing fiscal policy to pep up his 'sputtering' economy in 2001. Maybe it is also one reason why Alan Greenspan has spoken favorably of George W. Bush's proposed tax cut.

In 1992–3, a number of economists of both political persuasions agreed, both before and after the 1992 election, that the economy needed temporary fiscal stimulus. Two former Kennedy advisers, Professors Solow and Tobin, argued this case at a transition economic policy discussion with President-elect Clinton at Little Rock. But on the insistent advice of his new Treasury Secretary, Robert Rubin, President Clinton and his Democratic Congress rejected this proposal in favor of immediate tight fiscal discipline. Greenspan and his Fed then followed a monetary policy easy enough to offset the negative demand-side effects of the tight budget. Sometimes Clinton, Gore and Rubin seemed to attribute the great prosperity and growth of the 1990s entirely to their fiscal policy. But Greenspan was their indispensable ally. The tight-budget-easy-money mix was the key. The danger now in 2001 is that the new Republican president will return government and economy to the bad old policy mix of Reaganomics.

SIXTY BILLION STIMULUS NOW AND/OR TWO TRILLION OVER A DECADE?

When George W. Bush made a repeat of Reagan's income tax cut the central economic and fiscal issue of his campaign for president, he was not taken very seriously. The general public was not much interested. The economy was doing splendidly without it. Social Security and Medicare seemed higher priority uses of prospective budget surpluses. Even among Republicans only right-wing supply-siders chronically inimical to government seemed enthusiastic for big tax reductions.

Mr Bush, it turned out, meant every word of it and every number too. He was prepared to use any argument and any stratagem to get his proposal passed. The slowdown in the economy in 2001 provided, he thought, a great opportunity. He could now claim that his tax cut was needed to prevent or limit a recession. At the beginning of the year mainstream macro economists pooh-poohed this idea as outdated vulgar Keynesianism – has not Alan Greenspan taught us all that monetary policy, a much more efficient and flexible instrument, without such lasting costs and risks, can do the job? But bad news from stock markets convinced economists, business leaders, financiers, labor leaders and congressional Democrats that some fiscal stimulus is essential to save the economy. Greenspan, Volcker and Rubin, heroes of fiscal discipline and monetary policy in the 1990s, now endorsed some fiscal initiative.

The bad news for the president is the increasing realization that his 10-year back-loaded income tax cut is not the answer to the immediate ills of the economy. Its demand-side stimulus, even if made to take effect as of the beginning of 2001, is too long delayed and goes to the wrong people. What is needed is a one-shot dose of cash, directed to consumers most likely to spend it. The Ford administration put $8 billion out in April–June 1975, a 10 per cent rebate of 1974 income tax up to $200 per household. This was small but successful as far as it went. The design could be improved. Cash should be directed to consumers most likely to spend it promptly, the poor and the cash-poor, those whose spending is constrained by illiquidity. Many Americans who need help and would surely spend are not on income tax rolls. The whole population should be covered, not just income taxpayers.

A fiscal lifesaver of this kind would receive wide bipartisan support while leaving the permanent shape of the income tax up for more deliberate decision. The president likes the 'jump-start' metaphor, which ill fits his own proposal but possibly describes Senator Domenici's $60 billion injection of disposable income this year, like the economists' 1992–3 proposal that did not happen.

Perhaps the time has also come to revive consideration of a Kennedy–Johnson proposal from the 1960s. This is to enact legislation putting on the shelf a plan for temporarily cutting or rebating taxes or otherwise distributing spendable cash. The president might be empowered to put it into effect on a finding of economic need, or just to recommend it for expedited consideration by Congress. The point is to avoid the delay for debate and detail that can make fiscal policy a cumbersome instrument of business cycle stabilization.

OF THE PEOPLE, BY THE PEOPLE, FOR THE PEOPLE!

Like Reagan fiscal policy, that of the new Republican administration seems more a political and ideological attack on government than an economic reform. The overriding objective is once again to shrink radically the share and role of government – especially federal government – in the economic and social life of the nation. President Reagan described tax revenues as the 'children's allowances' of Congress. Reduce taxes, and Congress will have to spend less. In the period 1981–93, this strategy utterly failed. Democrats controlled the Congress. They fought a stalemate with the executive over whose programs would absorb the losses of revenues. Some tax cuts were reversed or offset, but mainly budgets moved heavily into deficit, the largest increases in federal debt (in dollars and relative to the economy) in peacetime history. At the same time, many meritorious public investments and social programs were crowded out by military buildups and tax cuts.

President George W. Bush has resumed the crusade against government: 'The federal surplus is not the government's money. It's the people's money and should be returned to the people. If it lies on the table, Congress will spend it.' Bush makes it sound as if we were ruled by an alien tyrant or a divinely ordained monarch. Is it not the people's government, of the people, by the people, for the people? It is American people who pay the taxes. It is American people who receive outlays in cash or kind and who benefit from public services. The federal debt is the people's debt, most of it owed by the people to the people. We the people also have solemn but unfunded obligations to future dependants on Social Security and Medicare. Two years ago both political parties solemnly put the Social Security Trust Fund in a 'lock box'. Clinton and Gore went farther, proposing to beef up the Social Security Trust Fund with part of the surplus elsewhere in the budget. President Bush is emptying the lock box, counting it and the Medicare fund in his general contingency reserve. Moreover, he himself has recognized a host of other national priorities: education, science and technology, environmental protection, health insurance, prescriptions. energy, poverty. He seems not to be budgeting for them, but all of them might well be more important than adding to the personal consumption of affluent Americans. The way the country has been prospering and growing, it is hard to complain that federal taxes are impoverishing us, or even that they were doing so when they were much higher in past decades

The surplus is the taxpayers' own money? The idea that the high incomes of wealthy Americans are due solely to personal qualities superior to those of other eras and other lands is arrogant and ridiculous. We are lucky to be Americans and to have benefited from a civilization to which our democratic government is an essential contributor.

PART IV

Political economy

23. Thoughts on indexing the elderly*

The Boskin Commission (BC) finds that the Consumer Price Index (CPI) reported by the Bureau of Labor Statistics (BLS) overstates inflation 0.8 to 1.6 per cent per year; the commission's best estimate of the bias is 1.1 per cent. Economists have long suspected that the CPI and other price indexes overstate inflation. The bias moved from academia to the national stage when, urged by Alan Greenspan, Congressional leaders began to realize that its correction could contribute mightily to solution of intractable fiscal and political problems. Cutting indexation of benefits by one percentage point could cut nearly in half the actuarial shortfall of the social security system over the next 75 years. Reckoning also the revenue gains from slowing the indexing of personal income tax brackets, the correction would do wonders for the unified federal deficit, for example saving one-third of the deficit now projected for 2006.

The technicians of the BLS are well aware of the shortcomings of their index and work steadily to correct them. Congress should provide the agency the resources it needs. (Reckless and short-sighted budget economies threaten the whole body of federal statistics.)

Enthusiasts for cutting indexation – including Chairman Greenspan and Senators Lott and Moynihan – don't want to wait for BLS's improvements in its index. They propose another commission of wise disinterested experts who would determine each year how much to lop off the BLS's CPI change for the purposes of official indexation. If the Boskin Commission had this responsibility right now, presumably the answer would be 1.1 percentage points. BC invites 'Congress and the President [to] decide whether they wish to continue the widespread over-indexing . . . If the purpose . . . is fully and accurately to insulate the groups receiving transfer payments and paying taxes, no more and no less, they should pass legislation adjusting indexing provisions accordingly' (Recommendation 16, p.86). BC elaborates, 'This could be done in the context of subtracting an amount partly or wholly reflecting the over-indexing from the current CPI-based indexing.' On the amount to subtract, presumably advice could be sought from the 'permanent (rotating) independent commission of experts' BC asks Congress to establish.

*   This chapter first appeared as 'Thoughts on Indexing the Elderly', *Federation of American Scientists Public Interests Report*, 50 (3), May/June 1997, 5–8.

Prior to 1973, Congress frequently raised social security benefits, using as a principal reason the need to keep up with inflation. Legislation in 1972 introduced CPI indexation from 1975 on, to discipline and depoliticize this process. Now to supersede the technical objectivity of the BLS with annual judgment calls is a grave step.

AN INDEX SUITABLE FOR ADJUSTING PENSIONS?

The CPI is in the statistical and political spotlight mainly because of its use in indexing social security benefits. An important issue is whether it is suitable for that purpose, as it is presently designed and calculated and as it will be reformed by the BLS following the recommendations of the Boskin Commission. Surprisingly, this question is barely mentioned either in the BC report or in the ensuing public debate.

I argue for an index consciously designed for social security. I contend that this will become increasingly necessary if and as the CPI is changed in accordance with BC proposals.

When indexation of social security benefits was introduced, little thought was given to whether the CPI was appropriate for the purpose. The CPI is an all-purpose series, originally intended to give general statistical-historical information, not to govern settlements of public obligations. CPI-W, the index used for social security, seeks to track changes in the cost of the average market basket wage-earners buy. The other CPI, CPI-U, does the same thing for urban consumers. Neither is conceptually appropriate for indexing the benefits of the elderly.

The general assumption has been that it is close enough, and BC agrees: 'Some have suggested that different groups in the population are likely to have faster or slower growth in their cost of living than recorded by changes in the CPI. We find no compelling evidence of this to date. . . .' (p.72). After citing two studies in support of their complacency, the commission notes a piece of evidence to the contrary. This is BLS's experimental CPI-E, measuring costs of the average market basket bought by persons aged 62 and older. From December 1990 to December 1995 CPI-E rose 0.35 percentage points a year faster than CPI-W. The difference is mainly due to health care, which, with a larger weight in CPI-E, recorded faster price increases than other CPI components. BC conjectures that, as health care inflation subsides and its upward bias is corrected, CPI-E will converge to CPI-W. This remains to be seen, and in any event there is no guarantee that other deviations between elderly and population-wide CPI movements will not arise in future.

The misfit between the standard CPI and its task of indexing social security will actually be magnified by some of the reforms the Boskin Commission is proposing. Most of them are quite appropriate for a general-purpose index, but some are quite inappropriate for social security indexation. The principal problems arise in corrections to the increasing costs of medical care.

FROM CPI TO COST OF LIVING INDEX

To understand this paradox, it helps to begin with BC's pervasive complaint, that the present CPI is not 'a true cost of living index' (p.1). Ultimately, BC seeks to convert the CPI into a cost of living Index (COLI). Recommendation 1 (p.78) reads: 'The BLS should establish a cost of living index as its objective in measuring consumer prices. All our specific recommendations are aimed toward this goal.'

This complaint and this ambition permeate the report, from Executive Summary and Introduction to Recommendations and Conclusion. The CPI is simply 'pricing a fixed (but representative) market basket . . . over time' (p.i.), whereas 'The change in the cost of living between two periods, for example 1975 and 1995, tells us how much income people would have needed in 1975, given the prices of goods and services available in that year, to be at least as well off as they are in 1995' (p.1). Again, 'A cost of living index is a comparison of the minimum expenditure required to achieve the same level of well-being (also known as welfare, utility, standard of living) across two different sets of prices' (p.20). BC recommends two indexes, 'one which is published monthly on a timely basis and is designed to maintain the spirit of the cost of living', and one 'which is published and updated annually and revised historically' to introduce improvements in data and methods (pp.78–79). It is easy to imagine the second index as the vehicle for and rationale for judgmental corrections of the CPI in indexation, but BC does not suggest this.

Three phases in metamorphosis of CPI to COLI can be distinguished, though they blend into each other. The first is for BLS to do better its present task of measuring changes over time in the prices of representative market baskets bought in cash transactions. Reforms include changing statistical formulas to eliminate bias; allowing more promptly for consumer substitutions among commodities and outlets; improved sampling and more accurate data collection. These reforms are not controversial. BC estimates that they would cut 0.51 percentage points from present CPI inflation.

The second category involves more adequate treatment of changes in quality of existing products and of gains in well-being attributable to introduction of new products, all still within the domain of cash market transactions. Examining the CPI, commodity by commodity, BC find 0.60 percentage points of upward bias.

The third category recognizes the contributions of a host of non-market changes in the physical and social environment to consumers' utility, welfare, well-being, or quality of life, and thus their relevance to estimates of cost of living. These changes are like improvements in product quality and introductions of new products but are not directly traceable to specific market transactions. BC regard these changes as strongly positive on balance. They look forward to research that will eventually put dollar estimates even on diffuse and in-kind quality-of-life events. No such estimates are in their 1.1 total bias now. However, it seems likely that having the third category in reserve makes BC more willing to resolve upwards uncertainties in the other categories.

MEDICAL CARE IS THE MOST IMPORTANT PROBLEM

To return to the particular problems of indexing the elderly, most items in the 0.6 points of bias of the second type concern quality improvements and product innovations. Many of the examples may not be fully appreciated or exploited by older consumers, for example computers, internet, automobiles, cellular phones, fax, compact disks. But the most important problem is treatment of the quality of medical care.

Allowing for quality changes that arise either from modifications of existing products or from introduction of new products is the most difficult task facing makers of index numbers. It is particularly problematic in the realm of medical care. Certainly reductions in the inputs, chiefly of professionals and hospitals, required for a given procedure, should be reflected in the index, offsetting rises in the hourly costs of those inputs. By analogy, as new procedures replace old, it is natural to look for the economies in inputs required to achieve the same outcomes. But quite frequently the outcomes of new procedures were just not attainable before. The new product does better for the patient and costs more, but since the inferior old procedures are no longer available, the patient does not have the choice of pocketing in dollars any imputed value of the change, whether she or an insurer or Medicare is paying the bill. Very frequently the quality gain, of a single advance in medical technology or of the synergy of many advances, is to extend healthy life. The BC report argues that quality-of-life negatives (pollution, crime, suicide, divorce) are more than offset by identifiable though incompletely measured positives, 'but most importantly by the major increase in longevity, which perhaps swamps everything else' (p.77).

SHOULD LONGER LIFE MEAN LOWER PENSIONS?

This may well be true in reckoning the cost of living for younger people and for the nation as a whole. The extensions of life, indeed of healthy life, afforded by the miracles of modern medicine are remarkable gains in human welfare. But it does not make sense to diminish indexation of old people's pensions on this account, because these most significant advances in social well-being actually accentuate the risks the social security system is designed to insure. This paradox is good reason to accompany reform of the standard CPI with creation of another index tailored to indexation of pensions.

Our health care system is determined to give every patient the most up-to-date care, however expensive. The elderly consumer of medical services has no feasible way to diminish his or her consumption of the bulk of those services in order to obtain extra cash for consumption of non-medical goods and services. That may be a tradeoff the society as a whole can make, but it is not available to one individual alone. When she leaves the hospital after the operation that prolongs her life, the octogenarian still has to buy groceries.

Social security was originally conceived as social insurance, universal and compulsory. The risk insured is that of out-living one's financial resources, of not dying before the money runs out. The monthly checks are meant to avert that fate, providing not just minimal subsistence but reasonable replacement of pre-retirement wages. In the 1930s when social security was enacted, the risk of outliving one's resources was still fairly new. Workers who voluntarily or involuntarily retired usually became charges on their own children. Social security was both adapting to and creating new demographic and social realities.

In practice, social security's income replacement objective is implemented by computing the participant's average history of social security-taxable earnings scaled up by a national *wage* index to the year he or she is age 62. This average is converted into annuity entitlements by a formula that is progressive in the sense that it treats participants disproportionately more generously the lower their wage histories. These dollar amounts are in turn indexed by the CPI relative to its level in the year the participant was 62. Broadly speaking, then, the price indexation is intended to stabilize the consumption value of annual benefits, once the wage-replacement value of the benefits has been set at the same ratios as for previous cohorts (an average of about 37 per cent.)

SHOULD NON-MARKET FACTORS BE INCLUDED?

In general, I believe, it is not appropriate to try to adjust cash benefits for non-market additions to or subtractions from 'quality of life', whether from medical care in kind or from natural and social changes in environment. The Boskin Commission is over-ambitious for itself and BLS if it expects to estimate a 'cost of living' index that will keep utility or well-being constant. Better to concentrate, especially in constructing indexes with dollars-and-cents implications, on measuring as accurately as possible changes in the costs retired people face in buying the consumption goods and services they acquire in markets for cash. BLS already tries to allow for changes in quality of specific products or their replacements, and they can do better. But it would be arrogant for bureaucrats or commissions of wise men and women to judge by how much improvements in general conditions of life offset increases in recorded market prices.

Let us not forget that indexation need not, should not, bear the whole burden of keeping benefits in line with needs. Congress can change the basic amounts of the benefits, and has often done so. Until now Congress has chosen not to diminish cash social security benefits because of Medicare and the increased effectiveness of medical treatments. Congress can change that policy, but it should not rely on the pretense that there is objective technical justification for eroding old folks' pensions annually by precise amounts.

24. The political threat to Social Security*

President Clinton has asked for a national debate this year on the future of Social Security. If the debate would match the high quality of the papers that Aaron and Shoven prepared for this symposium, we could be hopeful about the policy outcome. Right now, however, the greatest threat to Social Security as we know it is the campaign for extreme privatization, allowing workers to invest their payroll taxes for themselves in IRAs. As critics of Old Age and Survivors' Insurance (OASI) incessantly point out, those IRAs would very likely earn much higher returns on retirement than OASI can promise. If current payroll taxpayers opt out, the OASI Trust Fund won't be able to pay benefits due participants now retired or soon to retire. Advocates of privatization who entice workers with promises of stock market rates of return are inviting them to break the intergenerational compact on which the system depends.

These critics of Social Security also propose to convert OASI in whole or in large part into a defined-contribution (DC) pension system (like TIAA-CREF, beloved of academics). Social Security is instead a defined-benefit (DB) scheme. More important, it is social insurance, insurance against the general human risk of economic adversity in old age and incapacity to earn a living by employment. Social insurance requires universal participation, in which the premiums of the fortunate pay the claims of the unfortunate. This is the rationale for compulsory participation. Indeed, once society has recognized responsibility for aged citizens in distress, government has the right and duty to make sure that everyone who might benefit from this recognition makes provision against the contingency.

The advocates of extreme privatization and of full conversion to DC pensions would enable the more affluent to withdraw from Social Security as social insurance. An insurance system cannot survive the adverse selection of risks if the safest risks are allowed to opt out. The present DB system provides for progressivity in conversion of career payroll contributions into monthly pensions. These are entirely appropriate in social

* This chapter first appeared in H.J. Aaron and J.B. Shoven (eds), *Should the United States Privatize Social Security?*, MIT Press, 1999, pp.146–53.

insurance, but would be difficult or impossible in a DC system.
(Progressivity by federal subsidies augmenting each year missing or low
payroll contributions are advocated in the DC plan of Kotlikoff and Sachs,
but seem impractical.)

Demagogic and ideological delusions also threaten to wreck Medicare,
which also depends on 'community rating', in this case payment of insurance premiums by the healthy and affluent to pay the claims of the sick
and poor.

THE RATE OF RETURN MUST BE RAISED

The young and affluent may be attracted to secession from social insurance
because they misunderstand it. But it is understandable that they are dismayed by the rates of return their payroll taxes are likely to earn. Many cyn-
ically say that Social Security will not be there for them. OASI is largely a
pay-as-you-go system, which in its pure form yields a rate of return in
retirees' benefits over their earlier contributions just equal to the growth
rate of the system's revenues, employment times real wages. The slowdowns
beginning in the 1970s in both productivity growth and labor force growth
presage puny rates of return to future retirees. In contrast, the elderly of the
1990s have benefited from high rates of growth of labor force and real
wages and the expansion of the coverage of the system, now virtually complete.

As Aaron's paper shows, OASI can likely be saved in the sense of bridg-
ing the currently estimated gap, about 20 per cent, between the present
values of future revenues and future benefits. That can be done by a number
of sensible and reasonable modifications of benefits while essentially pre-
serving the present structure for most participants, for whom the replacement ratio of benefits to wages would stay about the same. Consequently,
the absolute real value of baby boomers' Social Security pensions would be
considerably higher than those of their parents. Nevertheless, the fact
remains that on average the replacement ratio and the rate of return will be
significantly lower in the future, especially for the young participants most
vulnerable to the siren songs of the 'reformers'.

RAISING TRUST FUND RESERVES AND
DIVERSIFYING ASSETS

Misgivings about the low rate of return on contributions is also the motive
for proposals to invest at least some of these contributions in assets with a

higher rate of return than government bonds, mainly common stocks. I don't recall any reform platform, DB or DC, that does not include this plank. Aaron is counting on diversifying the trust fund into stock market securities to fill 35 to 45 per cent of the gap. He would bring common stocks up to 40 per cent of reserves by 2015. The question is how big the reserves will be then and subsequently.

After all, rates of return on Trust Fund assets matter only to the extent that the Trust Fund has net assets. In a pure pay-as-you-go system that balance is negligible, and the return is just the growth rate of the system. Thanks to the 1983 Greenspan–O'Neill–Reagan reforms, so scathingly condemned by Shoven, we now have a nonnegligible and growing Trust Fund. In 1997, its assets were 165 per cent of outlays; they will rise to 350 per cent by 2010. But reserves will stop growing about 2013 and will be exhausted in 2032. If reform now would keep the inflow at a significant ratio to total annual benefit payments, improvements in Trust Fund earnings would make a big difference. This is a good reason for putting into effect as promptly as possible, long before they are urgently needed, many modifications of benefits and other reforms listed by Aaron and Shoven.

President Clinton's proposal, in the context of the politics of disposition of prospective budget surpluses, to 'save Social Security first' should be taken seriously. I take a meaningful interpretation to be that, in addition to the Trust Fund's own surplus, any surplus in the unified budget would be appropriated to the credit of the OASDI Trust Funds, that is, become a debt of the Treasury to the Trust Funds. (I realize that this means that part or all of the Trust Funds' own surplus might thus be counted twice. This is, like much other budget accounting, a political gimmick, for a better cause than most such gimmicks. Less generous to Social Security would be to credit any on-budget surplus to the Trust Funds.) The Trust Funds would invest these amounts in private stock and bond funds, owned and managed by the Trust Funds, not by individuals.

The larger the multiple of their liabilities the balances in the Trust Funds are, the greater the degree to which the pensions will reflect the Trust Funds' earnings, relative to the minimal pure pay-as-you-go payoff. In the extreme, fully funded case, participants would earn the rate of return to the Trust Funds portfolios less minimal administrative costs.

FUNDING? A SECOND TIER?

The vulnerability of the pay-as-you-go system to adverse demographic and economic shocks brought the problems of Social Security with which we are now struggling. OASI had developed into a DB pension plan and it became difficult and painful to find revenues to assure payments of the benefits defined. This was one reason for the growing popularity of DC plans, yielding whatever benefits could be paid from the accumulation of contributions.

Funding and DC, however, are not the same thing. The system could be funded in aggregate and distribute as retirement benefits only the income on the aggregate fund built up from its contributions. In this way, progressivity in the formula connecting contributions to benefits, as exists now, could be continued. For the participants, it would be a DB system, but periodic revision of benefits would be taken as normal rather than as a sign of crisis.

Likewise, the buildup of reserves, discussed above, would result in a partially funded, partially pay-as-you-go DB system.

An advantage of individualized DC accounts is to tie contributions and future retirement benefits tightly together in the participant's consciousness. Too often today workers regard Social Security contributions as burdensome taxes and don't connect them with the benefits they will eventually receive. Shoven points out that looseness in this identification makes payroll taxes bigger disincentives to work. (On the other hand, participants' skepticism that Social Security will 'be there for me' might encourage private and national saving.)

Shoven rightly criticizes the annual financial accounts the Social Security Administration (SSA) now reports to its clients. Their flaws could be substantially remedied without moving to DC.

It would take a half-century to install a fully funded system, individualized or aggregate. During the transition the working generations would have to support the elderly Social Security beneficiaries of the present pay-as-you-go system while also building up in advance the funds that would generate their own pensions. The extra national saving in this process would in principle supply additional national real capital, partially replacing the workers lost in the demographic slowdown. Kotlikoff and Sachs propose to accomplish this transition by a general federal sales tax.

Attention of more practical reformers has focused on what Shoven calls two-tier systems, with universal DC schemes supplementing but not replacing, at least not wholly replacing, the present DB OASI system. I am sympathetic to a second tier and I do not think the more modest of these proposals are so distant from Aaron's reformed one-tier DB system with augmented reserves invested in diversified portfolios.

As Aaron reminds us, there is no obvious differential advantage in economy-wide saving and investment in one or another of three possibilities: (1) individuals are refunded taxes and buy private securities, (2) the SSA buys private securities for each individual's account with his or her taxes, (3) the SSA buys private securities for its aggregate Trust Fund reserves. In all cases, the rest of the economy sells those securities and buys in their place the government bonds the Trust Fund would otherwise have held. The swap might be welfare-improving, however, if the OASI beneficiaries end up with higher yielding assets. Even though these are also riskier, they diversify the portfolios of less affluent workers and retirees in a desirable direction.

FOR GRAMLICH'S INDIVIDUAL ACCOUNTS PLAN

Among the plans reviewed by Shoven, my vote goes to the Individual Account (IA) proposal of another of my students, Ned Gramlich. I would gradually move the required percentage of covered earnings up from his 1.6 per cent to the Committee for Economic Development's 4.0. Also, I would welcome voluntary additional subscriptions, by workers or by employers, on their behalf. The IA and CED plans are really second tiers. The forced saving levies that finance them are additional to present payroll taxes; the plans are not substitutes for current OASI. They really can contribute to a net increase in national saving, unlike proposals to carve DC accounts out of traditional Social Security.

It is essential, in my opinion, that these new DC individual accounts be held and managed by the SSA, or by the new independent board Aaron proposes, that choices be confined to a few index funds, and that accounts be annuitized on retirement. I believe that fully privatized compulsory DC plans, with individuals investing for themselves hounded by mutual fund salespeople, would be a disastrous and expensive mess. I would reject any plan that one way or another, on whatever terms, makes payroll taxes cashable, or offers income tax credits, or creates IRAs, or goes into debt for most of a century. Besides their many other questionable features, Moynihan, Feldstein and the two personal security account plans strike me as what the English call 'too clever by half'.

I was relieved that in the end Shoven ranked CED first, ahead of his own variant of the personal security accounts proposal, though I prefer his rank number 5, Gramlich's individual accounts plan, to CED's proposal.

25. Fisher's introductory text*

Irving Fisher was a dedicated teacher – in classrooms, in books, and in the personal contacts by which he sought to educate presidents of the United States and influential business and government leaders throughout the world.

At Yale, Fisher liked to prepare for his students his own written expositions. He even wrote a calculus text for fellow students he was tutoring. Not surprisingly, when he assumed responsibility for the economics introductory course in 1910 he was dissatisfied with existing texts and wrote his own. He and a half-dozen other instructors taught from experimental editions for two years before he settled on the published version of *Elementary Principles of Economics* (1912). It was reprinted 10 times, the last in 1932, but never substantively revised.

Elementary Principles was not very popular outside Yale. However, much of the material survived, incorporated in the more conventional textbook published first in 1926 and in its fifth and final version in 1948, by Fisher's Yale students and colleagues F.R. Fairchild, E.S. Furniss and N.S. Buck. Their *Elementary Economics* was the market leader between the world wars.

Maybe Fisher's text was too good for the market. Anyway it is very different from other texts of his day and of ours. Fisher does not try to capture students' attention by covering contemporary events, controversies, and policies. He includes few statistics, none that have to be up-to-date to be useful. He does not tailor his expositions and illustrations too closely to the experiences and institutions of one country. He does not try to cover the entire domain of economics with its many applied fields; he urges students to take applied courses or explore those fields on their own.

Fisher tries to equip readers to think like economists. He stresses the basic concepts, not algebraic models and formulas. He does not train students to do synthetic numerical problems.

Why should a Principles text have to be revised every three or five years? Presumably the basic concepts and methods of the discipline are more durable than that. Rather it is the economic journalism which most textbooks combine with theory that compels frequent revision – perhaps to the

---

*   This chapter first appeared as 'Fisher's Introductory Text', in *AER Proceedings*, May 1997, 430–32.

profit of authors and publishers. A book like Fisher's does not build in obsolescence and does not need revision until the profession rethinks principles.

Are there any modern elementary texts in the same spirit? I am aware of two, Donald Nichols and Clark Reynolds (1971) and Edmund S. Phelps (1985). I am afraid their market success was similar to Fisher's.

Fisher suspects that his student readers are unconsciously confused about simple basic concepts. He would set them straight about the differences and connections between stocks and flows; capital and income; insolvency and illiquidity; wealth and saving; deficits and debts; price level and relative prices. He wants them to distinguish 'money' as used colloquially to refer to wealth or income from money as an asset with the definite properties of currency. He reminds them that bygones are bygones.

The book is unorthodox in its selection of topics and in their order and weight. He starts with 143 pages on capital and income accounting, individual and social. Then come 114 pages of his monetary theory. Only after half the book does he get to standard micro, supply and demand (which he deprecates [Fisher, 1912, p.145] as an overused 'glib' phrase that substitutes for 'real analyses'), and relative prices. After 96 pages he returns to economy-wide concerns, the theory of interest, and the distribution of income and wealth.

Fisher's textbook implements his conviction that he can make even his most esoteric results understandable to nonprofessional readers. The accounting chapters carry the message of *The Nature of Capital and Income* (1906); the monetary chapters expound the gist of *The Purchasing Power of Money* (1911); and the theories of interest and of distribution are based on *The Rate of Interest* (1907). Fisher's first great work, *Mathematical Investigations in the Theory of Value and Prices* (1892) is not represented in the textbook. This is surprising; one would expect Fisher to enjoy explaining to students how the economy can be regarded as a system of simultaneous equations; he had, after all, built an instructive mechanical–hydraulic model to depict general equilibrium.

As would be expected, this book is particularly strong in treatment of intertemporal choices and markets. According to Fisher, interest is 'by far the most important sort of price with which economics has to deal' (Fisher, 1912, p.354). But these chapters would have been better if written after Fisher's second book on interest theory, *The Theory of Interest* (1930). In the textbook, Fisher appears to subscribe to 'impatience' as the sole determinant of the rate of interest, neglecting the other blade of the scissors, opportunities, clearly awarded a parallel role in the later book. Here he scornfully dismisses as vulgar fallacies the concepts of productivity as a source of interest and the idea that the rate of return on capital could be a determinant of the interest rate. Like Joan Robinson later, he objects that the latter argument is circular, because the value of capital is itself determined by the rate of interest used to capitalize future earnings on capital goods. He ignores the fact that from the earnings or rents on reproducible capital can be determined a 'rate of return over cost' – Fisher's own term subsequently – independent of the interest rate.

In contrast to his rival John Bates Clark, Fisher does not regard interest as a return to a factor-of-production 'capital' comparable to labor and land. Interest is an allowance for time delays between inputs of labor and land and their outputs. Capital goods are essentially like other intermediate goods, part of the time-consuming nexus of ultimate inputs and final outputs of consumer goods. Sometimes, indeed, he seems to be expounding a labor theory of value (for example, Fisher, 1912, pp.77, 306), but all he means is that the utilities (he calls them 'desirabilities' for some reason) of consumption have to compensate for the disutilities of work. Only human beings, not machines and acres of land, have utilities and disutilities. (Fisher does play with the idea of human capital [p.139], but he sees the prohibition of slavery as a drawback to the concept.)

The main messages to freshmen are those of classical economics, with exceptions. Money is neutral – except during monetary transitions, where interest rates lag price changes (pp.359–62). This is the only mention of business cycles in the book. Markets generally work for the best – except that scale economies lead to cutthroat competition or collusion or monopoly and price discrimination. 'Make work' is a fallacy. Free trade and labor-saving progress benefit society, but they do hurt some workers in the short run. Inequality of wealth is mainly due to differences in thriftiness, thus differential impatience (Fisher allows himself thus to explain the prosperity of Holland, Scotland, England and France in contrast to the poverty of Ireland, China, India and Java, and of Negroes, peasants and American Indians everywhere.)

Nevertheless, there are some Fisherian heresies. What he calls 'unequal foresight' (p.362), anticipating asymmetrical information, can distort market interest rates. The efficiency of asset markets is impaired by those who would now be called 'noise traders'. Government regulation is essential to handle problems commodity markets do not solve: eugenics, alcoholism, unhealthful and unsafe hours and conditions of employment, and pollution, all subjects of Fisher crusades. Despite his theory of inequality, above, he sees a case for inheritance taxation and despises the very rich, whose irrational acquisitiveness he attributes to competitive spirals of 'vanity'.

Fisher is an ingenious architect of tables, balance sheets, diagrams and figures. They all assist his verbal arguments, though some require considerable intellectual effort. In the textbook he is especially fond of pictures of reservoirs connected by flows that equalize their levels, or sometimes do not, and of scales balanced by weights representing, for example, supplies and demands. But there is less curve-shifting than in a typical modern textbook.

Matrix tables for flows of funds and asset stocks (columns for sectors and rows for asset groups) would greatly improve Fisher's accounting chapters. Likewise Leontief input–output matrices would clarify his discussion of intermediate durable and nondurable goods.

The textbook appears in Volume 5 of the forthcoming collection of Fisher's works, where the editor, William Barber, reviews comments on the book from prepublication readers (especially Edwin Kemmerer) and postpublication reviewers. These were quite negative: the book is too difficult for beginners, and too eccentric. Its coverage is incomplete. Fisher was not impressed.

REFERENCES

Fairchild, F.R., F.S. Furniss and N.S. Buck (1948), *Elementary economics*, 5th edn (2 Vols), New York: Macmillan.

Fisher, Irving (1892), *Mathematical investigations in the theory of value and prices*, Transactions of the Connecticut Academy of Arts and Sciences no. 9, New Haven, CT: Connecticut Academy of Arts and Sciences; reprinted New York: Augustus M. Kelley, 1961.

— (1906), *The nature of capital and income*, New York: Macmillan.

— (1907), *The rate of interest*, New York: Macmillan.

— (1911), *The purchasing power of money*, New York: Macmillan.

— (1912), *Elementary principles of economics*, New York: Macmillan.

— (1930), *The theory of interest*, New York: Macmillan.

Nichols, Donald A. and Clark W. Reynolds (1971), *Principles of economics*, New York: Holt, Rinehart and Winston.

Phelps, Edmund S. (1985), *Political economy: An introductory text*, New York: Norton.

26. Review of *The Commanding Heights*

Yergin, the principal author judging from print size, attended Yale College and graduated in 1968 from Cambridge, where he also got an economics PhD in 1974. He got Pulitzer Prize for his 1990 book *The Prize: The Epic Quest for Oil, Money, and Power*, which by coincidence I reviewed here in my only other Sandwiching In. It is an excellent and fascinating book, I enjoyed reading and reviewing it.

This book lacks the natural coherence of *The Prize*. It is very ambitious, a history of political economy and economic policy for the second half of the 20th century for the whole world. It is both a narrative of actual events, country by country, and an account of the interrelated intellectual history, the revolution in economics, which in Yergin's view was decisive in bringing about an immense beneficent worldwide political and policy revolution. Perhaps one should say 'counterrevolution'.

Mainly this book is a panegyric for the 'free market' as opposed to government, not just to communism or even socialism but to what is described as the inordinate role of the state in capitalist countries, including democracies. Indeed, the great crusade since the 1970s, as the authors describe it, was aimed at 'mixed economies'. The 'Commanding Heights' of the title are the key, strategic parts of an economy, whose control gives government or market as the case may be control of the country's economic destiny. The authors attribute the phrase to Lenin, who excused his retreat in the early 1920s to the New Economic Policy, with many sectors still in private ownership and control, by alleging that the Bolshevik state retained the economic institutions that really mattered.

This does not seem to me a happy theme for a book that mostly concerns liberals v. conservatives in the USA, Labour v. Tories in the UK, Monetarists v. Keynesians everywhere, transitions out of communism, emerging economies, debt crises in Latin America, and so on.

There are many fascinating stories here, journalistically and entertainingly told. They cover episodes in the USA, the UK, France, Germany, the European Union, Japan, China, India, East Asia, Russia, Poland, the Czech Republic, Latin America, South Africa, even New Zealand. Leading personalities are emphasized, their lives, ideas and historical roles – intellectuals, politicians, entrepreneurs. Margaret Thatcher is the heroine. Jean Monnet, Milton Friedman, Friedrich Hayek, Keith Joseph, Jeffrey Sachs,

Yegor Gaidar, Leszek Balcerowicz and Tony Blair are principal heroes –
there are many others. The goats, the apologists for socialism and government, the targets of market reform, are interestingly and charitably
described – except for John Maynard Keynes, who becomes, almost against
the authors' will, the enemy incarnate, quite unjustifiably, I think.

As the authors tell it, the victory of market over government occurs
throughout the world, in several different ways. In the major industrial
democracies of Europe and North America, the 1970s were the crucial
decade. Keynesian economic policies, which looked good for the first
quarter-century after World War II, led to disaster and disrepute. They
were very inflationary, and at the same time unemployment rose, falsifying
the Keynesian theory that lower unemployment could be bought by accepting higher inflation. Friedman's monetarism and Reagan's supply side came
into their own. The public tired of 'tax and spend' and of 'regulate' too.
They recognized government as too big and too obtrusive, a burden rather
than a help, the problem not the solution. Thatcher and Reagan were victorious. The 1980s were the decade of market reform.

In the same spirit, Latin America learned from its debt crisis to stress
exports, accepted at last the discipline of international trade and finance,
and put its fiscal and monetary houses in order. Similar outward-oriented
policies unleashed the Asian tigers, imitating the miraculous model of
Japanese growth. Even African economies seemed to start growing, with
the help of market incentives.

In 1989, the Berlin Wall toppled and with it fell the most extreme enemy
of market capitalism, the ultimate victory for the revolution. After all, a
century and a half of history had been dominated by intellectual, ideological, political and military struggle between Marxism and capitalism. To
some historians, 1989 was the end of history. Would free market economies
now rise spontaneously from the ashes? The book celebrates the heroes of
a revolution that so far has had mixed results. The book begins with a triumphant metaphor, a big international outdoor market near Moscow. That
does not look like a happy choice today.

The end of the Cold War left the defeated economies in somewhat similar
circumstances to those of the devastated countries of Europe after World
War II. In those days no one had the romantic illusion that their economies
would rise from the ashes without planning, government and central coordination. Jean Monnet had spent the war planning for the day, and he was
ready to use the Marshall Plan when it was offered. His 'indicative planning', for France and neighbors in the coal and steel industries, casually dis-
missed as statist by the authors, got Europe on its feet again. Europe did
not try to establish the facades of capitalism – stock markets, convertible
currencies and so on – until the prerequisites of private property, laws of

contracts, accounting, bankruptcy law and transparency were re-established. The 1989 idea that, because the communist state was evil, ex-communist countries did not need governments, was a costly fallacy.

It was bad luck for the authors that the book went to press just when the East Asian currency crises were beginning. With the whole world economy infected, the market revolution seems less triumphant than they advertised. Japan and the Asian tigers are in deep and lengthy recessions or depressions. Brazil and other Latin American economies are precarious. Russia is a catastrophe. Western Europe is locked into double-digit unemployment. The USA and the UK look vulnerable. Right now the globalized financial free market seems to transmit instability and crisis, not prosperity and growth.

I take issue with the authors' account of the downfall of the 'mixed economy' in the 1970s. Clear thinking requires distinction between macro-economic policies and micro policies. By 'macro' I mean monetary policies of the Federal Reserve and other central banks, and overall fiscal policies – budget deficits, volumes of expenditure and taxes. These are Keynesian issues and policies, affecting economy-wide variables, interest rates, exchange rates, GDP, CPI, trade deficits or surpluses. By 'micro' policies I refer to details of regulations, taxes, government activities and expenditures, as they affect businesses, workers, collective bargaining, efficiency and productivity. The authors blur the distinctions. They assume that a Keynesian in macro policy would necessarily be a 'liberal' proponent of all kinds of micro interventions, from high taxes to rent controls, to trade union power, to farm subsidies, to nationalized electric utilities. And vice versa.

Did the 1970s prove that loose Keynesian macro policies had perverse results, causing both inflation and unemployment? Did they in consequence make the case for Friedman and monetarism. (Friedman is also a free-market apostle, but the two roles, macro (monetarism) and micro (free-market) are logically separable.) This misunderstanding is, alas, standard history, as in the book, but I think it is wrong. What did happen? The two oil shocks (see Yergin's *The Prize*) of 1973–4 and 1979–80 delivered mammoth upward price boosts. As they spread through the economy, the Federal Reserve drastically tightened monetary policy to fight inflation – a standard Keynesian policy that inevitably increased unemployment, to new post-World War II records. Keynesian policies did not cause the unprecedented supply-shock inflation. After Paul Volcker, Greenspan's predecessor as Fed Chairman, got inflation back down below 5 per cent, he abandoned any pretext of monetarism and geared his interest rate policies to noninflationary recovery from the 10 per cent unemployment of 1982 to the 5–6 per cent range at the end of the decade. The supply-side revolution had nothing to do with that recovery, and in every respect those tax cuts were an expensive failure, saddling the USA for 12 years with stubborn crippling budget deficits.

Yergin and Stanislaw are vague regarding the functions government needs to perform if a market system is to be successful. Often they seem to be indiscriminately favorable to eliminating government functions. There are important problems markets cannot solve on their own. Education? Environment? Third-party spillovers, what economists call externalities, seem to be more prevalent and formidable than ever, just when government or international efforts to cope with them are ideologically unpopular. Inequality and poverty? If we cannot modify the extremes of fortune generated by the market and perpetuated by inheritance, the consensual basis of the market economy may not survive.

Transparency? A big word in finance, also applicable to everyday life – not just the SEC (Securities and Exchange Commission) but also the Federal Trade Commission and the Food and Drug Administration and Health Maintenance Organizations.

In western Europe, governments and central banks deny that their chronically high unemployment rates are Keynesian problems, ameliorable by monetary stimulus to demand. They say the problem is structural, caused by trade unions and the welfare state. Yet they do not reform these institutions either. Mrs Thatcher was more courageous and ambitious. Her showdowns on these issues, especially her victory in the miners' strike, may indeed have contributed to better economic performance, which better monetary and exchange rate policy has been able to exploit. For the same reason, Ronald Reagan's tough stand against the striking air controllers in 1982 may have improved US performance.

Privatization has been a big part of the market revolution in countries other than the USA. We had few nationalized industries to begin with, but we have semi-privatized the post office. In other countries, denationalization has often been successful, creating efficiency and ending unjustified subsidies. However, over-hasty privatization in ex-communist economies has sometimes been hasty and corrupt, with major assets of public wealth transferred at bargain prices to insiders.

The Cold War was won by mixed economies, not mixed in Yergin's sense but in the functions of government and business in advanced democratic capitalist countries, where private enterprises predominate subject to government regulations and supported and modified by complementary public sector activities. The governments of capitalist democracies have been more than 'night watchmen'. They have guarded the interests of third parties to economic transactions, including the interests of future citizens. They have promoted education and research and basic science. They have guarded the public health. They have provided roads and parks and sewers and schools. They have prevented divisive extremes of wealth and income. They have preserved economic stability in volatile times. They have helped citizens endangered by natural disasters. They have made mistakes, but it is still true that the Cold War was not won by countries run for five decades on Friedman–Thatcher–Reagan principles. It was FDR and his activist tribe who saved us from economic and political disasters in 1932–3. It was a bunch of planners – Truman, Churchill, Keynes, Marshall, Acheson, Monnet, Shuman, MacArthur in Japan – whose vision made possible the prosperous postwar world and eventually won the Cold War. Yergin and Stanislaw need a bit more perspective.

27. On Minsky's agenda for reform

In economics, theory and policy are intimately related. Policy recommendations are derived from theory, and in turn theory is revealed by dicta regarding policy. Chapter 13 of Minsky's *Stabilizing an Unstable Economy* is an unusually complete design. Here is Hy Minsky's conception of a stable, prosperous, efficient, equitable capitalist system. It is the final chapter of his 1986 book, and I found it the most revealing exposition of Minsky's theory and his differences from other versions of Keynesian economics. It is an ambitious and comprehensive manifesto.

Minsky's objective is no less than to design a self-regulated system, one that does not depend on frequent discretionary policy moves, whether by central banks, finance ministries, regulators or legislatures. It is not that Minsky is fashionably advocating rules for policy makers rather than discretion. It is not that he is trusting an Adam Smith–Gerard Debreu Invisible Hand, although he does see an indispensable role for market competition and proposes a number of institutions to protect and promote it. It is not that he derogates the roles of government, either micro or macro. To the contrary, his self-regulating capitalist economy depends for its stability on Big Government, the source of macroeconomic built-in countercyclical variations of aggregate demand and thus of profits.

The federal government, according to Minsky, should account for about 20 per cent of full-employment GDP. Full employment he identifies with 6 per cent unemployment, although he surely and gladly would now revise that downward in the light of recent experience. Anyway, he rejects the current practice of monetary policy, guessing at the 'NAIRU' and trying to get there and stay there by variation of money-market interest rates. Instead, he wants the government to be the employer of last resort at a fixed minimal money wage rate, via a combination of New Deal-type measures, Works Progress Administration (WPA), Civilian Conservation Corps (CCC) and National Youth Administration (NYA). By this device, the built-in stability effects of fiscal policy are enhanced by the variations of applicants for the guaranteed jobs, and the nominal wage and price levels are stabilized. There are a good many practical difficulties in this proposal, but they are probably surmountable. Research on the idea continues right here at the Levy Institute of Bard College. Whether, as

Minsky hoped, this self-regulating mechanism dispenses with the need for monetary and fiscal responses to macroeconomic events is, I think, still uncertain.

Minsky thought that Big Government stabilizes because it is comparable in size to profits, the macro dynamo of capitalism. A more traditional Keynesian would explain built-in stabilizers by aggregate demand multipliers and the investment/saving nexus, but of course profits and aggregate demand move together, and so do saving and investment. So this may be distinction without difference.

Minsky expected and favored balancing the budget when the economy is operating at full employment, with deficits and surpluses reflecting only cyclical aberrations. Relying on his automatic government employment mechanism to stabilize nominal wage and prices – levels, not rates of inflation – Minsky opposed indexation of any government (or private) monetary transactions.

As we know, Minsky regarded capitalist financial markets and institutions as the principal agents of instability, and much of his new architecture is financial reform. Taking the Federal Reserve, or any other central bank, out of the business of macroeconomic stabilization, in accordance with the proposals just discussed, is one step. In Minsky's view, it is a dangerous mistake to try to stabilize the economy by affecting interest rates and asset prices; that itself feeds speculation. Minsky would have the Fed vary nominal interest rates much less, and for less macroeconomic purposes. Furthermore, his prescription of budget balance across business cycles would tend to hold federal debt constant relative to GDP and stabilize the interest rate term structure.

Yet Minsky foresees important roles for the central bank, some revived from earlier practice, some new. Minsky wants to revive the discount window as the major source of bank reserves, downgrading open market operations in federal debt instruments. (If current predictions of federal surpluses are correct, this may happen anyway in the next 15 to 20 years.) Minsky likes real bills, specific to-the-asset lending, and he thinks it would be healthy for the Fed and the commercial banks to join in this type of finance. It would be a good role for small banks and maybe even for regional Federal Reserve Banks (otherwise redundant).

Minsky would make the Federal Reserve responsible for the entire financial system, not just money markets and depository institutions. The Fed would supplant other state and federal regulatory authorities. All financial enterprises, not just banks, would have access to Federal Reserve loans and advances. Glass–Steagall and other arbitrary divisions of financial turf, most dating from early New Deal laws, would be erased. Tax laws and other regulations would preserve financial firms varying in size, purpose and location.

In Minsky's view, the corporation has been the source of most of the perils of instability in modern capitalism. The basic reason is the inherent riskiness of long-lasting special purpose physical capital assets. In comparison, wealth-owners want earlier liquidation. Equity markets appear to reconcile these differences, but only by inviting great waves of speculation. Minksy wants to remove the tax incentives for leveraging equity or long-term bond positions – deductibility of corporate interest. Indeed, he wants to abolish corporate income taxation and impute undistributed profits to individual share-owners as taxable by personal income tax. He decries any 'too big to fail' safety nets, easing the pain by simplifying bankruptcy proceedings. The speculative and Ponzi finance involved in so-called 'hedge funds' (not to be confused with Minsky's approved hedge finance) would doubtless persuade Minsky to advocate stronger measures. He would not shrink from having the Fed regulate adventurous financial enterprises. Recent events, like the débâcle of Long-term Capital Management (LTCM) show how rampant leverage can make it possible for firms of modest net worth to influence asset prices by their own transactions – they are not price takers when they have to unwind outrageous leverage.

Minsky advocated programs to diminish the inequalities of market outcomes among individuals. He greatly preferred programs with good incentive effects, like the employment supports mentioned above. For the same reasons, and others, he disliked means-tested transfers and recommended universal children's allowances, to be included in taxable incomes.

Economists and economic historians will for a long time debate the interpretation of the contrast between the high first 25 postwar years of growth and high employment, and the succeeding and disappointing quarter century that followed. Which was normal? Which was abnormal? The anti-Keynesian monetarist new classical view is that the policy errors of the first period led to the disasters of the second. The Keynesian view is that the theories and policies of the first postwar period were sound, that policy errors were made in the Vietnam war period and their consequences were compounded by incredibly adverse exogenous supply shocks in the 1970s, mainly the two big OPEC oil price increases. In this view, in normal circumstances something like the prosperity of 1945–69 could be obtained, though quantitatively less impressive, without drastic changes of policy. Minksy's viewpoint is different from both of these interpretations. He attributes the reversals of the early postwar prosperity to the inevitable evolution of capitalism, particularly capitalist finance. His Chapter 13 is designed to mitigate the vulnerabilities that produced these reversals. What would he think of the successes in the 1990s of mainstream Keynesian policies in the hands of Greenspan, without the help of much in the way of Minsky reforms? He would not care to extrapolate. He ends his book predicting that capitalists' destructive financial innovations could spoil even a Minsky-designed capitalist system.

28.   False expectations*

Celebrating the collapse of communism – its economic statism, its political despotism and its military threat – the West hailed the fall of the Soviet Union as a historic victory for free-market capitalism. The 150-year clash of ideologies symbolized by the names Adam Smith and Karl Marx was at long last over. Adam Smith had won.

In the euphoria felt as the Cold War was ending, the West expected the ex-communist countries to prosper under free-market capitalism. After all, it could only be their disastrous economic system that kept living standards of Soviet citizens so far below those of their Western neighbors. In Western countries themselves, right-wing antigovernment politics had gained in strength even before the end of the Cold War. Thatcherism and Reaganomics stand out. The collapse of communism increased the confidence and conservatism of these movements, and they cited the failures of extreme dirigiste regimes behind the Iron Curtain to promote their political agenda.

THE INVISIBLE HAND

Adam Smith's most famous passage is this: 'As every individual . . . endeavors . . . to employ his capital in the support of domestic industry, and so to direct that industry that its produce may be of the greatest value . . . [he] necessarily labors to render the annual revenue of the society as areas as he can. He . . . neither intends to promote the public interest, nor knows by how much he is promoting it. . . . [He] is in this, as in many other cases, led by an invisible hand to promote an end which was no part of his intention.' The Invisible Hand is certainly one of history's Great Ideas. Competitive markets in which prices, rather than queuing or rationing, equate demand to supply are marvellous mechanisms of social coordination. Like the wheel, the market is a widespread ancient human invention.

It is easy to see the powerful energy of self-interest working for the best when Henry Ford mass-produces cars, Edison lights the world, and Bill

*   This chapter first appeared as 'False Expectations' in L.R. Klein and M. Pomer (eds), *The New Russia: Transition Gone Awry*, Stanford University Press, 2001, pp.65–72.

Gates designs computer operating systems. The social benefits are well worth the fortunes these inventor-entrepreneurs garnered along the way. But as Adam Smith, a moral philosopher first and a political economist second, was well aware, there are perils to counting too heavily on the beneficent results of unmitigated self-interest. The Invisible Hand theorem has to be modified; governments in capitalist societies play essential roles in economic life. The market system works within social institutions that channel and guide self-interested energies into constructive activities. Without those institutions – which can never be perfect and may be weakened and perverted by crime and corruption – we are stuck with Hobbes's war of every man against every other, with outcomes quite different from the Invisible Hand theorem.

Laws and police are part of the answer, but a civilized society cannot survive if obedience to laws and other social norms becomes solely a matter of self-interest. It cannot survive, for example, if people pay taxes only if hedonistic calculus reveals that the probability-discounted penalty of being caught exceeds the probability-discounted gain from the violation. The glorification of self-interested behavior and the denigration of government in recent years bear some responsibility for recent trends. The anything-goes-if-you-can-get-away-with-it mentality is a recipe for anarchy. Enterprise can take the form of extortion by threat of violence. Alas, this kind of capitalism appears to be flourishing in Russia.

The Invisible Hand depends not only on preventing criminal activity but also on competition to convert self-interest into socially optimal outcomes. Undisciplined self-interest impels individuals and businesses to seek and protect monopolistic positions. Who would not like to control a toll booth through which economic traffic has no choice but to go? Maintenance of competition requires external vigilance in enforcing 'anti-trust' laws.

Governments often do economic harm by misguided interference with markets for the protection of particular interests and for the benefit of politicians and bureaucrats themselves. But blind campaigns for retrenchment of government expenditures and taxes are also very damaging. Wholesale destruction of the public sector in Russia, however understandable as a reaction to communism and its privileged bureaucracy, has been catastrophic.

Modern technologies are making constructive public sector activities more essential than ever. Public education must train workers in the skills needed in high-tech industries. Government coordination is required to create modern national and international systems of transportation and communication.

Individual and societal interests diverge in the case of 'externalities'. These are costs or benefits of an economic transaction that fall on neither buyer nor seller, but on persons not involved in the transaction. Businesses and individuals do not consider those spinoffs in deciding what and how much to produce and consume. Environmental damages resulting from production processes or from the use and disposal of products are well-known examples. Often these consequences cross national borders. On the other hand, businesses that train workers or invent new techniques or products may spin off to others valuable by-products for which they cannot enforce payment. It is an important function of governments to manage, when feasible and appropriate, these external costs and benefits.

REALLOCATION OF RESOURCES

In Russia, workers and other productive inputs must be substantially reallocated – shifted from activities where they are no longer needed to activities of social value. Immense reallocations are both today's necessities and tomorrow's hopes. Resources released from obsolete activities must be redeployed into new industries, new technologies, new products. Swords must be beat into plowshares, guns must be supplanted by butter. The winding down of military production is not the only reallocation required. As the civilian sector grows, its composition will be quite different. The goods and services freely chosen by consumers will diverge radically from the menu offered by Soviet planners.

It is a fallacy to expect this reallocation to occur on its own, much less quickly enough to satisfy the aspirations of an impatient public. That does not happen even in Western countries, with well-established capitalist and democratic institutions. Redeployment may be of immense social value eventually, but its initial impact is devastating to the many people who depend on the old activities for their livelihoods.

The United States also faces difficult and painful reallocations, though by no means as severe as those of Russia. We have political trouble shutting down the production of nuclear submarines, stealth bombers and aircraft carriers. We have similar trouble making trade agreements with our neighbors, Mexico and Canada, because freer trade might cost some jobs, even while it generates others.

The local pains, vested interests and political perils that obstruct such reallocations must be even greater in the ex-communist countries. Shock therapy strategy would suddenly create mass unemployment and leave it to spontaneous private enterprise to create new enterprises and new jobs. The new jobs would not happen very fast, and meanwhile the depression in aggregate demand would discourage potential entrepreneurs and investors. The scenario is not politically or economically viable. In the absence of

positive programs to provide jobs for displaced workers, it is not surprising
that workers continue to be employed and paid in obsolete and unproductive activities.

Consider what Jean Monnet did for France, Germany and Western
Europe immediately after World War II. Devastated by the war, their economies were in shambles. For the most part they had not been doing very
well before the war either. To revive the crucial industrial complex strad-
dling the French–German border, Monnet conceived and organized the
Coal and Steel Community. Industries and governments cooperated on
concerted, consistent plans to expand peacetime production capacities.
These plans envisaged optimistic but feasible levels of demand for coal and
steel products, which the expansionary activities of those very industries
could help bring about. To put the matter simplistically, coal companies
were induced to invest in expanded production capacity because they
became confident the steel industry would buy more coal; steel companies
similarly raised their capacity because they became confident the coal
industry would buy more steel. All the firms raised their sights above what
they would have expected without coordination.

In the same spirit, Monnet developed for France itself a system of 'indicative planning'. Private industries and public sectors worked out mutually
consistent plans of production and investment. These then could serve as
wholly voluntary guides for individual industries and enterprises. As in the
coal–steel case, each sector could expand without fearing it would be over-
extended because the rest of the economy would lag behind. Periodic exercises in indicative planning were useful in concertedly lifting the sights of
French entrepreneurs for two decades after the war, but the device became
unnecessary later.

Monnet s institutional inventions could be useful in transitions from
communist to market economies. But the animus against communism and
controls is so strong that anything that involves government participation
and seems to be 'planning', however indicative and voluntary, is rejected
out of hand.

FINANCE

A mature capitalist economy contains an immense variety of markets,
some well organized and others quite informal. Some are for goods and services, others for paper assets and debts. Those financial markets are very
exciting. They attract many of the best brains. The fantastic development
of computer and communications technologies has multiplied the speed,
scope and sophistication of financial transactions. The sun never sets on

trading in currencies, equities and bonds. Derivative instruments, offering new opportunities for arbitrage and speculation, are invented, it seems, almost every day. Developing countries once regarded their own steel industries and airlines as sources of national pride. Now the prestigious symbol is a stock exchange.

The 1980s in the capitalist world was the decade of the paper economy, encouraged by deregulation of both domestic financial institutions and cross-border financial transactions. Speculators and deal makers who hit jackpots came to rival multimillionaire sports stars as heroes to college students. It is no wonder that Russian youths equate capitalism with finance, deals, speculation and brokering.

The rush to incorporate Russia into Western financial markets was premature and damaging, except to those of whatever nationality who knew how to work the system for their own advantage. Western advisers stressed making the ruble fully convertible and the creation of unregulated financial markets, open to foreigners as well as to residents. Instead it would be better to follow the precedents of the 1940s and 1950s, the days of the Marshall Plan and the early IMF.

While it is important to ensure that foreigners who invest and sell in Russia are able to convert their ruble proceeds, it should not be guaranteed that everyone, resident or foreigner, can do the same at the commercial exchange rate. Foreign currency should be husbanded for use in purchasing investment goods.

The collapse of trade among Warsaw Pact countries and particularly among the republics of the Soviet Union has to do with uncompetitive industry. In similar circumstances in postwar Western Europe, the European Payments Union was set up. It allowed the Marshall Plan countries to discriminate collectively against the dollar, facilitating multilateral trade among themselves. This system, which worked extremely well, might be a model even at this late date. This, of course, does not justify restoring the inefficient Warsaw Pact trade mechanism or exchanging goods at uneconomic prices.

Foreign advisers and lenders also insist on government policies of financial stabilization. In practice, this means balancing government budgets, restricting central bank credit and currency issue, deregulating financial transactions, and stabilizing the foreign exchange value of the local currency. It certainly is important to keep inflation within limits. But the faith that monetary stability is a sufficient condition for reviving production, reorienting industry, and achieving the essential resource reallocations is a dangerous fallacy. The Russian central bank has been deservedly condemned for fueling hyperinflation by exorbitant printing of rubles. The purpose of its unrestrained issue of currency is equally deserving of condemnation. It is to enable old state enterprises to meet their payrolls even though they are now producing little of social value. The result is that Russia manages to maintain 'employment' while producing less and less gross domestic product. The bank should be, directly or indirectly, channeling credit to promising new ventures.

We should never forget that the overriding purpose of economic activity and of markets is to produce goods and services of value to individuals and to society. Financial markets are means to that end, not ends in themselves. The title of Adam Smith's 1776 book, *The Wealth of Nations*, conveys its principal message. Wealth does not consist in paper claims or even gold and silver per se but in commodities useful to consumers or capable of producing consumer goods and services. Smith sought to overcome the mercantilist instincts of sovereigns who geared their nations' economies and foreign trade to maximize accumulations of precious metals. Ex-communist economies need to produce real goods and services and develop markets where they can sell them. Excessive emphasis upon finances can be counterproductive, especially in adolescent capitalist economies.

FROM THE ASHES

In the euphoria of the moment, Western advisers all too often forgot that the economic victory in the war of systems was not won by ideologically pure free-market regimes but by 'mixed economies' in which governments played substantial and crucial roles. They forgot too that elaborate structures of laws, institutions, and customs, which evolved over centuries in existing capitalist countries, are essential foundations and frameworks for market systems.

Unfortunately, Westerners offering professional advice on the management of transitions to market capitalism – economists, financiers, business executives, politicians – encouraged false expectations. Their confidence in free markets and private enterprise had been reinforced by the political and ideological success of conservative antigovernment movements in their own countries. Their advice was in that same spirit: dismantle your government controls and regulations, privatize your enterprises, stabilize your finances, get governments out of the way, and just watch a new market economy rise from the ashes. It turned out not to be so easy.

29. Between a market-based and a caring society: what kind of socially responsible economy do we want?

In my opinion, the developed economies of the democracies of Western Europe, North America, Japan, Australia, and New Zealand are best described as *mixed economies*, certainly since 1950. They are market economies in that most transactions for goods, services, land and natural resources, and human labor are voluntary purchases and sales. They are capitalist economies in the sense that most non-human means of production are private properties whose uses are decided by the owners or their agents. But democratic governments have a great deal to say about these decisions and activities. Governments own many productive enterprises and provide (free or subject to user charges) goods and services to the public. These span many areas: public safety and defence, parks, museums, libraries, recreation, roads and streets, transportation, public utilities, communications, education, public health, medical facilities, research, insurance, financial institutions, and many more. Despite the recent waves of privatization, governments' weight in the economy remains substantial.

Likewise, governments regulate in considerable detail private market transactions and the permissible uses of private property: what goods and services may be sold and bought, when, with what information and warranty, and often within what range of prices; what persons may be employed, at what wages and hours, and for how long; how real properties may be used. Moreover, governments' taxes and transfers greatly alter the distributive impacts of markets on incomes and consumption. It is surely not true that government was more active in the economy in some idyllic era before World War II.

It was ridiculous when right-wing ideologues proclaimed the West's victory in the Cold War as vindication of extreme laissez-faire economic liberalism (European brand). It was in fact a victory of democracy and of mixed economies. The mistake was costly, because some enthusiasts for markets in the ex-communist countries and their advisers from the West

thought the transitions to market capitalism would come easily and automatically once the communist state was destroyed, forgetting that the successes of the West were built on public institutions developed over long
histories, traditions unfortunately absent behind the Iron Curtain. Facades
of Western capitalism like stock markets were prematurely built, without
the legal and regulatory safeguards. They could not do the job. Effective
governmental institutions are indispensable.

On the other hand, it is also ridiculous to ignore the roles of markets in
democratic capitalist economies. Even those with the biggest shares of
public ownership and control, and the most extensive welfare states, have
conducted most of their economic activity in private markets and private
enterprises. I think of Sweden, Germany, France and Britain.

'The market', applied to a whole national economy or to international
economic relations is a metaphor. Markets come in endless varieties, from
daily local personal fish markets on the docks to the production, refining,
transportation and distribution of petroleum throughout the world. In
some markets for well-defined homogeneous commodities or securities, the
bids of many suppliers and demanders are balanced continuously by ever-
changing prices. In others, the producer/sellers administratively set prices,
changing them from time to time in the light of their sales in competition
with similar products. In some industries economies of scale restrict the
feasible number of competitors, and result in monopoly positions, inviting
government regulation or public ownership.

At their best, markets are remarkable social tools, like traffic lights.
Without bureaucratic rationing, they enable scarce supplies to be channeled to those who most want them or can use them most effectively. To
make markets work, governments have to define and enforce contracts and
make sure that buyers and sellers have accurate information, prevent combinations in restraint of trade, and regulate unavoidable monopolies and
oligopolies.

Economists know that, even in the most propitious competitive circumstances, markets fueled by the rational self-interests of buyers and sellers
cannot fully achieve the optimal results extravagantly celebrated by ideological versions of laissez-faire liberalism. The reasons are 'externalities',
by-products of producing or consuming particular commodities that affect
third parties who are not involved in the market transactions at all. The
farmers' fertilizer drains into nearby lakes, spoiling their uses in fishing or
recreation, costs that neither the farmers nor the consumers of his crops
have any reason to consider. We are all more conscious of negative environmental externalities than previous generations were, partly because demographic and economic growth and technology have made them worse.
There are positive externalities too, for example the weather benefits of

reforestation. Our democracies, our mixed economies, try to do something about externalities. That is an essential function of government, ignored in communist societies. Since nature does not respect political borders, international agreements are required. And since long-range planning is necessary, the agreements are hard to come by, as in the case of global warming. It is ironic that the ideological anti-government backlash coincided in timing with these critical challenges that private markets and profit-driven enterprises, for all the good things they can do, cannot accomplish without governmental direction.

Our expert, M. Petrella, speaks of the power of the three institutions of world capitalism: market, enterprise and capital. But these institutions are not monolithic. There are diverse markets, enterprises and accumulations of capital. There is no single governing association of these institutions, either internationally or (in the advanced democracies, at any rate) nationally. Indeed, in important respects the diverse markets, enterprises and capitals discipline themselves by competition.

Democracies give political power to elected legislators and executives and establish the rule of law. On the politics of democracy falls the responsibility for contesting the powers and interests of the wealthy, and for acting on behalf of the common interests that are underrepresented in individualistic choices and pursuits. It is not easy, because wealth has political power in election campaigns and lobbying. Yet our market–capitalist democracies all provide social safety nets, most importantly for the basic needs of life, and accomplish substantial redistribution by progressive tax and transfer programs. Neither logic nor experience supports the view, too prevalent nowadays among both Right and Left, that successful capitalism necessitates severe inequality and sustained poverty, that a society with a decent welfare state cannot enjoy prosperity, full employment and growing living standards.

As World War II ended, the victorious allies, led by the United States, sought to establish international institutions that would consolidate peace without retribution, rebuild Europe and Japan, and establish international institutions to bring order to international commerce. The authors of these initiatives hoped to avoid the economic disasters that preceded that war: the Great Depression, high unemployment, trade warfare and protection, anarchy in international finance, and currency crises. The treaty of Bretton Woods established the International Monetary Fund and the World Bank. The Fund was to organize international currency relations; the Bank was to mobilize funds for reconstruction and development. The General Agreement on Tariffs and Trade (GATT) was to reduce barriers to trade, and in particular to encourage multilateral, as against bilateral, trade and clearing. Successive rounds of multilateral tariff reduction moved the world towards free trade.

The articles of agreement of the IMF required members to make their currencies 'current-account convertible'. That is, if, for example, a French winemaker sold his wares in Mexico for pesos, he should be allowed by the Bank of Mexico to convert them into francs or into dollars. Eventually this degree of convertibility was achieved throughout the world. These steps to liberalize trade were and are a good idea. Developing and emerging economies that sought to expand exports and external trade (Taiwan, Korea and other Asian tigers) prospered and grew, while countries that stressed import-substitution and protection (Latin America, India) lagged far behind. I cannot sympathize with those who regard reversal of the trend towards free trade throughout the world as a benevolent movement to benefit poor nations and poor people, and I am afraid I detect this sentiment in M. Petrella's paper. Insulation of developing and emerging economies from the competition and opportunities of world commerce is likely to benefit parochial 'crony' capitalists and bureaucrats at the expense of their less fortunate compatriots, keeping the country poor but the privileged class rich.

Complete convertibility – encompassing 'capital-account convertibility' – is another story. That would mean that anyone who had pesos, Mexicans included, could trade them in for dollars at the Bank of Mexico. In 1950 the United States dollar was the only currency ready for that, and some of the foreign exchange and capital transfer controls of western European countries were maintained well into the 1980s. Recently the advanced countries applied pressure to amend the IMF charter to require full convertibility of all members. This was part of the general pressure from governments and private financial institutions in the major countries to remove all obstacles to international movements of funds between them and developing, emerging and transition economies.

Premature financial globalization, involving countries that did not have the rudimentary prudential institutions to regulate banks and financial markets, was a great mistake. Fortunately the idea of amending the IMF articles in this way has now been abandoned, and even the US Treasury is looking for new international monetary architecture that will slow the movements of hot money and allow the central banks of the smaller economies to have some breathing room and some freedom to manage their own monetary policies. Evidently, we are not, after all, ready for a world of dollarization, euroization or yenization.

My own proposal, a small tax on currency exchange transactions, dates back to 1972. It is motivated by the need to orient participants in these markets to long-run considerations and the fundamentals of currency values, not to their values this afternoon or tomorrow or next week. How does the 'Tobin Tax' do this? Automatically and unobtrusively. If you make a round trip from euro to peso and return over a year or five years, as you will do if you are involved in a commercial transaction or in a serious business investment, a tax of 0.1 or 0.2 per cent, paid going and coming, will not discourage you. If you are a day trader you will pay the tax frequently, and it will make you wonder if the possible gains of your game with other speculators are worth while. With a round trip every week and a tax of 0.1 per cent one way, the loss of return is 10 per cent per year. That buffer between Frankfurt and Mexico City would prevent arbitrage that completely equalizes money market rates and would thus leave Mexico with some monetary autonomy. I am definitely not wanting to curtail net movements of funds from developed to developing countries for direct capital investment or equity purchases or long term business loans. Net transfers of saving in those forms can be of great benefit in raising productivity and living standards in poorer countries, but most foreign exchange transactions, in gross amounting to two trillion dollars a day, have nothing to do with such transfers of saving. Indeed the currency crises that speculative funds trigger set back those economies and retard overseas investment in them.

I would like to see the IMF require that each of its members levy a currency transactions tax, all at the same rate as decided by the Fund from year to year. Each country could decide for itself how to dispose of the revenues, how much to keep, how much to contribute to international purposes. I do not seek to establish international government. Contrary to the fears of some politicians in my own country, I am not proposing that the United Nations have power to legislate taxes on American citizens over the heads of Congress. For me, the Tobin Tax proposal was not a plank in a general platform for economic and social reform throughout the world, but a proposal for a specific purpose, improving the functioning of the international monetary system. While the IMF is the best vehicle for the purpose, I believe the tax is feasible if agreed by a smaller group of major financial powers. Unfortunately, the lords of finance, public and private, are so opposed to the tax that it has no chance in any form.

The tax is one of a number of changes in international monetary architecture that I favor, proposals that I think people who differ widely on other political issues could agree. These include flexible exchange rates rather than fixed pegs, except for countries that choose to give up monetary autonomy altogether and 'dollarize'; rules by small countries forbidding their banks, other financial institutions and nonfinancial corporations from having net short-term debtor positions in hard currencies; prudential regulations everywhere like those of advanced countries: bank capital requirements, limits on leverage, full disclosures (like US SEC regulations) by issuers of securities, bankruptcy rules; generous advance credit lines at

IMF for well-behaved countries, and substantial increases in IMF lending resources.

I agree with many of M. Petrella's complaints about the recent history and present state of the world economy. Inequality and poverty are much too great. Unemployment is much too high in Europe and Japan. Central banks in general have too much power; they are too independent of elected representatives of the people. Governments pay too much attention to the bond markets' verdicts on their fiscal policies.

However, I would emphasize different reasons for discontent, many of them revealed by the contrasts between macroeconomic policies and outcomes in the United States and those in Europe and Japan. Monetary and fiscal policies in Europe and Japan have been incredibly incompetent for at least one decade, perhaps almost two. The notion that macro policies should aim exclusively at price stability, with no attention to employment and economic growth, is a cardinal intellectual error, now frozen into ideology and constitutional structure. In the early 1930s, with capitalist economies collapsing, it was easy to believe the claims of Marxists and other critics of democracy and capitalism that the system was doomed by irreparable structural flaws. John Maynard Keynes showed that the correct diagnosis and prescription were much simpler and less revolutionary, and experience after World War II bore him out. History has been repeating itself, with Alan Greenspan the pragmatic Keynesian who has saved the American economy, achieving low unemployment without any of the predicted inflationary consequences.

Europeans sometimes excuse their poor macroeconomic performance, compared to that of the United States, by alleging that it is the inevitable cost of a humane economy, that low American unemployment is obtained only by forcing the poor into jobs with starvation wages, long hours, and 19th-century working conditions. This is not true. There are still safety nets in the USA, and regulation of wages, hours and working conditions. In my opinion, it is not humane but damaging for individuals and wasteful for the collectivity to consign cohort after cohort of school-leavers to unemployment, on the dole for much of their adult lives. Even if there is some truth in the orthodox European view that inflexibilities of labor markets have some responsibility for European unemployment, these conditions have not been imposed by some alien power but are amenable to reforms by the European Union and its member governments themselves, as they have long been. The big question mark about Euroland is whether these governmental bodies can find ways of handling their considerable economic problems. Certainly, they can not safely leave the whole policy show to the European Central Bank.

In technologically progressive economies, it is not possible to guarantee lifetime jobs to everybody. But M. Petrella is too pessimistic. A person who loses a job because of technological progress or import competition need not be jobless for life. The whole history of capitalism is the substitution of new techniques, products and jobs for old. We cannot stop progress in its tracks and employ people forever in obsolete tasks, where they cannot earn their wages. With good macroeconomic policy, the US labor markets succeed in putting people in new jobs without extended periods of unemployment. Europe is definitely pathological if the combination of its monetary policy and its labor market institutions cannot do the same. No doubt, severance pay, transition subsidies, and education and training need to be provided with government help.

30. Jan Tinbergen (12 April 1903–9 June 1994)*

Jan Tinbergen's life and work spanned the 20th century. He was the century's own economist, probably the most substantial contributor to the remarkable advances in economic science that occurred in these years. In 1968, the Bank of Sweden established the Alfred Nobel Memorial Prize in Economic Science, designed to be in every respect parallel to the original Nobel Prizes in sciences and literature. The initial prize was shared by Jan Tinbergen of the Netherlands and Ragnar Frisch (1895–1973) of Norway. These choices were so obviously merited that they were universally and enthusiastically applauded.

The major advance in economics during the 20th century was that it became more precise, more rigorous, more quantitative, more mathematical, more statistical – in sum, more scientific. A landmark in this development was the founding in 1931 of the worldwide Econometric Society, which began publishing *Econometrica* in 1933. Frisch and Tinbergen were important founders. Even more significant, they were the leading intellectual inspirations for the new quantitative methods of economic analysis. Tinbergen was later a leader of the Econometrics Institute of Rotterdam, founded in 1955.

Today econometrics has long since outgrown its status as a somewhat esoteric specialty. Almost all professional economics is econometric, almost all practitioners possess and rely on econometric skills.

Tinbergen began as a mathematical physicist. He received his doctorate in 1929 and joined the Dutch Central Bureau of Statistics. He served there for 10 years. He learned economics on his own, and already in 1930 published a famous article explaining observed cycles in production and prices of agricultural products. In 1933, he was appointed an adjunct professor (later full professor) in the Netherlands School of Economics (later named Erasmus University), from which he retired in 1973. Doubtless Tinbergen had many opportunities to migrate to prestigious universities abroad, but he stayed in his native land.

*   This chapter first appeared in *Proceedings of the American Philosophical Society*, 141, (4), December, 1997, 511–14.

Beginning in his student days, Tinbergen was an active political radical, deeply distressed by the poverty, inequality and injustice he saw around him, all exacerbated by the Great Depression. He gravitated into economics as a pragmatic empirical problem solver, an orientation that lasted all his life. In his final decade he was seeking ways to end the arms trade and to abolish child labor throughout the world. It was probably fortunate that Tinbergen became an economist innocent of the powerful 19th-century doctrinal traditions that then dominated economics teaching.

Tinbergen learned quickly that the problems that engaged him in his immediate neighborhood stemmed from national and international economic tides, that he could not really solve these local problems without understanding how whole economies worked and could be made to work better. He tackled the instabilities of agricultural markets, the fluctuations in business investments (for example, ship-building) and ultimately the cycles in entire national and international economies.

His scientific training led him to think of markets and economies as systems of algebraic equations linking economic variables to each other, and to estimate statistically the parameters of these equations. This path-breaking methodology is what became known as econometrics. Tinbergen was not inventing it for its own sake. He needed it on the job, to manage the practical empirical problems at hand. In 1936, he completed an econometric model of the Dutch economy and began to apply it in prediction and planning.

Meanwhile the League of Nations, seeking to understand the Great Depression, had engaged Professor Gottfried Haberler of Harvard to review critically various theoretical explanations of business cycles. In 1936, the League brought Jan Tinbergen to Geneva to test those theories empirically. By 1938 (!) Tinbergen and his team had completed a 48-equation macroeconometric model of the United States economy, estimated from data spanning the years from 1919 to 1932.

This model is the prototype of Lawrence Klein's 1950 model of the American economy and of a host of successors. Today macroeconometric models are everywhere, constructed for every national or regional economy or for the whole world, built and used by government agencies, international institutions, think tanks, business enterprises, investment bankers and academic economists. Some compete for customers. Some are guides for policy. Some are research tools. Their builders have much more data, infinitely more powerful computers and more reliable statistical methods than Tinbergen had. Yet his 1939 model still looks amazingly sophisticated both in its theoretical structure and in its statistical methods. It was a stupendous achievement.

On publication in 1939, Tinbergen's model encountered searching criticism from John Maynard Keynes. The exchanges in the *Economic Journal* (of which Keynes was editor) between these two giants are justly famous. Ironically, the model was very much a detailed empirical version of the revolutionary theory Keynes himself had espoused in his 1936 masterpiece, *The General Theory of Employment, Interest and Money*. Keynes respected and trusted Tinbergen, but he was afraid the new methods would be abused by less thoughtful econometricians and would be vested with excessive exactitude by unsophisticated readers. Keynes was right that Tinbergen's methods could not prevent numerical correlations from being misinterpreted as causations, a problem of which Tinbergen was aware and one that has dominated much of the subsequent history of econometrics. Keynes tended to throw out the baby with the bath water. Tinbergen argued effectively that important decisions of policy were sensitive to quantitative values of parameters and could not be made solely on qualitative theoretical presumptions or informal observations.

Policy! That was Tinbergen's central interest. Policy planning was the use to which he and his models were dedicated. In 1945, he became the first director of the Dutch Central Planning Bureau. He pioneered a new and fruitful subject, the formal theory of policy. He showed how a model must recognize some of its variables as objectives and some others as policy instruments, how a model of empirical reality connects feasible objective outcomes to settings of the various instruments, and how the most desirable of the feasible outcomes might be attained. Generally, policy makers need as many instruments as they have objectives, and sometimes even that does not guarantee the existence of a solution. One may not be able to optimize in every dimension, for example both employment and inflation. Besides expounding this theory and illustrating its application in various contexts, Tinbergen was busy putting it to practical use.

Gradually, he widened the focus of his applications from one single country to the whole world, from short-run problems of economic stabilization to long-run development and growth, and from advanced industrial economies to the poor underdeveloped nations of the Third World. He left the Dutch planning bureau in 1955, and associated himself with the United Nations, the World Bank, UNESCO and other international organizations.

He made many contributions to techniques of planning for development. He was always interested in workable procedures, not in theoretical niceties. Never one to believe that free market private enterprise economies will work without some intelligent central guidance, Tinbergen was not shy about identifying himself with planning, despite the word's growing political unpopularity. To him it was simply social rationality.

Tinbergen became an ardent internationalist, advocating augmented powers for regional and worldwide organizations, up to the United Nations. His goals were human life, health and happiness throughout the world. Inequality and economic injustice, among nations and among individuals, occupied much of his attention in the second half of his career. His final academic appointment, in 1973, was as Professor of International Cooperation at the University of Leiden, where he had earned his doctorate in physics 44 years before.

An account of Tinbergen's major achievements does not do justice to his versatility and fecundity. He made important, often seminal, professional contributions to the wide range of subjects he encountered in his research and teaching. He wrote, for example, on international trade, tariffs, commodity agreements and balances of payments; on national income accounting; on stock market prices; on trade unions. He wrote on statistical problems and methods and on technical issues of mathematical economic theory. These writings simply solidify the claim at the beginning of this memoir, that Jan Tinbergen was the 20th century's economist *par excellence*.

Index

Index